D1594112

Beckett and Joyce

Beckett and Joyce

Friendship and Fiction

Barbara Reich Gluck

Lewisburg
Bucknell University Press
London: Associated University Presses

© 1979 by Associated University Presses, Inc.

Associated University Presses, Inc.
Cranbury, New Jersey 08512

Associated University Presses
Magdalen House
136–148 Tooley Street
London SE1 2TT, England

Library of Congress Cataloging in Publication Data

Gluck, Barbara Reich.
  Beckett and Joyce.

  Bibliography: p.
  Includes index.
  1. Beckett, Samuel, 1906–   —Criticism and interpretation.
2. Joyce, James, 1882–1941—Influence—Beckett. I. Title.
PR6003.E282Z6658   848'.9'1209   76–50290
ISBN 0-8387-2060-9

to Simon

*without whom this never
could have been written*

Contents

Preface

For the majority of critics, the answer to the question of Joyce's literary influence on Samuel Beckett is the same now given to speculations about life on the moon: there is none. While, until recently, only a few[1] actually attempted to explore the issue, nearly every writer who has commented on Beckett's works has had a definite—and definitely negative—opinion on the matter. Dismissing what they disdain to investigate, most have vehemently denied the presence of any Joycean voice in Beckett's fiction. According to Colin Wilson, any comparison between the two authors is

> nonsensical. The only similarity is that they are both Dubliners. Joyce was preoccupied with language; Beckett's sense of language is about as lively as Hansard.[2]

Although more admiring of Beckett's skill with words, Christopher Ricks agrees that "it is only marginally useful to invoke the names of Joyce and Kafka [in discussing Beckett's literary origins],"[3] and V. S. Pritchett asserts: "There is far more to compare [in *Molloy*] with *Tristram Shandy* . . . than there is with Joyce."[4] Lionel Abel, who sees in Beckett's plays a symbolic representation of his psychological relationship with Joyce, nevertheless believes that "all of his [Beckett's] novels are . . . flights from Joyce—perhaps toward Kafka."[5] Finally, Beckett himself has taken pains to deny any artistic connection with his late friend: "I simply do not feel the presence in my writing as a whole of the Joyce and Proust situations."[6]

Of course, as D. H. Lawrence realized, it is the tale, not the teller, that should be trusted. A few critics, looking closely at Beckett's works, have detected Joycean echoes. "As a fiction writer Samuel Beckett derives from Proust and Joyce,"[7] Northrop Frye has flatly stated, and David Hayman refers to Joyce as Beckett's "literary godfather."[8] The most convincing testimony comes from a mutual friend of both Joyce and Beckett. Maria Jolas, wife of *transition* editor Eugene Jolas, implicitly challenges the views of Colin Wilson and reaffirms the close literary ties between Beckett and Joyce:

> when I read Sam today . . . his writing . . . seems to bridge the gap for me between now and Joyce. I hear the same soft Dublin voice, I sense the same vast cultural past, the same ferocious but as often very gentle irony, the same humanity and rare wit that makes me laugh out loud as I read. Like Joyce he is also a Christ-haunted man, not yet of the new barbarism.[9]

A. J. Leventhal, a longtime friend and sometime secretary of Beckett, is even more specific. He points out the significant stylistic impression that the works of Joyce made on Beckett: "Under the influence of Joyce and his own impishness one can see Beckett relying on the pun to put questions that he expects from his readers."[10]

Perhaps as a result of these testimonials by intimates, critics recently have begun to take a closer look at the Joyce-Beckett literary connection. H. Porter Abbott in *The Fiction of Samuel Beckett: Form and Effect* and Francis Doherty in *Samuel Beckett* both note resemblances between specific works of Beckett and Joyce. J. Mitchell Morse considers both authors practitioners of what has come to be known as "the French new novel" (*le nouveau roman*),[11] while Laurent Le Sage sees Beckett more precisely "as a living link between the young French authors and the foreign master James Joyce, whom they all revere."[12]

There are still, of course, many critics who see Joyce and Beckett as fundamentally opposite in technique and intent.

Martin Esslin makes the often-repeated point that Joyce's art and use of language are expansive while Beckett's mode is one of contraction.[13] Ruby Cohn discusses how similar the two authors are in their Irish cosmopolitanism, but nonetheless finally maintains the difference between them: "Joyce attempt[ed] to embrace all knowledge, all experience, all language; Beckett doubt[s] all knowledge, all experience, all language, and doubt[s] even the cartesian tradition of doubt."[14]

The truth, rather than lying between these two extremes, encompasses both of them. In the words of Francis Warner, whose chapter on Beckett I read only after this study was completed, Joyce and Beckett are complementary rather than contradictory: "they represent contrary but interdependent modes of vision and each completes the other."[15] Beckett *was* a disciple of Joyce, but a disciple who "has certainly gone his own way."[16] At first embracing Joycean verbal techniques,

> he beg[an] by parodying the inventories of *Ulysses* and the puns of *Finnegans Wake* and ends by devising a system of combinations and permutations more pure than any Joyce could have invented.[17]

Passing beyond a witty, derivative style to a brilliantly distinctive one, Beckett "charts, in regard to his own needs, the proximate attractions of Joyce and Proust; he is most influenced by what he discards."[18] For this reason, although there are undeniable fundamental differences[19] in their works, the Joycean devices that Beckett rejected are as important as the ones he retained.

Following a preliminary chapter on the personal friendship of Beckett and Joyce and the intellectual milieu surrounding them, I discuss Beckett's earliest literary efforts, his short stories and poems, and how deliberately they reflect Joyce's mature style, both by imitation and allusion (chapter 2). Chapter 3 focuses on Beckett's first novels, *Murphy, Watt,* and *Mercier et Camier.* These works represent a transitional stage in Beckett's

growing awareness of his own style and subject matter. The
verbal techniques are still strongly Joycean, but the underlying
philosophy shows Beckett's increasing dissatisfaction with his
mentor's *Weltanschauung*: the universe as a cyclical closed
system in which every object and event relates to every other
one, and the key to all is man's mastery of his own tongue—
language. For this analysis I am particularly indebted to the
work of one of the best of the Beckett critics, Hugh Kenner,
and the theories he developed in his book *Flaubert, Joyce and
Beckett: The Stoic Comedians* and, more recently, in *A Reader's
Guide to Samuel Beckett*.

With the publication of his novels *Molloy, Malone Dies,* and
The Unnamable, Beckett's divergence from Joyce becomes nearly
complete. For the trilogy narrators, words are lies, horrors that
are uttered only in the hope of ending a still greater torment—
the hell of a life unlived, an existence that meaninglessly goes
round in circles, perpetuating its pain and impotence by constantly approaching but never achieving an illusory end. Study-
ing these novels and some short stories of Beckett's in chapter
4, I attempt to present a rationale for Beckett's rebellion against
Joyce and for the literary path he chose instead. The fifth and
final chapter is concerned with Beckett's turn to the theater
and his qualified incorporation of the Joycean concepts he had
tried in vain to transcend. Forced to admit the circular nature
of time, Beckett is nonetheless adamant in his relentless opposition to it. Using the cyclical structure of *Finnegans Wake,* he
makes it serve his own ends: not to show the inherent harmony
and order of the universe, but rather to exhibit its discord and
disorder. Well-rounded plays in every sense, *Waiting for Godot*
and *Endgame* show that Beckett, although he relinquished the
punning Joycean prose of his early career, developed an equally
expert (if totally different) command of the written word; that
what he ultimately found in the works of Joyce was both a
form for his fiction and a shape for the chaos surrounding him.

This book could not have been shaped without the help of many persons. I would especially like to thank Professor William York Tindall of Columbia University for his constant encouragement and excellent advice; it was, moreover, his doctoral seminar on Beckett that first stimulated me to read one Irishman, connect him with the other, and love both of them. To both Professor Maurice Wohlgelernter of Baruch College and Professor George Stade of Columbia I am indebted for careful readings and perceptive suggestions. My gratitude also goes to George Reavey, a kind and generous man, who shared with me not only his considerable firsthand knowledge of, but also his correspondence with Beckett. Dr. A. J. Leventhal patiently answered my queries, and Patric Farrell brought the Irish brogue into my heart forever. Finally, I make a totally inadequate acknowledgment to a dear friend, Clara Kozol, who has set me a standard, in scholarship and in life.

Acknowledgments

My deepest gratitude goes to Mr. Samuel Beckett for allowing me to include the text of his poems "Home Olga" and "Gnome" as well as his prose piece "Text."

I should also like to thank Calder and Boyars Ltd and Grove Press, Inc. for permission to use material from the following works by Samuel Beckett:

Watt; All rights reserved. Reprinted by permission of Grove Press, Inc. Copyright © 1970.

Poems in English. Copyright © 1961 by Samuel Beckett. Reprinted by permission of Grove Press, Inc.

Murphy. First published 1938. Reprinted by permission of Grove Press, Inc. Copyright © 1970.

Molloy and *Malone Dies,* from *Three Novels.* Copyright © 1955, 1956, 1958 by Grove Press, Inc. Reprinted by permission of Grove Press, Inc.

Waiting for Godot. Copyright © 1954 by Grove Press, Inc. Reprinted by permission of Grove Press, Inc.

Beckett and Joyce

1

Friendship

Reeve Gootch was right and
Reeve Drughad was sinistrous!

Finnegans Wake (197.1)

At the end of *A Portrait of the Artist as a Young Man,* Stephen
Dedalus is about to leave friends and fatherland for "the reality
of experience."[1] Severing the ties of family, church, and country,
will, he paradoxically hopes, enable him to become an artist
and "forge in the smithy of [his] soul the uncreated conscience
of [his] race."[2] But this youthful attempt at flight, so boldly
and exultantly proclaimed, was destined to be, like that of
Icarus, both unsuccessful and short-lived. Stephen gets only as
far as Paris when his mother's illness suddenly summons him
home. In Dublin once more, almost all that he has to show for
his brief exile is memories of the old Fenian, Kevin Egan, and
the "rich booty" of "*Le Tutu,* five tattered numbers of *Pantalon
Blanc et Culotte Rouge* [and] a blue French telegram. . . ."[3]
    Nearly a quarter of a century later, another Irishman would
depart from Newhaven pier for the city of lights—with much
more success. Twenty-two years old, a graduate of Trinity
College in Dublin with Highest Honors in Modern Languages,[4]

Samuel Beckett was arriving in Paris to assume the post of *lecteur d'anglais* at the prestigious Ecole Normale Supérieure.

The Paris that greeted Beckett was indeed "a moveable feast."[5] Expatriate artists from all countries crowded the cafés and boulevards, especially those of Montparnasse on the Left Bank. Ernest Hemingway could be seen, writing the Nick Adams stories over a *crème café* at La Closerie des Lilas, a restaurant later frequented by Beckett himself.[6] Joyce and his family often dined on the excellent cuisine of Fouquet's, when they were not at Michaud's or the Deux-Magots. More than merely places to nourish the body, the cafés of Paris were informal literary salons where artists could meet each other and exchange ideas, stimulating their minds at the same time as the Pernods refreshed their palates. For the intimates there were the real salons—Thursday afternoons at Ford Madox Ford's; tea at Stella Bowen's studio; and the eighteenth-century French atmosphere of Nathalie Barney's gatherings in the rue Jacob, where guests like Proust, Valéry, Gide, Academicians, and "even a stray countess or two,"[7] contributed to the gracious and witty ambience. By far the most famous of these salons was that of Gertrude Stein, at 27 rue de Fleurus. Amidst Picasso- and Matisse-laden walls, visitors would sip fragrant liqueurs from crystal carafes in small glasses, watch Miss Toklas complete an intricate needlepoint pattern, and listen to the "Woman with the Face Like Caesar's"[8] hand down dicta on everything from Joyce ("He is a *good* writer. . . . His influence, however, is local")[9] to homosexuals ("they are disgusted with themselves")[10] and virginity ("To be a virgin is to be a virgin and not to be a virgin is not to be a virgin and not to be a virgin may be to be a virgin").[11]

As important as Gertrude Stein, if not more so, was another American, also a woman, Sylvia Beach, whose bookshop, Shakespeare and Company, at 12 rue de l'Odéon, was the literary headquarters for many of the literati of Paris. There, for a nominal fee, a struggling writer could join the rental library, or—if even that was beyond him—obtain a necessary loan or credit.

Along with the cafés, salons, and bookshops, the little maga-
zines formed the nucleus of Parisian artistic life. Of the latter,
transition was the most famous and influential.[12] Founded as
a monthly by Eugene and Maria Jolas and Elliott Paul in the
fall of 1926, its purpose was "to create a meeting place for all
those artists on both sides of the Atlantic who were working
towards a complete renovation, both spiritual and technical, of
the various art forms."[13] But *transition* quickly became more
than just an exile's review. In editorial philosophy and content
it reflected not only the expatriate's art, but his reasons for
coming to Paris as well. Disillusioned by the destruction of war,
people like Hemingway, Fitzgerald, Pound, and Pirandello were
even more disheartened by the society it had left standing.
Americans in particular fled the land of Harding and Coolidge,
exiling themselves from a nation that they believed had no
spiritual depth but just an industrial, commercial spirit totally
inimical to art, and from a public that, although it desired
nothing but a straightforward, provincial art (in the worst sense
of those words), itself seemed to embody only the qualities of
insincerity, hypocrisy, and sentimentality. In what Samuel Putnam terms an unprecedented "mass migration of writers and
artists . . . to a foreign shore,"[14] they came to "the Paris that
was our spiritual mistress, a wise and beautiful one, at a time
when our own America, or so it seemed, had turned a strumpet."[15]

Jolas saw the issue as one of even greater scope and import.
For him, as for Oscar Wilde thirty years ago, it was nothing
less than a battle against the philistine, that cultural dilettante
who had now succeeded in industrializing art and civilization,
depriving them both of all genuine emotion and reducing them
to a photographic and stagnant realism. "The artist," he proclaimed, "is the born enemy of the philistine in whom he sees
incorporated all the qualities which his metaphysical orientation
rejects. . . ."[16] All "must continue to oppose the present pluto-
cratic materialism"[17] and, by creating a new art, "help destroy
the ideology of a rotting civilization."[18]

As political as this sounds, it was not a Marxist revolution
that Jolas advocated, but a literary one. Intellectual, not political

anarchy,[19] was the goal, and he dedicated the pages of *transition* to this "Revolution of the Word."[20] Announcing the necessity for "a new symbolical language," Jolas argued that "the inroads made by the pragmatic forces have prostituted the language of poetry and deprived it of its autonomous, primal character. . . . The poet [i.e., writer] who gives back to language its pre-logical functions, who re-creates it as an orphic sign, makes a spiritual revolt, which is the only revolt worth making today."[21] In order to achieve this, in order to put a "new magic"[22] back in language and literature, it was necessary that "there be disintegration first."[23] For this is the natural process of language; always becoming, never static but dynamic and ever-changing, language is in eternal flux and the writer, in his handling of it, must be equally flexible. He therefore has "the right to disintegrate the primal matter of words imposed on him by textbooks and dictionaries . . . to use words of his own fashioning and to disregard existing grammatical and syntactical laws." In short, "the imagination in search of a fabulous word is autonomous and unconfined" and "the plain reader be damned."[24]

With this artistic credo, it was only natural that the writers Jolas championed were linguistic innovators, artists who, the verbal density of their work notwithstanding, were really trying to recapture an essential, unadorned speech: "By reestablishing the simplicity of the word, we may find again its old magnificence. Gertrude Stein, James Joyce, Hart Crane, Louis Aragon, André Breton, Léon-Paul Fargue, August Stramm and others are showing us the way."[25] These writers and *transition* itself would, in a sense, "show the way" to Beckett, who signed a somewhat similar manifesto in the March 1932 issue of the magazine. "Poetry is Vertical,"[26] as the statement was called, took its title from a comment by Léon-Paul Fargue that "on a été trop horizontal, j'ai envie d'être vertical." After declaring the primacy and independence of the poetic vision in significantly Beckettian terms ("the hegemony of the inner life over the outer life"), the proclamation went on to reject the classical ideal of Hulme and Eliot, "because it inevitably leads to a decorative reactionary conformity, to a factitious sense of harmony, to the sterilisation of the living imagination." Two paragraphs are doubly prophetic. One provides an excellent description of *Finnegans Wake,* which was being serialized in *transition* (as *Work in Progress*), and the style of which Beckett was then imitating:

> The transcendental "I" with its multiple stratifications reaching back millions of years is related to the entire history of mankind, past and present, and is brought to the surface with the hallucinatory irruption of images in the dream, the daydream, the mystic-gnostic trance and even the psychiatric condition.

Approving the direction of Joyce's art, Beckett, in signing the "verticalist manifesto," also anticipated the future concerns of his own fiction. Another paragraph of the proclamation speaks of "the final disintegration of the 'I' in the creative act"; from *Watt* to *Words and Music,* the physical deterioration of Beckett's heroes reflects the author's urgent search for his irreducible self —so as to reduce even that voice to pure silence.

Another signer of the verticalist proclamation was Thomas McGreevy, a colleague of Beckett's at the Ecole Normale, which was the gathering place for the Dublin intellectuals.[27] It was probably McGreevy who introduced Beckett to Joyce.[28]

Although there is no record of that first meeting between the older, already-famous author and the young English instructor who had yet to publish or write, it surely had none of the sinister overtones of Earwicker's confrontation with the Cad. Nor was there the sense of two worlds colliding that had marked Joyce's initial encounter with Yeats twenty-six years before.[29] On the contrary, Beckett and Joyce had much in common and were no doubt quick to realize it. Both had university degrees in modern languages,[30] a deep interest in literature with a particular passion for Dante, and, fellow countrymen, both were united in a desire to live apart from the city of their birth. Joyce, hating and loving his "dear dirty Dublin," found it impossible, for legal as well as personal reasons, to live there. Beckett's own attitude, similarly ambiguous, would eventually also be decided in favor of exile. (Temporarily in Dublin when World War II erupted in 1939, Beckett immediately returned to Paris, later commenting that he had done so because "I preferred France in war to Ireland in peace.")[31] Even with regard to religion, Protestant Beckett and Catholic Joyce showed a remarkable tendency to think alike. When questioned by Cranly about becoming a Protestant, Stephen Dedalus, echoing a statement that Joyce had once made, replied: "What kind of liberation would that be to forsake an absurdity which is logical and coherent and to embrace one which is illogical and incoherent?"[32] Beckett, raised a Protestant, has admitted that "Irish Catholicism is not attractive, but it is deeper [than Protestantism]."[33]

Given such mutual interests and opinions, it is not surprising that the relationship between the two men quickly progressed to the point where, within less than a year, Beckett was invited to join a group of Joyce's very close friends in a private celebration. On 27 June 1929, Joyce and his companions gathered to commemorate publication of the French translation of *Ulysses*, which had occurred the previous February, and the twenty-fifth anniversary of Bloomsday. The *Déjeuner Ulysse*,[34] as the luncheon was called, had been arranged by Adrienne Monnier, proprietor of La Maison des Amis des Livres, a bookshop that rivaled Sylvia Beach's for the literary crowd and that was, in fact, across the street from Shakespeare and Company.[35] As the site for the festivities, Miss Monnier chose Les Vaux-de-Cernay, a tiny village outside Versailles, because it fittingly contained the Hotel Léopold. The guests included Edouard Dujardin, author of *Les Lauriers sont coupés* and the writer whom Joyce credited with originating the interior monologue;[36] Paul Valéry; Philippe Soupault, who would later assist in the French translation of "Anna Livia Plurabelle"; Jules Romains, the novelist; Léon-Paul Fargue; Sylvia Beach; Thomas McGreevy; and Giorgio Joyce and his future wife, Helen Fleischman.[37]

Preferring an informal, relaxed atmosphere, Joyce had rejected the idea of speeches. As a result, the revelry was considerable and Beckett, in true Irish tradition, became highly intoxicated with both the occasion and the alcohol. On the trip back to Paris, after repeatedly requesting that Joyce stop the bus so that all could have another drink at a wayside cafe, Beckett was finally put off and left to pursue his own liquid desires.[38] Joyce later wrote of the incident to a friend, Valery Larbaud:

> There were two riotous young Irishmen[39] and one of them . . . fell deeply under the influence of beer, wine spirits, liqueurs, fresh air, movement and feminine society and was ingloriously abandoned by the Wagonette in one of those temporary palaces which are inseparably associated with the memory of the Emperor Vespasian.[40]

As influenced as Beckett could be by liquor, he was even more susceptible to intoxication by words, especially Joyce's. His first printed story, "Assumption," is written in a clearly Joycean style, a style that he vigorously defended in an essay, "Dante . . . Bruno. Vico . . Joyce," also published at the same time in the June 1929 issue of *transition*. In frank admiration of Joyce's achievement, Beckett's essay analyzes the philosophic and linguistic structure of *Work in Progress*: its "preordained [Viconian] cyclicism"[41] in which "all humanity [is] circling with fatal monotony about the Providential fulcrum";[42] the dualism of Giordano Bruno, who also held that all contraries are present in each other and all coincide in God, the universal monad; and the language which, while it simulated the primitive origin of speech as gesture, incorporated the sophistication[43] of linguistic synthesis, a device practiced by Dante in his *Divine Comedy*. Extolling the virtues of Joyce's verbal versatility and praising his prose, Beckett also denounced Joyce's detractors, whom he considered the very philistines Eugene Jolas so heartily despised:

> Here is direct expression—pages and pages of it. And if you don't understand it, Ladies and Gentlemen, it is because you are too decadent to receive it. You are not satisfied unless form is so strictly divorced from content that you can com-

prehend the one almost without bothering to read the other. . . .

Here form *is* content, content *is* form. . . . It is not written at all. It is not to be read—or rather it is not only to be read. It is to be looked at and listened to. He is not writing about something: he is writing something.[44] When the sense is sleep, the words go to sleep. (See the end of "Anna Livia") When the sense is dancing, the words dance.[45]

Joyce approved of the essay and, recommending it to Eugene Jolas,[46] had it "put in"[47] *transition.* He also arranged for it to be translated and published in an Italian review.[48] Nor did his interest cease when the essay was included in a book, *Our Exagmination Round His Factification for Incamination of Work in Progress,* a collection of twelve articles by friends and disciples such as Stuart Gilbert and Frank Budgen. By his own admission, Joyce was responsible for "the paper cover, the grandfather's clock on the title page and the word Exagmination."[49] More important, he acknowledges his responsibility for the content of the essays: "I did stand behind those twelve Marshals more or less directing them what lines of research to follow."[50] It is therefore likely that many of Beckett's insights into the *Wake* were given to him by Joyce although, since like Joyce he was fluent in Italian, they could as easily have come from his own reading.[51]

Beckett's wholehearted approval of *Finnegans Wake* and adulation of Joyce, as well as his proficiency in French and Italian, were no doubt responsible for Joyce's selecting him, along with Alfred Péron, in 1930, to translate the Anna Livia Plurabelle section into French. A first-draft version was completed, but by then it was fall and Beckett had to give up his role as "principal translator"[52] to return to Dublin and his teaching position at Trinity College.[53] The work was resumed by Paul Léon, Eugene Jolas, and Ivan Goll (a poet whom Joyce had known in Zurich)[54] under Joyce's own supervision, but a second draft still failed to satisfy the author. Philippe Soupault was recruited in November and he, Joyce, and Léon met every Thursday afternoon at 2:30 in Léon's apartment on the rue

Casimir Périer.[55] At a three-hour session, Léon read the English text and Soupault the French, which was then taken apart phrase by phrase. After fifteen such meetings a final draft was agreed upon and published with an introduction by Soupault in the 1 May (1931) edition of *La Nouvelle Revue Française*. It was, as Richard Ellmann has since written, "a triumph over seemingly impossible obstacles,"[56] the sound and rhythm as well as the sense of the original being reproduced with unbelievable accuracy.

Joyce was evidently pleased with Beckett's contribution and must have continued to associate him with A.L.P. For, in 1938, after finishing the last pages of the *Wake* (Anna Livia's "monologue"), he gave them to Beckett for his opinion. Beckett read them en route to the railroad station and, before departing, telephoned Joyce to confirm the emotional impact of the lines.[57]

In the course of writing *Finnegans Wake,* Joyce was aided by Beckett in a variety of ways. Although he was not, as is commonly supposed, Joyce's secretary,[58] Beckett was one of a number of aspiring young writers who, out of friendship and admiration for the author of *Ulysses,* read to the optically troubled Joyce and wrote down, at his dictation, passages for what was still called *Work in Progress.* An amusing incident that occurred at this time illustrates Joyce's method of composition and Beckett's reluctance to make it his own. One day, as Joyce was dictating to Beckett, there was a knock at the door. "Come in," said Joyce, and Beckett, who had not heard the knock, wrote it down. Upon rereading the passage, the error was caught, but Joyce decided to "let it stand." Beckett, according to Ellmann, was "fascinated and thwarted by Joyce's singular method."[59] Admiring the master, he would nonetheless do differently. Where Joyce's art tended to expansion and all-inclusiveness, Beckett's would move toward a contraction so absolute that it would eventually substitute silence and mime for the words themselves.

On still another occasion Beckett provided Joyce with actual literary inspiration. Joyce wished to incorporate his father's story of Buckley and the Russian General[60] into the *Wake* but

was at a loss to know how to do so. He told the anecdote to
Beckett, who wittily replied, "Another insult to Ireland," thus
giving Joyce the clue he needed.[61] The hint was so apt that
Joyce included Beckett's very words:

> For when meseemim, and tolfoklokken rolland allover our-
> loud's lande, beheaving up that sob of tunf for to claimhis,
> for to wollpimsolff, puddywhuck. Ay, and untuoning his
> culothone in an exitous erseroyal *Deo Jupto*. At that instullt
> to Igorladns! Prronto! I gave one dobblenotch and I ups with
> my crozzier. Mirrdo! With my how on armer and hits leg an
> arrow cockshock rockrogn. Sparro![62]

In some passages of the *Wake* Joyce seems to have gone even
farther and included not Beckett's words, but Beckett himself.
On page 64, line 31, there is a description of a person who suspiciously resembles the lanky young man of the Ecole Normale:
"Come on, ordinary man with that large big nonobli head, and
that blanko ber*becked* fischial ekksprezzion. . . ."[63] And only
a few pages earlier we read, "Sordid Sam, a dour decent de-
blancer [Dubliner?], the unwashed, haunted always by his ham
[home]. . . ."[64] At one point Joyce seems to be mocking Beckett's
puzzlement at his *Work in Progress*: "You is feeling like you
was lost in the bush, boy? . . . *Bethicket* me for a stump of a
beech if I have the poultriest notions what the farest he all
means."[65] At another, Beckett's early artistic attempts to follow
the style of his master—and their similar physique—are lightly
twitted: "Sam Dizzier's feedst. . . . He looks rather thin, imitating me."[66] Finally there is a reference to Beckett's alma mater
and an apparent allusion to his first work of fiction, *More Pricks
Than Kicks*: "Sam. . . . I bonded him off more as a friend and
as a brother. . . . Illstarred punster. . . . 'Twas the quadra sent
him and Trinity too. . . . He'll *prisck*ly soon hand tune your
Erin's ear for you."[67]

The *Wake* is a polyglot book, and while Joyce knew five
languages fluently and had a familiarity with several more, there
were some that he did not know at all. One of these was ancient
Greek, and there is a record of at least one occasion on which

Beckett provided his friend with the necessary information on a postcard.[68]

Beckett would also read aloud to Joyce and, since his mind "had a subtlety and strangeness that attracted Joyce,"[69] they had many long conversations that were, however, marked more by silence than by speech. As Ellmann entertainingly describes it:

> Beckett was addicted to silences,[70] and so was Joyce; they engaged in conversations which consisted often of silences directed towards each other, both suffused with sadness, Beckett mostly for the world, Joyce mostly for himself. Joyce sat in his habitual posture, legs crossed, toe of the upper leg under the instep of the lower; Beckett, also tall and slender, fell into the same gesture. Joyce suddenly asked some such question as "How could the idealist Hume write a history?" Beckett replied, "A history of representations."[71]

This tendency to silence assumes vital significance in Beckett's novels, where Molloy, Malone, and the Unnamable are all striving for an end to speech; in the plays, "pause" or "silence" is one of the most frequent stage directions.[72]

Although both were writers, their discussions rarely centered on literature, a subject Joyce disliked and avoided—unless the work in question was his own.[73] After once listening to some intellectuals converse at a party, Joyce remarked to Beckett, "If only they'd talk about turnips!"[74]

Beckett's visits and conversations with Joyce did not go unnoticed, especially by Joyce's daughter, Lucia. A high-strung and nervous girl, Lucia quickly fell in love with the tall blue-eyed Irishman, but unfortunately for her the passion was not returned. Out of a kindness that came naturally to him, Beckett took Lucia to restaurants and theaters, and was present at her last dance recital, an international competition held at the Bal Bullier in Brussels on 28 May 1929. Lucia appeared dressed in a "shimmering silver fish costume"[75] of her own design. Although she did not win first prize, she did captivate many of the audience who shouted, "Nous reclâmons l'Irlandaise," to the great pleasure of Joyce.[76]

Even though he "sometimes felt he should have more than a casual interest in this tortured and blocked replica of genius,"[77] Beckett was unable to feel anything more than friendship and affection[78] for the daughter of his friend. Unfortunately, his well-meant attentions only increased Lucia's emotional involvement, and it was finally necessary to tell her that he came to the apartment to see her father.[79] Lucia felt the rebuff keenly, and took out her frustration on her family. At least one fight with Nora was "precipitated by an irrational suspicion that her mother had broken up her friendship with [Beckett]."[80] Shortly after this, in March of 1932, Lucia became engaged to Alex Ponisovsky, the young brother-in-law of Paul Léon, but she still thought more about Beckett than her fiancé.[81] The engagement was "forgotten" when Lucia suffered the first of many bouts of schizophrenia. Beckett, however, remained in her memory, and when in 1935 she was invited by Harriet Weaver to come to her in London for a visit, Lucia eagerly accepted, partly motivated by the hope of seeing Beckett, who was then there.[82]

Beckett's pity and concern for his friend's mentally ill daughter have not left him even now. In 1961 he was interviewed for the French journal *Les Nouvelles Littéraires* by Gabriel d'Aubarède, who mentioned that he had known the two children of James Joyce. "Ah!", Beckett replied, "vous avez connu Georges et cette pauvre Lucia?" When d'Aubarède asked him, "Pourquoi pauvre Lucia?" Beckett simply made "un geste intraduisible."[83] Even more recently, Patric Farrell reports that he and his wife spent Bloomsday of 1965 in Paris with Beckett, who inquired about Lucia (then, and now, at Saint Andrew's Hospital, Northampton, England). Learning that the Farrells planned to visit her, he urged them to take with them some perfume or other feminine fineries. Lucia was somehow misinformed and believed that Beckett was also coming to see her. When that hope was dashed her elation turned into depression.[84]

His inability to have a romantic relationship with Lucia did not affect Beckett's friendship with her father. At about the time that he disillusioned Lucia about the nature of his interest in the family, Beckett wrote an acrostic on Joyce's name for him. "Home Olga," as the poem is called, was written in 1932, but, because it is little known and is not included with Beckett's published poems, I present it in full here:

J might be made sit up for a jade of hope (and
      exile, don't you know)
And Jesus and Jesuits juggernauted in the haemor-
      rhoidal isle,
Modo et forma anal maiden, giggling to death in
      stomacho.
E for the erythrite of love and silence and the
      sweet noo style,
Swoops and loops of love and silence in the eye of
      the sun and view of the mew,
Juvante Jah and a Jain or two and the tip of a
      friendly yiddophile.
O for an opal of faith and cunning winking adieu,
      adieu, adieu;
Yesterday shall be tomorrow, riddle me that my
      rapparee;
Che sarà sarà che fu, there's more than Homer knows
      how to spew,
Exempli gratia: ecce himself and the pickthank agnus—
      e.o.o.e.[85]

The title, an anagram of Homo Logos (Word Man), and a pun on *homologous*, implies the connection between Joyce and Christ that Beckett will make more explicit in the poem. It has two other possible sources as well. Lawrence Harvey reveals that there was a private joke, known to intimates in Paris in the early thirties. At a party in Ireland, so the story goes, a bored husband abruptly fetched his wife's coat and his own and, saying "Home Olga!" whisked her away without even permitting her to say goodbye. "At subsequent parties the phrase signalled ennui and became a covert call for relief and regroupment at a pre-selected cafe."[86] Beckett also may have had in mind *Finnegans Wake* itself. Page 256, line 11, contains the phrase "Home all go" (possibly a reference to the "Home Olga!" joke) and it is followed three lines later with "For here the holy language" (256.14), which itself is appropriate to the Joyce-Christ identification.[87]

The poem begins with Joyce's—and Beckett's—expatriate state. "Exile" is mentioned specifically in the first line, and is suggested throughout the acrostic by references to Stephen Dedalus's other two weapons: "silence (ll. 4 and 5) and "cunning" (l. 7). Ireland and the reasons for flight to the Continent are given in lines 2 and 3: Catholic ("Jesus and Jesuits juggernauted") and sterile (an "anal maiden"), the land of Cuchulain and Parnell is no longer an emerald but a "haemorrhoidal isle" (l. 2), where its citizens are "giggling to death in stomacho" (l. 3). This last may be an allusion "to a certain atmosphere then prevalent in Dublin pubs, described by Beckett as 'miserable, provincial sneering and quipping at everything.'"[88] "Jesuit" recalls Buck Mulligan's epithet for Stephen, "fearful jesuit,"[89] and Leopold Bloom is, by analogy, (Jesus) Christ. Line 2, then, suggests the world of *Ulysses* as well as the land it savagely indicts.

Dante, along with Ibsen, was Joyce's literary idol, and Beckett, in line 4, appropriately uses an allusion to the Florentine ("the sweet noo style") to characterize Joyce's own technical innovations. The very next line may portray a more contemporary master-disciple relationship—that of Joyce to Beckett. If we read "I" for "eye" and "son" for "sun," the sense of line 5 becomes this: Beckett is, metaphorically speaking, a son to father Joyce for whom he has "Swoops and loops of love."[90] And, indeed, line 6 goes on to present Joyce as God the Father. "Jah" from "Yahweh" denotes the Judaeo-Christian deity, "Jain" is a reference to the Indian religion of Jainism, and the "tip of a friendly yiddophile" recalls again the God of the Old Testament whom Stephen Dedalus dubbed a "collector of prepuces."[91] It is equally important to recognize that "eye of the sun" is close to "Oxen of the Sun," and that the pronunciation of "sun" brings to mind the entire father-son theme of *Ulysses*. "A Jain or two," when coupled with the "giggling" of line three, sounds suspiciously like the two girls in *Finnegans Wake*. Beckett, like Joyce, wrote on not one but many levels.

The thrice-repeated "adieu" in line 7 shows Beckett's familiarity with *Chamber Music*;[92] it comes, in fact, from one of Joyce's favorite poems in that collection, the one that begins "Bid adieu, adieu, adieu,/ Bid adieu to girlish days" (no. XI).[93] Line 8 continues the temporal theme, but significantly restates it in Joycean-Viconian terms: "yesterday shall be tomorrow." In the words of one critic, "The implication is of a Viconian, cyclical resurrection, presumably through the Logos that tells tales (pickthank)."[94] As Lawrence Harvey points out, the second part of the line, "riddle me that my rapparee," echoes a passage from the end of the "Anna Livia Plurabelle" section that Beckett had helped to translate: "Latin me that, my Trinity scholard, . . ."[95] But Harvey fails to realize the real humor of the parody. Not only is Beckett imitating the *Wake,* but he is playing on the very line that Joyce included as a reference to him. He is truly a "Trinity scholard," and at the time was helping Joyce not with Latin but with another classical language, Greek.

Combining Dante and Vico, Joyce's two passions, Beckett next uses Italian to reiterate the Viconian philosophy. "Che sarà sarà che fu" (l. 9) ; because he knows this, Joyce is superior to that other blind (Greek!) writer, Homer. (And, by implication, *Ulysses* is a better book than the *Odyssey.*) Greater than the author of the *Iliad,* Joyce, a homo logos par excellence, is the peer of no less than the Son of God. "Ecce himself" (l. 10) puns on "Ecce homo" and uses the Irish idiom ("himself") to do so. As did the fifth line, the last line of the poem turns to Beckett's relationship with Joyce. If Joyce is Jesus, then Beckett is a lamb following his Shepherd, a "pickthank agnus."[96] Like both Joyce and Vico, Beckett liked to round things out. And so the poem ends with the commercial abbreviation, "e.o.o.e." for "errors or omissions excepted"—or, "ecce" with the "c's" made into spheres.

On 22 July 1932 Joyce wrote to Stuart Gilbert that he had shown the acrostic to Eugene and Maria Jolas:

The latter thought it poor, the former thinks it acid and not funny. I think it is all right—though if I may suggest anything, it seems to me "tickled to death" is better than "giggling to death" though the "g" is nearer "j."[97]

Aside from this slight criticism, Joyce seems to have been pleased by the poetic tribute and it was published on the occasion of his fifty-second birthday in 1934.[98]

While Harvey is mistaken in seeing the poem as "an admirer's farewell to the master,"[99] the acrostic did mark a separation between the two writers, albeit a geographical one. For, after a brief stay in Paris in the summer of 1932, during which time he did translations and wrote *Dream of Fair to Middling Women* at the Trianon Hotel on the rue de Vaugirard,[100] Beckett returned to Dublin via London. He remained there with his family until his father's death in June 1933. Deeply affected, Beckett left for London where he lived for nearly two years, and then, after having visited his mother for a few weeks in Ireland, again embarked for the Continent. This time he spent the next two years traveling around Europe, particularly in Germany.[101] By October of 1937 he had settled once more in Paris, at the Hotel Libéria on the rue de la Grande Chaumière in Montparnasse. The following spring he would move to a seventh-floor studio at 6 rue des Favorites, where, with the exception of the war years, he would stay until 1961. In Beckett's own words, these "Wanderjahre" were a time of "lostness, drifting around, seeing a few friends—a period of apathy and lethargy."[102] A poem of his, published a few years earlier, suggests that the journeying was perhaps partly motivated by a reaction against the academic life:

> Spend the years of learning squandering
> Courage for the years of wandering
> Through the world politely turning
> From the loutishness of learning.[103]

When Beckett returned to settle in Paris he met Peggy Guggenheim, who provides a fascinating if questionable picture of what he was like in the thirties. Calling him Oblomov, after the title character in Goncharov's novel who also used to stay in bed till well into the afternoon,[104] she goes on to describe Beckett as

> a tall, lanky Irishman of about thirty with enormous green [!] eyes that never looked at you. He wore spectacles, and always seemed to be far away solving some intellectual problem; he spoke very seldom and never said anything stupid. He was excessively polite, but rather awkward. He dressed badly in tight-fitting French clothes and had no vanity about his appearance. Oblomov accepted life fatalistically, as he never seemed to think he could alter anything. He was a frustrated writer, a pure intellectual.[105]

Beckett, she says, "had an enormous passion for James Joyce"[106] and was "a sort of slave"[107] to him. Though he "had little vitality and always believed in following the path of least resistance . . . he was prepared to do anything for Joyce." This annoyed Peggy, because Oblomov was "always leaving [her] to see his great idol" and consequently she was "very jealous." "Joyce," she concludes, "loved Oblomov as a son."[108]

In 1937 the lives of Joyce and Beckett crossed in a strange fashion. Oliver St. John Gogarty, Joyce's arch-enemy who had "evicted" him from the Martello Tower, wrote a volume of memoirs entitled *As I Was Going Down Sackville Street.* The reviewer in the London *Times* found the book full of "Celtic exuberance and high-spirited contrariness" and "well calculated to disconcert the conventional reader of social memoirs."[109] *Disconcert* proved to be a mild word for what ensued, for in the book Gogarty had included a ballad about "two Jews . . . in Sackville Street." The entire song was highly derogatory, but there were two especially defamatory stanzas:

> They kept a shop for objects wrought
> By masters famed of old,
> Where you, no matter what you bought
> Were *genuinely* sold.

> But Willy spent the sesterces
>   And brought on strange disasters
> Because he sought new mistresses
>   More keenly than old masters.[110]

There were, indeed, two Jews, Henry Sinclair and his late brother, William, who had kept an antique shop on Sackville Street. As if the ballad were not enough to enrage them, Gogarty also spoke of their grandfather,

> an old usurer who had eyes like a pair of periwinkles on which somebody had been experimenting with a pin, and a nose like a shrunken tomato, one side of which swung independently of the other. The older he grew the more he pursued the immature, and enticed little girls into his office.[111]

Henry Sinclair sued Gogarty for libel and applied for an injunction against further publication of the book, which was granted. The trial, in November 1937, was the sensation of Dublin, with people queuing up early in the morning in order to be allowed to observe it. Beckett was a witness for the prosecution, testifying that he had been able to identify Sinclair from the passages in the book. J. M. Fitzgerald, Gogarty's lawyer, tried to discredit Beckett's testimony by pointing out that William Sinclair's widow was his aunt,[112] and that he, Beckett, had written obscene books, such as an essay on "Marcel Prowst"[113] and a blasphemous collection of stories (*More Pricks Than Kicks* —the title was too shocking to be pronounced in court) that had been banned in Ireland within six months of its publication.

While Gogarty had clearly written a libelous book, the trial itself did not seem to be any the less slanderous. Albert Wood, the attorney for Sinclair, vilified Gogarty in his opening statement as having "a pen dipped in the scourings of a putrid and amoral mind."[114] Fitzgerald, not to be outdone, in his speech singled out Beckett as belonging "to a coterie of bawds and blasphemers," and said "he might well have stayed in Paris."[115] And whereas Fitzgerald made anti-Semitic remarks throughout the trial, Wood blatantly appealed to a prejudice in reverse by intimating to the jury that unless they decided in favor of Sinclair they would be guilty of anti-Semitism themselves.[116]

The trial finally ended with Sinclair victorious. Further publication of the book was prevented and Gogarty was forced to pay £900 for damages to the reputation of Henry Sinclair, as well as all court costs. Beckett returned to Paris with a bitter taste in his mouth, confirmed both in his opinion of Ireland and in his decision to live abroad.

Gogarty was bitter, too, and remained so for many years thereafter. In 1956 he wrote to Ulick O'Connor in reference to a talk given on the Third Programme of the BBC. O'Connor had praised Beckett's play *Waiting For Godot,* and Gogarty expressed regret that he had done so, saying, "It's nothing but a long wail."[117]

Although there is no record of Beckett's discussing the trial with Joyce, it is highly likely that he did. Henry Sinclair was an old friend of Joyce's and it was either he or his brother William who had lent Joyce ten shillings on his elopement with Nora.[118] Joyce remembered the favor and years later paid it back by including the donor in *Ulysses.* During the course of the day, Bloom reminds himself to "have a chat with young Sinclair. . . . Well-mannered fellow."[119] With his strong interest in old friends and his ever-present desire to settle old scores, it is questionable in which event Joyce took more pleasure—the Sinclairs vindicated or Gogarty defeated.

After the trial was over, Beckett was once more in Paris. On a night in December 1937 he was stabbed in the ribs on the Avenue d'Orléans. The assailant, an unknown madman, had no apparent reason for the attack; Beckett refused to press charges, even though the knife had punctured a lung and he had to be hospitalized. Lucia, Nora, and Joyce visited him,[120] and the last, concerned over his friend's condition, telephoned doctors in London.[121]

An incident that occurred at this time illustrates how Beckett refused to exploit his relationship with Joyce. While Routledge was negotiating for the English publication of *Murphy,* the

Viking Press of New York heard about the book and became interested in bringing it out in America. It was suggested to Beckett that he ask Joyce to intercede on his behalf with Viking, but Beckett refused to do so. He also made it clear that he did not want any one else to ask Joyce for the favor either.[122]

When *Murphy* did come out later that year, Beckett gave Joyce a copy and he responded with a limerick beginning "There was a young fellow called Murphy. . . ."[123] In fact, Joyce thought so highly of Beckett's first novel, that he committed the passage on the disposal of Murphy's body to memory.[124]

On February 2 Radio Eireann marked Joyce's fifty-sixth birthday with a program dedicated to him. Many friends, including Beckett, gathered at Joyce's apartment to hear the broadcast and then went on to the Jolas flat for a prearranged dinner party and more celebration. Beckett, according to Peggy Guggenheim, had been "in a state of great excitement about suitable gifts. He went with me and made me buy a blackthorn stick. As for his own present, he wished to give Joyce some Swiss wine, Joyce's favorite beverage."[125] Whether because of the wine or not, the party, like the *Déjeuner Ulysse* eleven years earlier, was a great success. There was dancing—by Joyce—and singing until 3:00 A.M. After seeing the still-singing Joyce home, the guests all went out for a nightcap before retiring.[126]

Such pleasant evenings were soon to end. Hitler was pursuing his quest for power with great success, and the political situation was increasingly ominous. Beckett, more aware of world events than one might think, discussed the Nazi persecution of the Jews with Joyce. But the man who had created Leopold Bloom could only remark that such acts of intolerance were not new.[127] Perhaps viewing the world from a Viconian height necessitated such a loss of perspective; in an eternally unchanging round of existence, no crisis or fall seems worse than any other—and there is always the rise to come.

Joyce did, however, have personal problems that demanded his attention and concern. Despite his fame and the simultaneous publication on 4 May 1939 of *Finnegans Wake* in New York and

London, he was, as always, in financial difficulties. Beckett, to whom he confided that it might soon be necessary for him to teach, made inquiries and discovered that the University of Capetown in South Africa needed a lecturer in Italian. Joyce considered the possibility for a few days, but decided against it when he heard how frequent thunderstorms were there.[128]

The political storm soon displaced all other disturbances, and even Joyce was forced to pay it heed. By October of 1939 the situation in Paris had gravely deteriorated. Joyce's friends had either already left the city or were planning to leave. Nora felt housekeeping to be an unnecessary burden and the Joyces decided to transfer themselves to the Hotel Lutétia. Beckett helped with the moving and went with Joyce to the flat for some books. "Extremely nervous," Joyce "jumped to the piano and sang at the top of his voice for half an hour. 'What is the use of this war?' he demanded of Beckett, who thought it had a use and a reason; Joyce was convinced it had none."[129]

Giorgio and his wife, Helen, had separated. When she became ill, their son, Stephen, was cared for by his grandparents. In November Joyce sent Stephen away from Paris, to the village of Saint-Gerand-le-Puy near Vichy, where Maria Jolas had resituated her Ecole Bilingue. Mrs. Jolas invited the Joyces and Giorgio to come there for Christmas. Before he left, Joyce, who had been drinking and spending heavily, told Beckett, "with something like satisfaction in his voice, 'We're going downhill fast.' "[130] Beckett himself was subsequently asked down for the holidays. "By now, for Joyce, Sam had become a close friend and his presence at that moment of personal distress and general anxiety was particularly welcome."[131]

The Joyces also spent Easter of 1940 with Mrs. Jolas and Beckett again came down. When he arrived, Joyce mentioned their going to Moulins for the church services, but the plan was never carried out.[132] It was at this time that Joyce arranged for Valery Larbaud to cash a check for Beckett, who was also in financial straits.[133]

Although he did not know it then, that holiday of spiritual

rebirth and personal celebration[134] would be Beckett's last sight
of Joyce. When his friend died in Zurich on 13 January 1941,
the war prevented Beckett from attending the funeral. He has
since, however, kept in contact with Joyce's family. Despite
Lucia's romantic disappointment, Giorgio remained friends with
Beckett, as apparently did his son Stephen, at whose wedding to
Solange Raytchine on 15 April 1955 Beckett was best man.[135]

There is one curious postscript: some time after Joyce's death,
Beckett was authorized to inquire in Ireland about the possibility
of transferring Joyce's remains to Dublin. Alan Simpson detected "perverse pleasure" on Beckett's part when he related
that "the answer had been no."[136] Joyce, like Beckett, is still an
exile.

2

Apprenticeship: 1929-1934

Imitation is the sincerest form of admiration, and Beckett's unequivocal approval of Joyce's *Work in Progress* (as expressed in "Dante . . . Bruno. Vico . . Joyce") soon reflected itself in his own literary efforts. For the next five years, 1929 to 1934, in a conscious and deliberate attempt to emulate Joyce's style, Beckett filled his prose and poetry with puns, witty analogies, multilingual allusions, and occasional but unmistakable references to Joyce's own works. Not so readily apparent, but perhaps more significant with regard to the future novels and plays, is the presence in these early writings of peculiarly Joycean themes and motifs. All this is not to imply that Beckett's first stories and poems are totally derivative and devoid of any originality. On the contrary, characters such as Belacqua Shuah and Ruby Tough are immediately recognizable as unique literary creations, different in concept and execution from any of Joyce's—and, indeed, from any other author's. What is to be emphasized, however, is that at no other time in his writing career would Joyce's stylistic influence so overtly dominate Beckett as it did in the 1930s.

Before we consider Beckett's first poem, "Whoroscope," it might be well to glance at his second venture into literary criticism, an essay on Marcel Proust written in 1930, just one year after his tribute to Joyce was published in Eugene Jolas's *transition*. In this short book,[1] Beckett confines himself to a discussion of Proust's concept of time—a subject that was equally central to Joyce's own *Work in Progress*—with a brilliant exposition of the two Proustian corollaries, involuntary memory and habit. While entirely consistent with the theme of time as it is presented in *A la recherche du temps perdu*, Beckett's interpretation is even more revealing of his own thoughts and theories. Time, for Beckett as it certainly was for Joyce and probably for Giordano Bruno, is a "double-headed monster of damnation and salvation" (*P*, p. 1), a "condition of resurrection because an instrument of death" (*P*, p. 22). But, whereas Joyce contemplated the inevitable round of birth, death, and rebirth with the gaiety of Yeats's Chinamen, taking the eternal sequence as a guarantee of eternal life ("Phall if you but will, rise you must"),[2] both Proust and Beckett, while "respect[ing] the dual significance of every condition and circumstance of life" (*P*, p. 52), nevertheless saw time as a "cancer" (*P*, p. 7), an agent of destruction and decay that traps man in a prison of unending change and deterioration:

> There is no escape from the hours and the days. Neither from tomorrow nor from yesterday. There is no escape from yesterday because yesterday has deformed us or been deformed by us. The mood is of no importance. Deformation has taken place. . . . We are not merely more weary because of yesterday, we are other, no longer what we were before the calamity of yesterday. (*P*, pp. 2–3)

The effect on the individual is to make him "the seat of a constant process of decantation" (*P*, p. 4), forever altering his personality, forever making him "other."[3] While this at first seems to resemble Joyce's Viconian mutations, there is a vital difference. Earwicker, an allegorical figure, is literally Everyman: he is Finn MacCool, King Mark, Wellington, Adam, and a hundred other figures of fact and fiction all rolled into one. And he is all of them *at the same time*! In the Beckettian and Proustian worlds, however, there is no such stasis of personality, only the struggle to achieve it. Proust's people stop time by transcending it through involuntary memory, which recalls the past from a stimulus in the present (e.g., the famous example of the madeleine, which re-creates Combray for narrator and reader alike). This Proustian effort "to rescue and preserve the self from time was Beckett's cue. For him, as for Proust, the self fought steadily to avoid immersion in nonentity, to assert identity."[4] Where Joyce would glorify motion in time, exulting in the stillness that is the unalterable center of the "vicociclometer,"[5] Beckett would see only time's snare: the change that corrupts the human self, condemns it to become, but prevents it from ever being. More than a difference in method between allegory and nonallegory, these views of Joyce and Beckett on time are distinctions in philosophy and *Weltanschauung*. The result is two literatures that, while they both contemplate a circular universe, do so from divergent vantage points. Paradoxically, although he will eventually reject Joyce's approach, Beckett will strive for the stasis that is inherent in his friend's system. Plus ça change, plus c'est la même chose.

There is little in the critical content of Beckett's essay to suggest any influence of Joyce. Indeed, the aristocrats of Proust's novels and the middle-class Dubliners of Joyce's have as little in common as the authors themselves did,[6] so it is not likely that Joyce would have read the Frenchman with any great degree of attention. But Beckett obviously read Proust with Joyce in mind, for he does not fail to mention Madame de Cambremer, "whose name, as Oriane de Guermantes observes to Swann, stops just in time" (*P*, p. 38). The sentence is one that Joyce would have noticed, and *le mot de Cambronne*—the same one Mme. de Guermantes was thinking of when she made her remark to Swann—figures prominently in *Finnegans Wake*.

In addition to the hidden puns in Proust's work, Beckett included those of others and his own in the essay. By mistake, the original Chatto and Windus edition excluded the introductory quotation from Leopardi, "E fango è il mondo," that the Grove Press reprinting later restored. A. J. Leventhal, a close friend of Beckett's, writes that "this should not have been omitted if only out of piety to the memory of Joyce who loved it because of the possible *double entendre*."[7] Later in the essay Beckett refers to two Proustian characters as "the Duchesse de Caca or the Princesse de Pipi" (*P*, p. 58). The scatological puns are ones that Joyce would have appreciated, and Beckett must have been fond of the first one himself because he used it again in *Molloy*.[8]

Finally, there is one curious coincidence. On page 56, Beckett mentions Dostoevski's novel *Crime and Punishment*, commenting that it is "a masterpiece that contains no allusion to either crime or punishment." Joyce, once teased by his son Giorgio, who pretended to think more highly of the Russian's work than that of his father, replied to the same effect.[9]

"Whoroscope" (1930)

Winner of Nancy Cunard's Hours Press competition for a poem on time, "Whoroscope" nearly was not. Beckett wrote it the night before the contest deadline and deposited it in Miss Cunard's mailbox at dawn. Although he based the 98-line poem on Adrien Baillet's seventeenth-century biography of Descartes, Beckett's real subject was time itself, lifetime to be exact. René Descartes, Seigneur du Perron, could not tolerate an egg that had been sat on for less than eight days, and preferably ten. Using this fact as the metaphorical crux of his poem, Beckett transformed Descartes's own life, "*ab ovo* to death,"[10] into metrical art.[11]

Both Eliot and Joyce provided the young poet with inspiration. Taking a cue from *The Waste Land*, Beckett included more than two pages of learned footnotes on the more obscure lines. But if the scholarly supplement is Eliotesque, the stylistic substance is pure Joyce. Even the title, A. J. Leventhal admits, "might possibly have been different if there were no Joyce living in the quarter."[12] As it is, the word *Whoroscope*, while being the kind of pun Joyce relished and actually used,[13] is also functional in that it suggests the irony of the poem and anticipates its last line: Descartes, fearful of astrology, concealed his birthdate so that his horoscope could never be cast; his death was indeed a "second/starless inscrutable hour" (ll. 97–98) .

Notwithstanding Frederick Hoffman's contention that " 'Whoroscope' is much involved in the kind of dream elaboration that Joyce was developing,"[14] Joyce's real literary influence lies in the punning style that Beckett uses throughout the poem. John Fletcher notes that "lame puns like 'prostisciutto' (i.e., 'ham'/ 'harlot') and 'Jesuitasters' attempt to imitate Joyce,"[15] but the technique is both more pervasive and more wittily employed than these examples would indicate.

Because, in Beckett's own words, "the shuttle of a ripening egg comb[ed] the warp of [Descartes's] days" (Notes, p. 16) , most of the poem's puns and images center upon food, especially those associated with eggs. "In the name of Bacon will you chicken me up that egg" (l. 66) , cries Descartes. Earlier there are references to the "Porca Madonna" (l. 8) , "a little green fry or a mushroomy one" (l. 12: omelettes) , "hen-and-a-half ones" (l. 19) , "burning liver" (l. 25) , "fruit" (l. 31) , "fish fork" (l. 88) , and "a sack-of-potatoey charging Pretender" (l. 9) .

Intertwined with the food imagery are references to Catholicism, Descartes's faith and the predominant one of Ireland as well. Beckett's religious puns, like Joyce's, are both witty and aggressive. He plays on a phrase from St. Augustine's *Confessions,* "He tolle'd and legge'd," in line 75, and manages to parody simultaneously Descartes's famous philosophical axiom, "cogito, ergo sum," and Augustine's syntactically similar but lesser-known one, "si fallor, sum," in "Fallor, ergo sum" (l. 73) . There is a blasphemous allusion to the Virgin as the "Porca Madonna" (l. 8) , and, between sly references to "Jesuitasters" (l. 51) and Christ as both fish and hen ("Kip of Christ hatch it!" l. 49) , a Joycean (and ancient) pun on "one sun's drowning" (l. 50) . La Flèche, the Jesuit college Descartes attended, is mentioned as "the crypt of the arrow" (l. 41) , and his pilgrimage to the Loreto Shrine is also included (ll. 46–47) . Passing from Old to New Testaments, line 69 goes from "Moses" to the "crucified" Christ, and, by line 76, Beckett has dressed Augustine in a "redemptorist waistcoat" (an allusion to his sudden conversion). The father-son theme is present in religious terms (see l. 50), and there is a brief mention of Descartes's own father, Joachim, whose name also suggests the biblical Joachim, husband to Anna and father of the Virgin Mary. Queen Christina of Sweden is characterized by a triple barrage of religious epithets. As "Rahab of the snows" (l. 91), she is the harlot of Jericho, and her refusal to allow Descartes to remain in bed till noon earns her the additional titles of "murdering matinal pope-confessed amazon" (l. 92) and "Christina the ripper" (l. 93).

"Chalice" and "tray" in line 64 not only suggest the Communion service, but provide the real key to Beckett's Joycean method in this poem. Both strands of imagery, condiments and Catholicism, are fused and re-fused in the allusion to the Eucharist, lines 60 to 64. "The watery Beaune," a red Burgundy of France, is wine to the wafer of "stale cubes of Hovis" (a whole-meal bread). But, as in *Finnegans Wake*, there is reversal. "Beaune," pronounced "bone," could also refer to the body of Christ, and "Hovis," or "eau de vie," to His blood.[16]

By permitting the egg of Descartes to hatch into the many food references of the poem, Beckett was duplicating Joyce's technique in the "Lestrygonians" episode of *Ulysses*, where Bloom's lunchtime hunger determines the imagery of the chapter.[17] By obliquely alluding to the Eucharist in terms of secular food and drink, Beckett was again imitating Joyce, whose constant teas, cocoas, biscuits, and rolls are all meant to evoke the presence or absence of spiritual communion. Finally, Beckett, like Joyce, constructed a work of several levels of meaning, all related and all interacting. The blood motif in "Whoroscope" was also, in a sense, a pervasive element in Descartes's own life. His illegitimate daughter, Francine, was "scourged by a fever to stagnant murky blood" (l. 35); he had attended La Flèche, where the heart of Henry IV resided after almost being lost, prematurely, to a Jesuit assassin; and, while he did not completely agree[18] with William Harvey's theory of the blood's circulation, Descartes thought the British scientist had "scored a triumph, and . . . should be recognized and honored as its discoverer."[19] (Descartes also had a private theory on Christ's body and blood in the Mass. He believed that wine and wafer underwent a process of "natural transubstantiation" whereby their surfaces remained the same, but their essence was miraculously transformed.)

Descartes's final association with the life fluid came in death. A medical practice of the time was blood-letting, or bleeding, in cases of severe illness. When Descartes lay dying, his physician wished to follow this procedure, but the philosopher refused to give his consent until the last moment. For a scholarly man, his was indeed a bloody end.

Echo's Bones and Other Precipitates (1935)

As Beckett's first poem exhibited definite Joycean techniques, so too his first volume of verse[20] is marked by puns, foreign words, religious imagery, and themes of exile and physical movement. Such poetic concerns and devices are, of course, also present in the works of nearly all Beckett's contemporaries, especially Ezra Pound and T. S. Eliot, to name only two outstanding examples. But Beckett's personal relationship with Joyce and the obviously close study he gave to the master's works, make it more than likely that Joyce's was the predominant literary influence on him.

The book's title, evidence of the literary turn of Beckett's mind, is derived from the myth of the nymph Echo. According to Longus, a Greek romancer of the second or third century A.D., the story is one of crime and punishment. Echo, having spurned the love of the god Pan, was torn limb from limb. Fragments of her body were buried in the earth and given the power of song. Ovid's more famous version of the tale traces Echo's fate to her clever duplicity. Loyal to her lord, she chattered and covered up Jupiter's amours with the other mountain nymphs. Juno, angered at this aid to adultery, made Echo love Narcissus, who loved only himself. The nymph pined away in unrequited love; only her bones and voice were left to sing on.

The thirteen poems of the collection are not fragments resulting from precipitate writing. Carefully crafted with attention to language and structure, they contain scattered details from the author's personal life, one of Beckett's rare violations of his own privacy. In this he differs significantly from Joyce, who, though a reticent man in life, was extremely vocal about that life in his art, using it and reusing it throughout his works. Beckett, on the other hand, although he utilizes the events of his life in his novels and plays, does so much more subtly than Joyce. Nor does he depend on them to such a great extent, and the actual experiences are often subordinate to the emotions they aroused. One such personal reference is especially interesting because it is presented in Joycean style with Ulyssean overtones. In "Sanies I," Beckett, returning to his home in the Dublin suburb of Foxrock, recalls his birth:

> back the shadows lengthen the sycamores are
> > sobbing
> to roly-poly oh to me a spanking boy
> buckets of fizz childbed is thirsty work
> for the midwife he is gory
> for the proud parent he washes down a gob
> > of gladness
> for footsore Achates also he pants his pleasure.
> > (ll. 26–31)

Language like "roly-poly oh to me a spanking boy" suggests the "Hoopsa, boyaboy, hoopsa!" with which the Oxen of the Sun chapter in *Ulysses* begins. Indeed, at the end of the poem Holles Street itself is mentioned (l. 49). Joyce's chapter is punctuated by the carousing and ale-drinking of the medical students and Stephen Dedalus; Beckett almost seems to acknowledge this when he says "buckets of fizz childbed is thirsty work" (l. 28).

The examples of *Dubliners* and *Ulysses* can also be discerned in the local color of the poems. Reading them is like taking a walking tour of Dublin. Sites and thoroughfares mentioned include: the Portobello Private Nursing Home, Parnell Bridge, canal, the Fox and Geese (a pub), Chapelizod, Kilmainhaim, the Liffey ("Enueg I"); O'Connell Bridge and Guinness's barges ("Enueg II"); Portrane, Donabate, Turvey Swords, and Holles Street ("Sanies I"); Butt Bridge, Bull Island, Poolbeg Lighthouse (all *Portrait* and *Ulysses* territory), Victoria Bridge, Ringsend Road, Sandymount, Irishtown, and Merrion Flats ("Serena III"). One poem, "Serena I," is set in London, but, although we read of the British Museum, Regents Park, Tower Bridge, and St. Paul's Cathedral, the atmosphere is that of Ireland and *Dubliners*. Beckett writes of a sterile, suffering world, "pressed down and bleeding" (l. 7), in which animals and humans alike are imprisoned[21] and man is brother to "the common housefly" (l. 47).

Always an outsider, especially when in his native land, Beckett, like Joyce, is an eternal exile. But whereas Joyce's exile dates from 1904, Beckett's started the day he was born. "Exeo in a spasm," he says in "Enueg I," referring to his departure from the Portobello Private Nursing Home, but suggesting his emergence from the womb as well. The poem then goes on to present a series of images all of which are states of exclusion from a desirable place, as if, subconsciously, Beckett wanted to be able to remain in Ireland. A child playing in one field is separated from another field where the narrator stands. "I was in that field before and I got put out," he explains, and, although he desires readmittance, he is afraid to attempt it. In the next section, "a lamentable family of grey verminous hens" is

> perishing out in the sunk field,
> trembling, half asleep, against the closed
>   door of a shed,
> with no means of roosting.
>
> (ll. 52–54)

And on the hill into Chapelizod there stands

> a small malevolent goat, exiled on the road,
> remotely pucking the gate of his field.
>   (ll. 63–64)

Ireland, all this seems to imply, is a country that exiles its own children, whether they leave for the Seine or choose to remain by the Liffey. Dublin itself, a circular city whose river recirculates "by a commodius vicus . . . back to Howth Castle and Environs,"[22] is an enclosed trap out of which not even the poet can break. For the narrator's journey, south out of Dublin, then west and back along the Liffey quays into the city proper, is a circle, ending where it began. Lawrence Harvey interprets this as an allusion to Dante's circles of Hell,[23] but the structural and thematic motif of circular return is one that Joyce used throughout his works. *Dubliners* starts and ends with death and sisters, and the sixth story, "Two Gallants," contains just such a looping stroll with both Lenehan and Corley returning to meet at the corner of Merrion Street. "Grace," which is structured according to the tripartite division of *The Divine Comedy*, contains many "rings" and "circles" of spectators, and in "The Dead" Gabriel Conroy tells of the old family horse, Johnny, that went "round and round" King Billy's statue.[24] *A Portrait of the Artist as a Young Man*, progressive and circular at once, begins with one father, Stephen's own, and ends with three: Mr. Dedalus, Christ, and the "old artificer."[25] In *Ulysses*, Joyce's circles once again provide significance and structure. Bloom's day is a double circle: around Stephen, whom he finally centers on, and back to Molly, who is his center and to whom his thoughts ever return. In addition, many individual chapters end where they began. By having Bloom leave Molly and, after some early morning shopping, return to her, Joyce mirrors the structure of the whole book in "Calypso." After his encounter with Gerty MacDowell, Bloom muses on the June many years ago when he courted Molly and concludes: "The year returns. History repeats itself."[26] "Circe" starts outside Bella Cohen's brothel with Cissey Caffrey and Privates Carr and Compton, all of whom are there for a reprise some hundred and seventy pages later. And of course, Molly's monologue encircles everything, going from "Yes" to "Yes . . . yes . . . yes . . . yes . . . yes . . . yes . . . yes . . . Yes," one for each of the eight sentences in the chapter.[27] In *Finnegans Wake,* Joyce accomplished what mathematicians have been unable to. Using Vico's four cycles of history, he squared the circle, creating "an engine with only one wheel. No spokes of course. The wheel is a perfect square."[28] Reading the *Wake* also becomes a circular operation: the last sentence is but the first part of the first. Again, it must be remembered that Joyce's circles are joyous as well as commodious. All-inclusive, they reaffirm birth and life in the face of inevitable but not permanent death. For Beckett, however, the circle of time and life is a cruel trap, a death that separates one from the real life beyond.

As if to stress the imprisonment that is existence, other poems, in addition to "Enueg I," are circuitously constructed. "The Vulture" goes from sky to sky, but the freedom this implies is false: all is "offal." "Enueg II" begins and ends with the face of the moon, still another natural circle, while "Alba" significantly progresses from "morning" to mourning (the last line is "and bulk dead").

Puns proliferate. "Enueg" could be "a new egg," an anagram for "genug" (German: enough), or a reference to a troubadour lyric form.[29] Lawrence Harvey finds climatic puns in "Sanies I." After the "sweet showers" of Chaucer in line one, comes the "Portrane" ("poured rain") and Beckett's own admonition: "Donabate" ("don't abate").[30] The title itself can denote a discharge, and in the first section we find "trees bleeding voiding . . . the highway" (l. 6). Later on there are "sparkling beestings" (l. 32: "beesting" is the first milk from a mammal after parturition). "Spy Wedsday," in line 22, links marriage to the betrayal of Christ by Judas, "since wedlock prepares the way for the Good Friday crucifixion of being born."[31]

"Sanies II" is slightly reminiscent of "Whoroscope" and

"Home Olga." Here, "red eggs" cause "henorrhoids" (l. 5).
"Frescoward" (l. 16) is a Joycean portmanteau word, and
Shakespeare's sonnet 116 is parodied in line 26: "suck is not
suck that alters. . . ."

The "damfool . . . bleating to be bloodied" in "Serena II"
(ll. 8–9) suggests a young horse or "dam-foal," and "able-bodied
swans" (l. 21) catches up the reader who would say "swains."
"Divine dogday" ("Malacoda," l. 22) combines hot summer days
and religious holiday in Joycean fashion.[32] The last poem,
"Echo's Bones," contains the triple pun "gantelope," which
mixes gauntlet, gant ("glove"), and antelope into one word.

Like Joyce, Beckett associated the color green with corruption
and decay. The old josser in "Encounter" has green eyes, and
the sea in *Ulysses* is described as "snotgreen." In "Enueg I," the
"stillborn evening" turns "a filthy green/manuring the night
fungus" (ll. 26–27), and "The great mushy toadstool" is "green-
black" (ll. 55–56). "Enueg II" contains the bizarre "green tulips"
(l. 24), and the bawd in "Dortmunder" "sustain[s] the jade
splinters/the scarred signaculum of purity . . ." (ll. 6–7). True,
the larches of Beckett's childhood are green in "Sanies I," but
"the sycomores are sobbing" (l. 26).

As Joyce did throughout *Portrait* and *Ulysses*, Beckett relates
sex and religion in "Dortmunder." The "red spire of sanctuary"
(l. 2) is without a doubt a church illuminated against a fiery
sunset, but red suggests other places as well. Indeed, two lines
later we come upon the "violet lamp . . . of the bawd" (l. 4), or
the whore of Babylon, who is symbolized by that color. "Scroll"
(l. 10) and "Habbakuk" (l. 12) further support the biblical
imagery, but the bawd's "signaculum of purity" is "scarred" (l.
7) and, unlike Echo, she does not sing but "puts her lute away"
(l. 14).

In these poems Beckett begins to include words from foreign
languages. Eliot, in *The Waste Land* and his Sweeney poems,
was the first modern to seize upon this device, but it was employed to more humorous ends by Joyce in *Finnegans Wake*.
Just back from a stay in Germany, Beckett included some of

that country's native words in "Sanies I": "Ritter" (l. 4), "müde" (l. 9), and "Stürmers" (l. 42). In "Sanies II" he becomes even more multilingual, mixing Italian, Latin, and French with a sophisticated English vocabulary:

> quick quick the cavaletto supplejacks for
>   mumbo-jumbo
> vivas puellas mortui incurrrrrsant boves
> oh subito subito ere she recover the cang
>   bamboo for bastinado
> a bitter moon fessade à la mode.
>   (ll. 34–37)

Echo's Bones, then, are poetic precipitates of many of Joyce's literary techniques. Self-contained, they incorporate the structural and thematic motif of circular movement that pervades Joyce's entire work and that will come to dominate Beckett's own canon of novels and plays.

Text; "Sedendo et Quiescendo" (1932)

An interesting prologue to Beckett's short stories is the brief prose passage entitled simply "Text."[33] The 34-line piece, published in *The New Review* of April 1932 is given in full below:

Text

	Come come and cull me bonny
	bony doublebed cony swiftly my
	springal and my thin Kerry twin-
	gle-twangler comfort my days of
5	roses days of beauty week of red-
	ness with mad shame to my lips of
	shame to my shamehill for the
	newest news the shemost of she-
	news is I'm lust-be-lepered and un-
10	well oh I'd rather be a sparrow
	for my puckfisted coxcomb bird to bird
	and branch or a coalcave with goldy
	veins for my wicked doty's poty-
	stick trimly to besom gone the hart-

15   shorn and the cowslip wine gone
        and the lettuce nibbled up nibbled
        up and gone nor the last beauty day
        of the red time opened its rose and
        struck with its thorn oh I'm all of
20   a galimaufry or a salady salma-
        fundi singly and single to bed she
        said I'll have no toadspit about this
        house and whose quab was I I'd
        like to know that from my cheerfully
25   cornuted Dublin landloper
        and whose foal hackney mare toing
        the line like a Viennese Taubchen
        take my tip and clap a padlock on
        your Greek galligaskins before I'm
30   quick and living in hope and glad
        to go snacks with my twingle-
        twangler and grow grow into the
        earth mother of whom clapdish and
        foreshop.

One reading is enough to discover that Beckett has here essayed a lyrical and direct imitation of Joyce's *Finnegans Wake* style. Marked by symmetry and repetition, the passage opens with the words "Come come" and closes with "grow grow" ("go go"), contraries that recall Bruno and predict Beckett's 1968 dramaticule, *Come and Go*. Verbal duplication continues via phonetics—"bonny bony"—and soon we have a "doublebed" for a "thin . . . twingle-twangler" who will, nevertheless, go "singly and single to bed" (l. 21). "Days of roses" (ll. 4–5) will be matched up with wine some ten lines later; "beauty week" (l. 5) is reduced to "beauty day" (l. 17); and "redness" (ll. 5–6) becomes a shorter "red time" (l. 18). The world is mutable, "nibbled up nibbled up and gone" (ll. 16–17), and Beckett presents us with a consistent but shifting animal and vegetable imagery that suggests the Protean transformations of the dog in the third chapter of *Ulysses*. A "cony" (l. 2), or rabbit, changes to a "Kerry" cow or bitch (l. 3). The speaker would rather be a "sparrow" (l. 10) or a bird with "goldy veins" (ll.

12–13), perhaps Yeats's golden bird of Byzantium, but seems to become a squab (l. 23: "whose quab was I . . ."), and then a "foal hackney mare" (l. 26) before he finally changes into a small Viennese dove (l. 27). "Hartshorn" (ll. 14–15), or royal fern, "cowslip" (l. 15), and "lettuce" (l. 16) all go to make a mixture ("galimaufry," l. 20) or "salady salmafundi" (a salmagundi is a salad plate) that recalls the "funferall" of *Finnegans Wake*. Lines 28 to 34 are a description of the "lust-be-lepered" (l. 9) speaker making love to his "springal" (l. 3): he will "grow grow into the earth mother" (ll. 32–33), who carries the almsplate or "clapdish" associated with the leper.

While not so witty as *Work in Progress, Text* has internal cohesion and a lilting musical rhythm not unworthy of the French translator of "Anna Livia Plurabelle," or of Joyce himself. It will remain Beckett's most serious and extreme attempt to emulate Joyce's style, but, although *Text* proved his ability to write in such a manner, it probably also convinced Beckett that Joyce's techniques could not be entirely his own. "Sedendo et Quiescendo," a short story published at this time, does not have the verbal density of *Text,* and many of the sentences are more contrived than functional, but Beckett's prose does exhibit Joycean characteristics to the extent he found congenial in *Echo's Bones.*

Included in the March 1932 issue of *transition,* the story has as its hero Belacqua Shuah, the central character of *More Pricks Than Kicks,* which volume of short stories Beckett would publish two years later in 1934. In this story[34] Belacqua has arrived in Germany for a reunion with his girl friend, the Smeraldina-Rima, whose passionate love letter to him is included in *More Pricks Than Kicks.* We witness their meeting at the railroad station, and read of their cab ride back to her (?) apartment. That is the entire action, but there are several descriptive digressions, inserted, one suspects, more for style than for content. The language is playful and punny, mocking the romantic nature of the reconciliation: "The bright beer goes like water through the near-sighted Frankfort porter," (p.

13), writes Beckett, in obvious parody of Eliot's *Waste Land* lines on Mrs. Porter and her daughter.[35] Later he speaks of "A sentimental coagulum, sir, that biggers descruption" (p. 17), and "Augen Celeryice" (p. 18). Like Joyce, he can pun in two languages at once: "the others do the streets but I go and *dien* in the *furchtbar* . . ."; "I'll send you a *Schein* when I have a *Schwips*" (p. 17; italics mine). *Ich dien* or "I serve" is the motto of the Prince of Wales, but Beckett may also be punning on Stephen Dedalus's—and Lucifer's—oath of nonallegiance: "*non serviam*"). German is mixed with French and English for a polyglot effect much as in the "Sanies" poems or *Work In Progress* itself:

> Cosi fan tutti with the magic flute (p. 13) viewed from a very special Blickpunkt . . .
> Vie de taxi. Je t'adore à l'égal (p. 14) Ausgang, on the right Rouletabille. . . . Crémieux (p. 15)
> whorchen (p. 18).

Joycean allusions play their part in this derivative prose, and at one point Beckett baldly asks, "do you recognize the style?" (p. 19). The Smeraldina-Rima, like Molly Bloom, has "two great melons" for buttocks (p. 13), and Belacqua seems guilty of a sin, the vicarious nature of which is akin to Earwicker's:

> you see he led a fairly small fleshly maiden I might have said Jungfrau into the wood I might have said Wald and creeped and peeped at the Sabbath fornications instead of. (pp. 18–20)

Some references seem to be to Joyce himself: "I once wrote a poem . . . on him" (p. 15) most probably refers to "Home Olga", and "Randygasp of ruthilarity in honour of private joke" (p. 19) is unmistakably similar in sound to the *lilliata rutilantium* refrain of *Ulysses*. In spite of some excellent passages, however—"he was continent and he was not sustenant" (p. 19) is one—the story is diffuse and lacks a real thematic center. Beckett showed good judgment by not including it in

More Pricks Than Kicks, a superior book that will be considered next.

More Pricks Than Kicks (1934)

Out of print for many years, *More Pricks Than Kicks* has been reissued by Grove Press in their complete edition of Beckett's works. The stories, strange to anyone who has read just the trilogy or *Comment c'est,* but not to those who have sampled the delights of *Murphy,* have worn well. Light, bright, and sparkling, they show the comic side of Beckett's nature and reveal his literary debt to Joyce. Like Joyce's first published book, Beckett's is also a collection of short stories with Dublin as an important background. Unlike *Dubliners,* however, which is really a portrait of a city as a paralyzed and provincial metropolis, *Pricks,* although it uses the geography of Beckett's birthplace,[36] and occasionally mocks it, actually centers upon its hero, Belacqua Shuah, whose dominating presence—and absence (in "The Smeraldina's Billet Doux" and "Draff")—binds the ten stories together. The book's unity is further reinforced by the repeated presence of certain individual characters: Alba Perdue, McCabe the murderer, Hairy Quin, and a blind beggar in a wheelchair. This device, giving the effect of a real world with real people, is one that Beckett probably borrowed from Joyce. McCoy, Power, Cunningham, Joe Hynes, and Tom Kernan are just some of the *Dubliners* who reappear in *Ulysses*; and, of course, we have two books in which to follow the fortunes of Stephen Dedalus.

Dubliners moves from the death of Father Flynn to all "The Dead" of Dublin. *Pricks,* equally circular, begins with the deaths of a lobster and murderer, and ends with Belacqua's own demise. A comparison of Joyce's last story and Beckett's first reveals a remarkable similarity of technique as well. "Dante and the Lobster," though it has a totally different theme from "The Dead," is also structured around several motifs that, like the snow, subtly change their meaning as they reoccur. And there is even a Joycean epiphany of sorts at the end. Because

of these and other curious points of resemblance, a close examination of the two stories will be undertaken. First, however,
a few words on Beckett's hero, Belacqua Shuah.

An eccentric citizen, as we shall see, Belacqua is alienated
in mind and body not only from Dublin, but from all human
intercourse whatsoever. (It is one of the ironies of the book
that this asocial being marries three times and has at least two
affairs.) Although Frederick Hoffman believes that Belacqua is
"more or less based" on the similarly disaffected Stephen Dedalus,
he is closer to the truth when he adds that Beckett's hero lacks
the passionate joy and guilt in love of Joyce's.[37] Not so priggish
as Stephen, Belacqua also does not respond so intensely to the
world around him. The ringing challenge of Stephen's last diary
entries could never be his. At the same time, both young men
are, to some extent, autobiographical reflections of their creators.
Many of Stephen's experiences in *Portrait* were Joyce's own, and
Belacqua, like Beckett, adores Dante, is a strange partygoer,
and exercises a marked degree of indolence. Moreover, his initials
are the reverse of Beckett's.

"Dante and the Lobster" opens with Belacqua puzzling over
the moon passage in *The Divine Comedy.* So impenetrable is
the poetry that he is "stuck in the first of the canti," "so bogged
that he [can] move neither backward nor forward" (*MPTK,*
p. 9). This image of paralysis, to be further developed, recalls
the initial page of *Dubliners* and, indeed, the entire theme of
that book. Beckett's increasing concern with stasis and motion-
lessness may, in fact, owe a great deal to Joyce's moral history
of their native city.

The first sentence of Beckett's story also combines the contraries that Joyce and Bruno loved: "It was *morning* and
Belacqua was stuck in the first of the canti in the *moon*" (italics
mine).[38] Second, besides calling the reader's attention to the
tight time scheme of the story—an Aristotelian unity, it will
comprise morning, noon, and night of one day—that first line
and a half contains the dominant image of the tale. "Moon,"
circular like Dante's Hell and the "rounds" (*MPTK,* p. 11) of

bread that Belacqua will shortly have for his lunch, here
represents a self-enclosed enigma or "demonstration . . . of the
real facts" (MPTK, p. 9) that Belacqua's brain cannot penetrate
without help. Later, through the Cain and Abel motif, the moon
will become associated with murder, sin, and punishment, and
still later, when dusk falls and the moon rises, it will betoken
the questionable mercy of night and Divine Providence.

The stroke of noon interrupts Belacqua's studies, and he
proceeds to prepare his lunch. This midday meal, together with
his purchase of the lobster and the Italian lesson, constitutes
the crux of Belacqua's day. A tripartite division that parodies
The Divine Comedy, it also recalls Joyce's similar structuring
of his short story "Grace." If the meal represents the Inferno,
it is no surprise that Belacqua prefers his toast burned, perhaps
to correspond to the burning of sinners in Dante's Hell. But
the toast, blackened through and through, is also a "burnt of-
fering" (MPTK, p. 13), like Bloom's scorched kidney. Seasoning
the toast with enough salt and pepper to burn his own mouth
out, Belacqua takes it with him to a neighborhood grocery,
where he obtains his customary slab of rotten Gorgonzola cheese.
Leopold Bloom also has a Gorgonzola cheese sandwich (not
burnt) at Davy Byrne's. Could Belacqua's meal be a parody of
Bloom's breakfast and lunch? There are other details that suggest that Beckett may have had this in mind. Both Joyce and
Beckett minutely describe the preparation of the respective meals.
Bloom takes great care to cook his kidney properly, and it is
an accident that he does not remove it from the fire in time.
Beckett, on the other hand, deliberately sets out to ruin the
toast, and whereas Bloom cuts away the burnt portion of the
meat and gives it to the cat, Belacqua consciously refrains from
leaving even crumbs for the sparrows.

After finishing his lunch in a pub, Belacqua buys the lobster
he and his aunt will have for dinner, and then proceeds to
his three o'clock Italian lesson with the Signorina Ottolenghi.
Her office, being the front room off the hall, is associated in
Belacqua's mind with a vestibule. It may also be Beckett's

symbolic equivalent for Dante's antepurgatory, with the Ottolenghi as Belacqua's Vergil or guide. The lesson is interrupted
by the entrance of a French professor, Mademoiselle Glain, who
informs Belacqua that she has just prevented her cat from
tearing apart the package he left in the hall. After she leaves,
Belacqua turns to his teacher and asks, "Where were we?"
"Where are we ever?" cried the Ottolenghi, "where we were, as
we were" (*MPTK*, p. 20). Stasis and paralysis, like the snow of
"The Dead," are uniform over Ireland.

The lesson finished, Belacqua travels to his aunt's house.
There he learns what the man had meant when he said the
lobster was "lepping fresh" (*MPTK*, p. 18). In a parody of
Joyce's epiphany, with superficial but significant religious overtones added,[39] Belacqua discovers that the lobster is not dead.
"Christ!" he said, "it's alive" (*MPTK*, p. 21). Paralyzed, perhaps
by the shock of the news, Belacqua remains motionless as his
aunt takes the lobster into the kitchen to boil it. Apparently
"mercy and Godliness" (*MPTK*, p. 21) cannot, as he had hoped,
exist together. McCabe's petition for mercy is denied; he will
die in the morning. The lobster, after surviving the French-
woman's cat and Belacqua's "witless clutch" (*MPTK*, p. 22), will
also be killed. And, as Beckett himself comments at the end of
the story, "*it* is not" (*MPTK*, p. 22) a quick death. Indeed, if
Dante's *Comedy* ends with a *Paradiso*, Beckett's concludes with
an *Inferno*. From the bliss of the Italian lesson, Belacqua is
sent downward, "into the bowels of the earth, into the kitchen
in the basement" (*MPTK*, p. 22) of his aunt's house. An Italian's circles give way to an Irishman's. Dante's progression yields
to Joyce's cyclical movement—or stasis. But Beckett's pessimism
alters Joyce's schema too: instead of ending with rebirth, as
the author of *Finnegans Wake* always does, "Dante and the
Lobster" ends with death and a symbolic descent into the under-
world.

The superb Joycean coordination of motifs (moon, murder,
mercy) in this first story, does not, unfortunately, extend to
the nine others in the volume. Joyce's influence, however, is

noticeable everywhere. "Fingal," an account of Belacqua's outing with his girl friend Winnie Coates, is set in a Ulyssean landscape. Parodying Molly and Bloom on the Hill of Howth, Belacqua and Winnie are making love on the Hill of Wolves. Looking across at the Fingal coast, he sees "a magic land . . . a land of sanctuary" (*MPTK*, pp. 24–25), whereas she sees "nothing but the grey fields of serfs and the ramparts of ex-favourites" (*MPTK*, p. 26). And truly it is land barren to the point of nothingness, "its coast eaten away with creeks and marshes, tesserae of small fields, patches of wood springing up like a weed, the line of hills too low to close the view" (*MPTK*, p. 24). But perhaps this is what attracts Beckett's hero.

When Belacqua sights the round tower of the Portrane Lunatic Asylum, and Winnie reveals that she knows a doctor there, they decide to pay a visit. On the way, they pass several Martello towers, like the one Stephen shared with Mulligan and Haines in *Ulysses*.

Once at the asylum, Belacqua leaves Winnie in the somewhat lecherous hands of her friend, Dr. Sholto. He is supposedly going down to check a "point in connexion with the Church" (*MPTK*, p. 31) and will meet them later at the main gate. In reality, Belacqua appropriates a bicycle and heads straight for the tower, which Winnie learns from Dr. Sholto is the one that Swift kept his Stella in. Swift and his two girls are constantly referred to in the *Wake*, and by associating them here with a Joycean tower that he is extremely anxious for his hero to visit, Beckett may be making a subconscious statement about his feeling for Joyce and/or Joyce's art. This is only a suggestion, and there is no doubt that the central significance of the story is Belacqua's attempt, like Murphy's later one, to escape the pressures of the macrocosm by retiring to the small microcosm of the mind: a lunatic asylum.[40] However, the Joycean innuendoes are fascinating.

"Ding-Dong," the third story in the volume, is a treasury of motifs and symbols from Joyce's works. Unlike "Dante and the Lobster," this story begins with movement. Belacqua, we are told, believed that the best thing he had to do was to move constantly from place to place. . . . He was pleased to think that he could give what he called the Furies the slip by merely setting himself in motion. . . . The mere act of rising and going, irrespective of when and whither, did him good. (*MPTK,* p. 36)

The simplest form of such motion is that of departure and return, or, as Beckett puts it here, "boomerang, out and back." In spite of this internal imperative toward action, paralysis often afflicts Belacqua, and he finds himself in a stasis similar to the one he experienced reading Dante's canti of the moon: "he found he could not, any more than Buridan's ass, move to right or left, backward or forward" (*MPTK,* p. 39). Such stasis becomes, in turn, a circular movement that is really a marching in place: "Itself it went nowhere, only round and round, like the spheres, but mutely" (*MPTK,* p. 39). The title of the story might provide the music that the spheres lack, but by suggesting the pendulum swing of a clock, it too reinforces the idea of repetitive, meaningless motion.

On the day of the story, Belacqua is out walking and, although the stroll is not circular, it does appropriately describe the path of a boomerang:

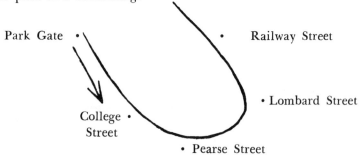

Park Gate •   • Railway Street

                                                      • Lombard Street

                College •
                Street
                          • Pearse Street

Passing the Palace Cinema on Pearse Street, Belacqua notices a little girl lying in the street. She had, we are told, been run over as she hastened home with a newly purchased loaf of bread.

In a paragraph that rivals *Dubliners* for baring the selfish soul of a city, Beckett relates how none of the people standing in line for the movie would move to lend assistance.[41] Only one girl, "debauched in appearance and swathed in a black blanket" (*MPTK*, p. 41), leaves the line—and this is for the purpose of securing the bread. "When she got back to the queue her place had been taken of course. But," adds Beckett in savage irony, "her sally had not cost her more than a couple of yards" (*MPTK*, p. 41).

In Lombard Street Belacqua stops for a drink at a pub, and is there accosted by an old woman with a radiant face (the "poor old woman" that is Ireland?) who is selling "seats in heaven . . . tuppence apiece, four fer a tanner" (*MPTK*, p. 45). Fascinated, he listens to her sales pitch: "Heaven goes round . . . and round and round and round and round and round" (*MPTK*, p. 45). Because he is embarrassed and conscious of all eyes on him, Belacqua finally buys two tickets. After pocketing the change and blessing him, the woman leaves; Belacqua does likewise a short time later. This incident both supports the circle imagery of the story and furnishes its meaning as well. Dante's Belacqua, the source for Beckett's hero, was guilty of indolent procrastination throughout his life. For this he was condemned to wait in antepurgatory and watch the spheres revolve for as many years as he had lived on earth. But the old woman's gestures and words refer to more than a canto of *The Divine Comedy*. Vico also imagined a circular universe and the four tickets offered to Belacqua could correspond to Vico's three ages plus a recorso (Joyce considered them as four ages). At the very least the story demonstrates a consistent circular imagery[42] reminiscent of the *Wake*, and it seems to express a Beckettian desire for a Joycean heaven that is constant motion without progress.

"A Wet Night," the next story, is the most overtly Joycean of all. In it Belacqua goes to a Christmas Eve party that bears a strong resemblance to the Morkan sisters' annual social. As Ruby Cohn writes:

The hostesses in the one ["The Dead"] are sisters and niece, and in the other, mother and daughter. In both works there are festive tables and lingering descriptions of good food; there are free flowing spirits both liquid and verbal; there are musical renditions, both vocal and instrumental, punctuated with lust and longing. Even Joyce's Protestant Mr. Browne finds a foil in Beckett's Jesuit priest.[43]

But Beckett is more than imitating Joyce's story; he is good-naturedly mocking it. Instead of a nationalist like Miss Ivors, he includes a Communist, and Gabriel's efforts in his speech to resurrect the past are parodied by the partygoers' poems in Old French and about Calvary. A brief concert on the viol d'amore is substituted for the piano recital of Mary Jane, and whereas Bartell D'Arcy sang "The Lass of Aughrim" with skill and feeling, Larry O'Murcahaodha "tore a greater quantity than seemed fair of his native speech-material to flat tatters" (*MPTK*, p. 80).

Belacqua, in direct opposition to Gabriel who is protected by his galoshes, enters soaked to the skin, and when he leaves Alba after seeing her home, he discards his shoes, in this respect somewhat resembling Greta Conroy, who despised the rubbers her husband made her wear. Finally, there is a direct parody of Joyce's final paragraph on the snow:

> and the rain fell in a uniform untroubled manner. It fell upon the bay, the littoral, the mountains and the plains, and notably upon the Central Bog it fell with a rather desolate uniformity. (*MPTK*, p. 83)

Other Joycean touches include allusions and puns. Maestro Gormeley is a "violist d'amore with his instrument in a bag" (*MPTK*, p. 65). The sexual nuance is combined with a reference to the first page of *Finnegans Wake*: "Sir Tristram, violer d'amores. . . ." Later on we meet a "popular Professor of Bullscrit and Comparative Ovoidology" (*MPTK*, p. 65), and there is "asinine dumfusion" (*MPTK*, p. 75) when Belacqua arrives. The Poet recites some verse, the fifth line of which exhorts:

"rocket of bloom flare flower of night wilt for me" (*MPTK,* p. 60). This recalls the simultaneous climax of Leopold Bloom and the firecracker rocket in the "Nausicaa" chapter of *Ulysses.* Moreover, the syntax of "rocket of bloom . . . wilt for me" is similar to that of the litany of the Daughters of Erin in "Circe": "Kidney of Bloom, pray for us. . . ."[44] Subsequent lines of this poem employ cyclical imagery that suggests Bloom's circular day:

> the tranquil act of its cycle on the waste
> from the spouting forth
> to the re-enwombing . . .
> till the clamour of a blue bloom
> beat on the walls of the womb. . . .

It is significant that the poem itself is a circle of sorts, starting with "the water/the waste of water" and ending "the waste of/the water." Finally, on page 82 there is mention of Joyce's beloved Feast of the Epiphany, and shortly after that a fifty-five letter word that is certainly meant to parody the hundred-letter thunder of *Finnegans Wake:* "Himmisacrakrüzidirkenjesusmariaundjosefundblütigeskreuz!"

"Love and Lethe," a wryly humorous story of a suicide pact that fails to achieve its goal, is atypical of Beckett in that the hero turns from death to love. Although there is no direct kinship with any of Joyce's works, the hilltop tryst of Belacqua and Ruby Tough again suggests that of Molly and Bloom, and, like the boys in "Encounter" who seek the Pigeon House and adventure, Belacqua does not find what he expected, except insofar as *"l'Amour et la Mort . . . n'est qu'une mesme chose"* (*MPTK,* p. 100).

"Walking Out" presents ingenious possibilities. In this story of a broken bride but a (verbally) consummated marriage, Beckett borrows from Joyce personally as well as literarily. Belacqua, we learn, likes to spy on people in the park, much as Earwicker does in the *Wake.* His desire to do so, and by so doing to obtain what he calls *sursum corda,*[45] causes Belacqua's fiancée, Lucy Stone, to ride out after him and be crushed by a

Daimler driven by "a drunken lord" (*MPTK,* p. 110). Horribly mutilated, she is nonetheless alive, and their subsequent marriage turns out to be quite successful, possibly because there is now no need either for a sexual relationship or for Lucy to take the cicisbeo (lover) that Belacqua had urged.[46] "They sit up to all hours playing the gramophone, *An die Musik*[47] is a great favorite with them both," writes Beckett. The reader, remembering the authorial comment that ended the previous story of Belacqua and his girl Ruby Tough—"May their night be full of music at all events" (*MPTK,* p. 100)—can only smile.

Lucy, like Wordsworth's Lucy Gray, is associated with nature and premature death. Her life, doomed as it is, does admit a brief period of marital bliss, but in paralysis and death a quatrain of the Lake poet could apply to Lucy Shuah, née *Stone*:

> No motion has she now, no force,
>   She neither hears nor sees,
> Rolled round in earth's diurnal course,
>   With rocks, and stones, and trees.[48]

There is another possible source for Beckett's most ill-fated heroine. Lucy, in name and physical fate, recalls Joyce's daughter Lucia, whose mind, like Lucy's body, was terribly crippled. Moreover, the description of Belacqua's fiancée bears a striking resemblance to the girl who longed to become engaged to Beckett: Lucy is "dark as jet and of a paleness that never altered, and her thick short hair went back like a pennon from her fanlight forehead" (*MPTK,* p. 105). By having Belacqua marry Lucy in spite of her shattered condition—and his own questionable ardor—Beckett may have been subconsciously exorcising some of the guilt he had felt over his abandonment of Lucia. G. C. Barnard, in his book on Beckett,[49] sees an even more general influence on the part of Joyce's daughter. Lucia, he claims, is responsible for much of Beckett's interest in schizoid people and lunatic asylums. Whatever the truth, the story does illustrate Beckett's belief that stasis, here in the form of physical paralysis, can bring happiness. It is also, needless to say, an example of the humorous debunking of romanticism by exaggeration and ridicule that seems to concern Beckett so much in these stories.[50]

"What a Misfortune" finds Belacqua, after the inevitable death of Lucy, about to take a second wife, one Thelma bboggs, who is not beautiful but has "a most cherharming personality" (*MPTK*, p. 117). The preparations for the marriage and the ceremony itself constitute the story and make for a biting social satire on middle-class mores. It is not the kind of story that Joyce, who preferred parody and puns, would have written, but Beckett had him in mind anyway. On page 126 there is a reference to the "Purefoy triplets," a joke, since Mrs. Purefoy is not mentioned in *Ulysses* as having had any multiple births. At the end, when Belacqua and his bride are driving off, she asks him where his lapel flower, a veronica, has gone. "Gone west" (*MPTK*, p. 151), he replies, and, although the saying is a common metaphor for death, it does recall Gabriel Conroy's ambiguous decision at the conclusion of "The Dead."

Puns are not frequent in this story, but there are twisted clichés that smack of Joycean wordplay: "Say what you will, you can't keep a dead man down"; "that would be doing the dirty on man's innocency" (*MPTK*, p. 140).

"The Smeraldina's Billet Doux" is a love letter to Belacqua from his German *Liebchen*, Smeraldina. A Molly Bloom type of monologue, it is ungrammatical and marked by misspellings as well as by a total lack of punctuation. Joyce himself apparently thought letters important, for he included them in his works. *Ulysses* has Boylan's letter to Molly, Milly's to her "Papli," and Martha's to Bloom, alias Henry Flower. *Finnegans Wake* has *the* letter which, coming from the litter or dump, is not only the *Wake* itself but all literature. Beckett's story does not make any such grand epistolary claims. Its humor derives from the contrast between Smeraldina's violent protestations of love for Belacqua and her admission that she is going dancing with someone else that very night, between the illiterate nature of her letter and the inexplicable allusion to Goethe's *Faust*: "Meine

Ruh ist hin mein Herz ist schwer ich finde Sie nimmer und nimmer mehr (Goethes *Faust*)" (*MPTK*, p. 155).

"Yellow," though it is only the penultimate story in the book, brings the volume full circle. Somewhat like McCabe, who "would get it in the neck at dawn" (*MPTK*, p. 21), Belacqua will die during an operation on a neck tumor.[51] Enforcing the irony, Beckett makes use of a joke in which a parson, acting in an amateur theatrical production, refuses to say the words, "By God! I'm shot." Through an accident, he *is* shot, and expires on stage with the now authentic cry, "By CHRIST! I *am* SHOT!" (*MPTK*, p. 172). Beckett, commenting on Belacqua's death from an overdose of anesthetic, similarly cries, "By Christ! he did die," (*MPTK*, p. 174), and this in turn recalls Belacqua's own shock upon finding the lobster alive: "Christ!" he said, "it's alive" (*MPTK*, p. 21).

Joycean touches include one pun, "Belacqua cut the surgeon" (*MPTK*, p. 174); a twisted Blake quotation that also suggests Giordano Bruno, "between contraries no alternation was possible" (*MPTK*, p. 163); and two question-and-answer passages reminiscent of the "Ithaca" episode in *Ulysses*: "What were his tactics in this crisis?" (*MPTK*, p. 162) and "How did he proceed to put this plan into operation?" (*MPTK*, p. 164).

Opposites, as in the *Wake* and Beckett's first story, play an important part. Belacqua, facing the possibility of death, must decide whether to follow the example of Heraclitus and weep, or of Democritus and laugh. The night nurse soon gives way to the day nurse who, upon learning that Belacqua is having growths removed from neck and toe, guffaws, "Top . . . and bottom" (*MPTK*, p. 168).

"Draff," as the title implies, concerns the remains of Belacqua. His not-so-grieving widow, the Smeraldina, buries Belacqua in a flower-lined grave with the help of her husband's friend Capper "Hairy" Quin, who, it seems, will undertake to comfort Smeraldina permanently. On the drive back from the funeral, the parson is kicked out of the car. " 'Wouldn't he give you the sick' said Hairy 'with his Noo Gefoozleum?' " (*MPTK*, p. 189), a possible allusion on Beckett's part to the New Bloomusalem in *Ulysses*. Two pages earlier, Hairy makes what could be another Joycean allusion: " 'O G.P.I. . . . where are thy rats?" The initials might stand for General Paralysis of the Insane, a phrase and abbreviation to be found in *Ulysses*, where there is also a rat at a funeral (Paddy Dignam's).

Puns pepper the story in Joycean manner. "Capper Quin arrived on Tiptire . . ." (*MPTK*, p. 179), we are told, and "No gardener has died within rosaceous memory" (*MPTK*, p. 191). Thelma, Belacqua's second wife, finally did "go west" after all: she died of "sunset and honeymoon" (*MPTK*, p. 175). And Belacqua himself came—literally—to a bad end: his undertaker's name is "Malacoda." Ireland and the Irish Revival come in for a few sarcastic asides. Gaelic has "no words for . . . big ideas" (*MPTK*, p. 186), and, after describing Hairy Quin, Beckett concludes, "Even Ireland has a few animals, now generally regarded as varieties, which have been ranked as species by some zoologists" (*MPTK*, p. 180). This mockery of his own country will be even stronger in Beckett's first major novels, *Murphy* and *Watt*. The next chapter's discussion of these works will show that, although the stylistic and thematic influence of Joyce remains strong, Beckett is beginning to assert his own literary individuality and use what he learned from his mentor for his own artistic ends.

3

The Joycean Shadow: *Murphy, Watt, Mercier et Camier*

Just as his early poems and short stories tested Beckett's command of Joyce's stylistic techniques, so his first attempts at a novel permitted him to explore thematic concerns that are equally central to *Ulysses* and *Finnegans Wake*. In *Murphy, Watt,* and the recently (1970) published *Mercier et Camier,* Beckett continues to indulge his Joycean predilection for puns and witty dialogue, but the focus is now on a philosophical concept that engrossed Joyce's attention for the last years and the ultimate literary achievement of his life. The idea of the universe as a closed system, containing within itself, *ab origine,* all possible people, objects, and events, and merely recycling them *ad infinitum,* appealed to Joyce's innate need for order and harmony. For Beckett, however, the fact that the sun would always shine, "having no alternative, on the nothing new,"[1] presented a horrible truth, one that, though always forced to acknowledge, he would never cease to rage and rebel against. Beckett would also revolt against the looking-glass realism of *Dubliners* and *Ulysses.* While the characters and situations of his first three novels are recognizably human, they are by no means conventional, and the beginnings of a comical and Kafkaesque superrealism can already be discerned. Finally, even the puns are starting to yield to Beckett's own, more elaborate, comic techniques.

Murphy, Watt, and *Mercier et Camier,* then, represent an intense examination of Joycean themes at the same time that they exhibit the strong but waning presence of Joycean language and technical devices.

Murphy (1938)

Murphy, written in the 1930s when his master's stylistic influence over Beckett was at its height, is the most overtly Joycean of the three novels. Both book and hero probably owe their name to the fact that Murphy is one of the commonest patronymics in Ireland, something like Smith in England. Indeed, when the narrator of "An Encounter" wishes to hide his identity and that of his friend from the old josser, he chooses "Smith" for himself and "Murphy" for his companion. "Shakespeares were as common as Murphies. What's in a name?"[2] says Stephen Dedalus to Leopold Bloom.

Beckett's seedy solipsist may also have been suggested, if in name only, by a minor character in *Ulysses.* Joyce's own Murphy, unlike Beckett's, has a Christian name, or at least initials: W. B. Murphy is obviously a humorous allusion to William Butler Yeats, but Murphy suggests Morpheus, and we meet the storytelling sailor in the chapter ("Eumaeus") that is written in old narrative, an exhausted and sleep-inducing style with split infinitives, dangling participles, and sentences that seem to go on forever. Moreover, on their way out of the cabman's shelter on Butt Bridge, Stephen and Bloom notice that the sentry, one Gumley, is now asleep or, in Joyce's words, he is "wrapped in the arms of Murphy."[3] Beckett's magnetic if somewhat phlegmatic character, who delights in rocking himself into a trance and who finally falls asleep never to wake up, might be the result of unconscious associations on the part of his author with this episode of Joyce's odyssey. As tenuous as such a hypothesis is, it is strengthened by a fascinating verbal coincidence. Wylie, asked by Neary to define Murphy's appeal for women, cites the latter's "surgical quality" (*M*, p. 62). Bloom and Stephen, after leaving the shelter, proceed to the kitchen of 7 Eccles Street where they experience communion through cocoa, and where the reader learns that Bloom's hand possesses "the operative surgical quality."[4]

Finally, one character may represent Joyce himself. Austin Ticklepenny has a first name that is a variant of Joyce's middle one, and he even tells Murphy to call him Augustin (*M*, p. 94). Moreover, like the author of *Chamber Music*, he is a "Pot Poet" (*M*, p. 84). However, there is no reason to associate Ticklepenny's fawning attitude and homosexual behavior with Joyce. Most probably, as A. J. Leventhal has said, the identification is unfounded.[5]

Whether or not Joyce recognized Beckett's borrowings, there is no doubt that he appreciated *Murphy*'s humor and thought highly of its author's achievement. Richard Ellmann reports that Joyce wrote a bad limerick beginning, "There was a young man named Murphy," and later paid Beckett the compliment of memorizing the passage on the disposal of Murphy's body.[6] Perhaps the biggest proof of Joyce's esteem are the many references to *Murphy* in *Finnegans Wake*. Since they are not present in either the first-draft version or the installments that appeared in *transition*, it is very probable that Joyce inserted them after he had read Beckett's novel. A comparison of the different texts shows that this was indeed the case.

"The Ballad of Persse O'Reilly" in chapter 1 contains the lines, "With the bailiff's bom at the door,/(Chorus) Bimbam at the door" (*FW*, 46.8–9). In the *transition* version these two lines read: "With the bailiff's bum at the door,/Bumbum at the door."[7] Joyce's vowel changes, seemingly trivial, create a definite allusion to the Clinch twins, Bim and Bom. Page 59, lines 5–7, refer to Mrs. F . . . A . . . (Rebecca West) "recoopering her cartwheel chapot (ahat!—and we now know what thimbles a baquets on lallance a talls mean). . . ." Although "recoopering" was present in the *transition* text, the French "chapot" was not. Neither was the "thimbles a baquets" phrase. Joyce probably added both when he realized (after 1938) his own prophetic reference to Beckett's strange character, Cooper, who, besides not being able to sit down, cannot remove his hat. Parodying Thomas Beckett's name suggests again that Sam is also present here. The Rabelaisian catalogue of Earwicker's names on pages 71–72 contains "Awl Out" (*FW*, 72.2), a definite play on the park cry refrain "All Out" that runs throughout *Murphy* and ends the book. There is another possible reference to Bim and Bom Clinch in line 3 ("A Ban for Le King of the Burgaans and a Bom for Ye Sur of all the Ruttledges"), and lines 6–7 could refer to a story in *More Pricks Than Kicks*: "Enclosed find the Sons of Fingal." Finally, on page 205, line 16, the "Mericy Cordial Mendicants' Sitterdag-Zindeh-Munaday Wakeschrift" is mentioned, certainly an allusion to the Magdalen Mental Mercyseat, since the *transition* version of this line is simply "Beggars Sitterday Journal."[8]

Written in a bright, witty, and elliptical style, *Murphy* is filled with cliché variants, variations of proverbs and folk sayings, twisted quotations, and misplaced literalism.[9] "In the beginning was the pun" (*M*, p. 65), and this first novel continues the fanciful Joycean wordplay begun in "Whoroscope."[10] Mr. Kelly ponders a "sad pun" on Celia's name: *"Celia, s'il y a, Celia, s'il y a"* (*M*, p. 115), and Murphy tries to amuse Celia with the following riddle: "Why did the barmaid champagne? . . . Because the stout porter bitter" (*M*, p. 139).[11] "Murphy on the jobpath . . . is . . . a fragment of Job" (*M*, p. 70), and his suit "felt like felt rather than cloth" (*M*, p. 72). Miss Carridge, his landlady, has "insmell into her infirmity" (*M*, p. 132), and can only wish her troubles were "a little less penetrating" (*M*, p. 144). It is winter and "night's young thoughts had been put back an hour" (*M*, pp. 73–74; a pun on Edward Young's poem "Night Thoughts") when the old boy commits suicide, causing Celia to set up a "niobaloo" (*M*, p. 139). In the meantime, Neary is bedridden, thinking of his latest *"voltefesses"* (*M*, p. 200).

Returning to the technique of "Dante and the Lobster,"

Beckett has again employed the device of recurrent motifs. Here, however, such repeated elements as Miss Carridge's smell, Cooper's inability to sit or take off his hat, and Ticklepenny's homosexuality operate more as a humorous burlesquelike refrain than as actual symbols in the manner of Joyce's snow. The characters themselves possess a large measure of caricature, even Celia who, convincing as she is, does recall the stereotyped fig-ure of the prostitute with a heart of gold. "All the puppets in this book whinge sooner or later" admits Beckett, with the exception of Murphy "who is not a puppet" (*M*, p. 122).

Just as the realism of the characters is undermined by their exaggerated physical traits and buffoonery, so the realism of the setting is mocked by an almost too-precise rendering of space and time. Situated in the recognizable cities of Dublin and London, the novel boasts basically realistic characters and situations. The initial reality of the setting is, as in *Ulysses*, emphasized by deliberate references to specific streets and sites, and by a scrupulously detailed chronology of events. Even the dates of the Old Boy's seizures (Shrove Tuesday and Derby Day) are given. At the same time, however, continued astrological references mock the realistic time scheme, and so does Murphy's own desire to move beyond the confining physical facts of exis-tence into the timeless and (for him) real world of the mind.[12] Raymond Federman interprets this quasi-realistic structure as a "rejection of traditional realism in favor of a more abstract and fanciful type of fiction [that] draws toward the paradoxical affirmation that the validity of fiction lies in its aesthetic fraudulence."[13] Michael Robinson agrees, going so far as to term *Murphy* "in part a Joycean parodic comment on the nature of fiction."[14] While this may be viewing the novel in the light of the later trilogy, it is certainly correct to say that in *Murphy* Beckett has combined the realism of *Ulysses* with the surrealism of the *Wake*.

As well as being the most overtly Joycean of his novels, Beckett's *Murphy* is also the most obviously Irish—or anti-Irish—and in this too Beckett was imitating Joyce. Although he left Dublin as a young man, Joyce never allowed his native country to leave his heart. A European resident for 37 of his 59 years, Joyce remained a Dubliner wherever he lived. Wavering "between affectionate fascination . . . and mistrust,"[15] Joyce could never forgive England and Rome for their treachery to Ireland; however, neither could he forget his own countrymen's betrayal of Parnell and other patriots.

If Ireland was political death to its heroes, it was a spiritual assassin to its writers, whose only hope for creative achievement lay in exile. "Isolation is the first principle of artistic economy," says Stephen Dedalus,[16] and Joyce himself often echoed that opinion.[17] Indeed, all Joyce's heroes are exiles, Stephen from home, church, and country, Richard Rowan from Ireland, Bloom from Molly, and HCE, by virtue of his sin and fall, from God. But physical exile is not only a major theme of Joyce's works, it is the very condition that made those works possible. Therefore, as anti-British as he was, Joyce later came to resent the possibility of Irish independence, acutely perceiving that political autonomy, while a national gain, would mean a personal loss to himself: "Tell me why you think," he asked Frank Budgen, "I ought to change the conditions that gave Ireland and me a shape and a destiny."[18]

Beckett's attitude toward Ireland is at the same time more tolerant and less forgiving than Joyce's. He too rebelled against the constrictions of Irish life, confiding to Israel Shenker, "I didn't like living in Ireland. You know the kind of thing— theocracy, censorship of books, that kind of thing. I preferred to live abroad."[19] Finding himself in Ireland when World War II erupted in 1939, Beckett immediately returned to Paris, later commenting that he "preferred France in war to Ireland in peace."[20] Alan Simpson credits much of Beckett's disgust with Ireland to his friendship with Joyce. Seeing how their native country treated the author of *Ulysses*, Beckett could not but agree that Ireland is "the old sow that eats her farrow."[21] At the same time, however, his exile appears to have little of the extreme emotional ambivalence that marked Joyce's separation from the emerald isle. Dublin for Beckett, one suspects, is more dirty than dear,[22] and, writing mostly in French since 1945, he has assimilated himself into European life more so than Joyce ever did.

If Beckett's love for Ireland is not so consuming as Joyce's, neither is his hatred. *Murphy* mocks the author's birthplace, but does so with more risibility than rancor. Mr. Kelly, upon learning that Murphy is from Dublin, cries in horror, "My God!" (*M*, p. 17), and Wylie, departing for London, comments "It is always pleasant to leave this country" (*M*, p. 129). The turf in Miss Counihan's fire "was truly Irish in its eleutheromania, it would not burn behind bars" (*M*, p. 131), while Miss Counihan's exceptionally anthropoid appearance is, like all things, relative: "It was only in Dublin where the profession had gone to the dogs, that Miss Counihan could stand out as the object of desire of a man of taste" (*M*, pp. 196–97). Wylie praises Cooper and debunks Ireland simultaneously: "I say you know what women are . . . or has your entire life been spent in Cork" (*M*, p. 206). Neither does London escape Beckett's wit: "London was less conscious of her garbage [than Dublin], she had not given her scavenging to aliens" (*M*, p. 274). Even in translation Beckett did not neglect a chance to strike out against his country's narrowness. Murphy, urged by Celia to find a job, is threatened with her departure if he doesn't. "Murphy knew what that meant. No more music." Beckett then adds an authorial aside: "This phrase is chosen with care, lest the filthy censors should lack an occasion to commit their filthy synechdoche" (*M*, p. 76). In the French edition this last passage becomes:

> Cette phrase, loin de la rédaction *en anglo-irlandais*, fut choisie avec soin, de crainte qu'il ne manquât aux censeurs l'occasion de pratiquer leur synechdoche.[23]

As Ruby Cohn correctly explains, "The translation is not into English but into 'Anglo-Irish' . . . to lash out at the censorship of the Irish. . . ."[24]

If *Murphy*'s language, leitmotifs, surface naturalism, and humorous criticism of Ireland all are in the Joycean vein, the book itself nevertheless embodies an implicitly anti-Joycean philosophy. By positing a dualism of mind and body that will become central to his works, and explicitly resolving it, as did Descartes and Geulincx before him, in favor of the mind, Beckett is attacking the very crux of Joyce's attitude toward life. For Joyce, although he had abandoned the Catholic religion of Ireland and his childhood, did not relinquish the Christian habit of seeing all history as part of a single unified scheme of order. Harmony and communion were, moreover, not only personal needs, but the aim of his fiction as well. In *Portrait*, Stephen Dedalus is finally united with the urges and qualities that impel him to leave Ireland and devote himself to the secular vocation of art. *Ulysses* gives him a spiritual father in Leopold Bloom who, after a partial communion with Stephen via Epps's cocoa, returns to Molly and perhaps is able to achieve union of a sort with her.[25] *Finnegans Wake,* though it celebrates the eternal conflict of opposites, glorifies even more the union of those opposites into one: Shem and Shaun, forever fighting against each other and Earwicker, will forever make peace by uniting to become their father.

The separation of the mental from the physical as anything but a temporary state was abhorrent to Joyce. *Ulysses,* more than any of his works, proclaims the unity of man's brain with his body. Each chapter, written in a different verbal (or mental) mode, takes its cue from a specific organ or part of the body—kidneys, lungs, heart, and so on. In "Lestrygonians" the organ is the esophagus and the technique peristaltic; in "Oxen of the Sun" both foetus (organ: womb) and the chapter undergo a nine-part embryonic development. Although the book ends "superficially" with the flesh, even here the mind is present, for Molly's episode is perhaps the most famous interior monologue and example of stream of consciousness in all literature. And just as Bloom is the all-around man, so *Ulysses* is the complete book of man—the whole greater than the sum of its parts and the technical virtuosity of each chapter subordinate to the greater harmony of all eighteen.

But if unity is the end of Joyce's work, that in itself presupposes a certain disharmony or clash of opposites. Indeed, one of the themes of *Ulysses* is a fundamental discrepancy between the physical and the spiritual, the mental and the material, a discrepancy that may very well have been a source for the similar although more extensive conflict in Beckett's own fictional world. Stephen's spiritual reluctance is contrasted with Mulligan's mocking compliance, his artistic idealism with Deasy's prejudice and materialism. But by far the greatest contrast is with Bloom. Separated by "name, age, race, creed,"[26] Bloom and Stephen represent separate temperaments, the scientific and the artistic. Moreover, where Bloom is a physical man, eating "with relish the inner organs of beasts and fowls,"[27] Stephen is extremely uncomfortable with the fleshy nature of man, especially his own body. "Who chose this face for me? This dogsbody to rid of vermin,"[28] he asks in "Telemachus," and it is significant that no organ of the body is associated with any of the first three chapters (Stephen's). In the "Proteus" episode Stephen tries to shut out the entire physical world by closing his eyes. Finding that it can't be done ("There all the time without you: and ever shall be, world without end"[29]), he settles for the symbolist approach: earthly phenomena are not important for their own sake but for the hidden meaning they conceal—"Signatures of all things I am here to read."[30]

If the world of flux is repugnant to Stephen's mental and aesthetic orientation, it is the basis of Bloom's relation to life. Richard Ellmann perceptively notes that "Bloom's thoughts always begin close to the ground, as Stephen's all begin in air."[31] This is true even at the very end of *Ulysses,* where there exists "a certain analogy" between them, "as if both their minds were travelling, so to speak, in one train of thought."[32] For example, at the beginning of the "Eumaeus" episode Bloom and Stephen, though walking side by side, are far apart in their thoughts. As they go past the warehouses of Beresford Place, Stephen thinks of Ibsen, "associated with Baird's, the stonecutter's, in his mind somehow"[33]—perhaps through Ibsen's *The Master Builder*—while Bloom's is a characteristically physical response: he senses with "internal satisfaction the smell of James Rourke's city bakery." Moreover, even during their simultaneous urination in the garden, which for at least one critic is "the moment of symbolic union,"[34] Joyce is careful to make clear the essential difference between Stephen and Bloom. The trajectories of their micturition are, we are told, parallel but "dissimilar: Bloom's longer, less irruent, . . . Stephen's higher, more sibilant."[35] And when Stephen finally departs there is "the union of their tangent, [but] the disunion of their respectively centrifugal and centripetal hands."

Despite their sharing a few moments of intimacy together, Bloom and Stephen nevertheless remain essentially opposites. To Joyce they represented, among other things, the scientific and artistic temperaments. Joyce's friend Frank Budgen put it another way: "Bloom is while Stephen is becoming."[36] This interpretation is echoed by S. L. Goldberg in his excellent study of *Ulysses.* For him, Bloom's "freedom and maturity stand as actuality to Stephen's mere potentiality; his wisdom to Stephen's knowledge; his love to Stephen's bitterness; his acceptance of life to Stephen's uneasy division; his stasis to Stephen's kinesis; his waking to Stephen's nightmare."[37] Still another critic sees still another contrast, that between the spontaneity and impulse of Hellenism, represented by Bloom, and the rational, self-contained approach of Hebraism, embodied in Stephen.[38] Finally, Richard Ellmann argues that the principle of contrast, taken by Joyce from Giordano Bruno, underlies not only the content but the form of *Ulysses,* with each episode or group of episodes structured around a different conflict: body/soul; space/time; land/water, and so on. Thus, although the basic tendency in Joyce's work is toward unity, there is a deep-rooted thematic and stylistic opposition of forces that may well have influenced Beckett's own dichotomy.

But where Joyce contemplated—and created—intricate order,

Beckett, admiring the genius of his friend, saw only chaos and
fragmentation. Joyce's characters may be exiled from country,
religion, or wife, but Beckett's experience a deeper alienation.
Completely asocial, they are separated not only from any society
but—a more crucial and difficult gap to overcome—from themselves, their own identity. Hence a schism between the two
major divisions of man, his exterior and his interior, his body
and his mind.

This estrangement, which dominates Murphy and his book,
has its roots in Beckett's earliest works. "Whoroscope" speaks,
perhaps symbolically, of the separation between the white and
the yolk of Descartes's egg; in "Fingal" we are told that Belacqua
"scoffed at the idea of a sequitur from his body to his mind"
(*MPTK*, p. 29) ; and in "Yellow" Belacqua appeals to his mind
to help him deal with the fear of a physical operation. It is then
no wonder that Beckett found Descartes a congenial philosopher
to study. Approximately eight years after he wrote a monograph
on the Seigneur du Perron and devoted a prize-winning poem
to him, Beckett published *Murphy*. In this first novel Descartes
is alluded to specifically. Murphy has a Dutch uncle, Mr.
Quigley, who, as Descartes did, resides in Holland. After telling
Celia the answer to his riddle, Murphy collapses in hysterics
"on the dream of Descartes linoleum" (*M*, p. 140) . But the real
importance of Descartes lies not in these superficial references,
but in the philosophical problem he bequeathed to Murphy and
Beckett: the separation of mind and body. Unlike Descartes,
who believed that the two met in the pineal gland, Murphy
draws no such conclusion. Not particularly anxious to discover
how the body communicates with the mind (or vice versa),
Murphy is eager only to escape the one for the other. Closer to
Arnold Geulincx than to Descartes, Murphy's attitude toward
physical reality implies the seventeenth-century Occasionalist
thinking that, because it can act on itself without the necessary
intervention of God, the mind is superior to the body and is the
place where the inner self and true reality are to be found.
Whereas for Descartes thinking was the irrefutable proof of the

self's existence—"*Cogito, ergo sum*"—for Beckett it *is* that existence. Fleeing the big buzzing confusion of the macrocosm,
Murphy finds his heaven not outside himself but in the microcosm of his mind. Joyce, no doubt experiencing cerebral delights
in creating his fictions, nevertheless retained an equal joy in the
reality of the physical universe.

Although both authors[39] use the image of the circle to express
their attitudes toward time and the world, that image, as we
have seen, signifies different things to each author. Just so, the
circle itself encompasses a different world for Beckett than it
does for Joyce. Substituting faith in cyclical recurrence for
the Anglicanism of Eliot and the occultism of the Theosophists,
Joyce, like the seventeenth-century metaphysicians, regarded the
universe as complete, self-contained. "It was good, he felt, to
contemplate a formal pattern and to be where he was not
alone."[40] But where the philosophers of Donne's time saw the
micro- and geocosm as reflections of the larger macrocosmic
pattern of the universe, Joyce saw history and the universe as
patterned after man—specifically, after the social nucleus of the
family. Beckett, an ahistorical writer, also centers his circles upon
man, but only a part of man: his mind. Acknowledging a circular
order to the universe, Beckett's man is desperately trying to
escape that large circle by living in the smaller one of his head.
More than a difference in scope, the circles of Beckett and Joyce
signify radically different attitudes toward the physical world
that both must live in. Joyce, accepting it, creates a fiction of
affirmation; as does Molly Bloom, he says yes to everything.
Beckett, on the other hand, negates the value of external reality,
renounces the imprisoning circle of physical existence for the
freedom conferred by a purely mental life.

Murphy is interesting not only for its extensive use of the
circle metaphor, nor because, as does *Finnegans Wake*, it posits
a universe that is both circular and closed. In writing this first
novel, Beckett was actually setting up the philosophical and
figurative horns of his dilemma: on the one hand there is the
macrocosm of the world—an impossible place in which to live—

and on the other there is the microcosm of the mind, an equally impossible place to enter totally, except through the ultimate rejection of the physical world: death.

All, in *Murphy*, is a closed system. Even the dialogue seems to circle endlessly around a verbal fulcrum. "You are all I have in the world . . . you . . . and possibly Murphy," says Celia to Mr. Kelly on page 11. Seven pages later she repeats the first part of her speech, "You are all I have in the world," and Mr. Kelly finishes it for her: "I . . . and possibly Murphy." The first example of the closed system is romantic involvement:

> Of such was Neary's love for Miss Dwyer,[41] who loved a Flight-Lieutenant Elliman, who loved a Miss Farren of Ringsakiddy, who loved a Father Fitt of Ballinclashet, who in all sincerity was bound to acknowledge a certain vocation for a Miss West of Passage, who loved Neary. (*M*, p. 5)

Love requited, then, becomes a "short circuit."

Astrology, the system in which Murphy places such faith, is also closed, based on a finite number of planets that follow predestined, orbital courses. The Magdalen Mental Mercyseat and its patients are, likewise, a world unto themselves. "Self immersed [, they are] indifferen[t] to the contingencies of the contingent world" (*M*, p. 168). The padded, womblike cells they occupy are covered completely with "pneumatic upholstery," so that one felt he was a "prisoner of air." "No system of ventilation appeared to dispel the illusion of respirable vacuum. The compartment was windowless, like a monad . . ." (*M*, p. 181). Even Murphy's hours of duty, or "rounds," are self-contained: he works from 8:00 A.M. to 8:00 P.M., with a two-hour break from 12:00 to 2:00 P.M.

Life itself is a closed system. As Wylie[42] observes:

> the syndrome known as life is too diffuse to admit of palliation. For every symptom that is eased, another is made worse. The horse leech's daughter is a closed system. Her quantum of wantum cannot vary. (*M*, p. 57)

Or: "Humanity is a well with two buckets, . . . one going down to be filled, the other coming up to be emptied" (*M*, p. 58). The advantage of such a stasis is that if things cannot improve, they also cannot get much worse. "They will always be the same as they always were" (*M*, p. 58). Bloom, in the "Lestrygonians" chapter of *Ulysses* also muses on the circular course of the stream of life:

> Things go on same; day after day: . . . . Mina Purefoy swollen belly on a bed groaning to have a child tugged out of her. One born every second somewhere. Other dying every second. Since I fed the birds five minutes. Three hundred kicked the bucket. Other three hundred born.[43]

At the end of Beckett's book the "inner circle" (*M*, p. 264) of Murphy's friends comes to inspect the charred remains of his body. It is Celia, much to Miss Counihan's disappointment, who identifies him from a birthmark on his buttock. " 'How beautiful in a way,' said the coroner, 'birthmark, deathmark, I mean rounding off the life somehow, don't you think, full circle . . .' " (*M*, p. 267).

Chief of the major circles is Murphy's mind, "a large hollow sphere, hermetically closed to the universe without" (*M*, p. 107). Even Murphy realizes "that his mind was a closed system, subject to no principle of change but its own, self-sufficient and impermeable to the vicissitudes of the body" (*M*, p. 109). In a way, Murphy's mind is synonymous with the external world: "Nothing ever had been, was or would be in the universe outside it but was already present . . . inside it" (*M*, p. 107). But there is a vital difference. Because they are extra-physical, none of the three mental zones is subject to the restrictions of time and space. The first, or light zone, contains forms parallel to those of the external world, but capable of being arranged according to Murphy's own wishes and whims. The second, or half-light zone, permits Murphy to contemplate forms that do not exist in reality, and the third, dark, zone provides the supreme pleasure and freedom: As is *Finnegans Wake* it is a

flux of forms, a perpetual coming together and falling asunder
of forms . . . nothing but forms becoming and crumbling
into the fragments of a new becoming, without love or hate
or any intelligible principle of change. . . . Here he was not
free, but a mote in the dark of absolute freedom . . . a point
in the ceaseless unconditioned generation and passing away
of line. (*M*, p. 112)

While Murphy's mind, along with astrology, asylum, and life
itself, is the main focus of Beckett's circle imagery, there are
other, minor spheres.

Murphy himself, by virtue of his mind and because he is the
object of many people's desires, is a closed system. "Our medi-
ans . . . meet in Murphy" (*M*, p. 213), says Wylie. Murphy's
clothing, like his mind, is "hermetically closed to the universe
without." The jacket is "a tube in its own right," and the entire
suit is made of nonporous material: "It admitted no air from
the outer world, it allowed none of Murphy's own vapours to
escape" (*M*, p. 72).

Celia, meeting Murphy for the first time, slowly rotates before
him, and "when she came full circle" (*M*, p. 14), she found his
eyes fixed upon her. She then walks away, but after a short stay
at the river, she *circles* back to Murphy, who is still standing at
the juncture of Cremourne Road and Stadium Street.

Neary, in Mooney's bar[44] awaiting news of Murphy from
Cooper,

> sat all day, moving slowly from one stool to another until he
> had completed the circuit of the counters, when he would start
> all over again in the reverse direction. (*M*, p. 56)

The circular motion and reversal suggest *Finnegans Wake,* but
Yeats's gyres are perhaps also present. Furthermore, Neary himself is a closed system; he sleeps with his feet crossed, because "he
had some vague theory about his terminals being thereby connected, and his life force prevented from escaping" (*M*, pp.
207–8). In the end Neary comes to need Murphy as the only
person he can trust. However, as Beckett points out, his need

"had to lose with reference to the rival what it gained with reference to the friend" (*M*, p. 117). "Humanity is a well with two buckets. . . ."

Murphy's daily dilemma, in what order to eat his biscuits, introduces a new kind of circle. The five biscuits could be consumed a total of a hundred-and-twenty different ways, if Murphy could conquer his prejudice for the ginger and against the anonymous. Such calculations of the possible permutations within a finite number of objects belong to both mathematical set theory and Beckett's second novel, *Watt,* where they will provide him with style as well as substance. Here, however, they are used to promote a more general idea of the closed system. After the dog Nelly has kindly relieved Murphy of the necessity for any decision by eating all but one of the biscuits, Beckett comments that "Wylie might have consoled himself with the thought that the Park was a closed system in which there would be no loss of appetite" (*M*, p. 102).

The final, and perhaps ultimately most significant, circle is the chess game between Murphy and that other human closed system, Mr. Endon. Continually played but never decided, this game is started in the morning and "evening found it almost as level as when begun" (*M*, p. 187). Because each player consciously and deliberately refrains from checkmating the other, there can never be an endgame. What his last chess match with Mr. Endon does produce, however, is more important for Murphy than victory. Indeed, it is a defeat of sorts. First, the game removes Murphy to the nearly timeless realm of his dreams: "Time did not cease, that would be asking too much, but the wheel of rounds and pauses did" (*M*, p. 246). Second, gazing into Mr. Endon's eyes, Murphy sees, "in the cornea, horribly reduced, obscured and distorted, his own image" (*M*, p. 249). He sees himself, but Mr. Endon does not. For the real meaning of the closed system, the meaning that Murphy now learns, is that each person is imprisoned, isolated in his own being. Communication—and part of Murphy's tragic/comic flaw is that he is still sufficiently of this world to desire human relationships—is impossible. "Mr. Murphy is a speck in Mr. Endon's unseen" (*M*, p. 250). It is this knowledge, as much as anything, that causes Murphy's "suicide."[45]

The last scene in the novel poignantly reinforces the lesson. Celia is helping Mr. Kelly fly his kite in the park. The kite soars into the white-flecked sky and disappears from view. "Mr. Kelly was enraptured. Now he could measure the distance from the unseen to the seen, now he was in a position to determine the point at which seen and unseen met" (*M*, p. 280). But the string snaps and the kite "vanishe[s] joyfully in the dusk" (*M*, p. 282), without Mr. Kelly's ever seeing the point at which the kite would swim into human vision. There is no way, then, to break out of the circle of this world into that of the mind. There are only the unseen and the seen, two closed systems that never meet, except through death. The symbolic figures of line (here: kite) and circle will recur throughout Beckett's works, a continual contrast that is, paradoxically, a union. For both circle and line are infinite, one forever revolving, the other eternally extended, without beginning, without end.

Although this sounds completely antithetical to Joyce's view in *Ulysses* (p. 666), there is a curious similarity between the conclusions of the two works. Bloom and Stephen—if they do not actually fuse as Joyce's Linati schema and Richard Ellmann suggest—do, in the final chapters, follow "parallel courses," even to the point of urinating in two parallel streams. And parallel lines do not, of course, ever meet (except, perhaps, in Einstein's physics).

Watt (written 1942–47; published 1953)

Watt,[46] like *Murphy*, bears a certain punning resemblance to Joyce's works. Just as Beckett had punned on the names of Miss Carridge, Rosie Dew, Celia, and Lord Gall of Wormwood, so now the very title (and hero) of his book is a play on words. Watt may be named in honor of Wat Tyler, the leader of the fourteenth-century Peasant's Rebellion, and, indeed, Arsene makes this connection (*W*, p. 48). But Watt is also a homonym

of the interrogative *what?* and so is symbolic of the hero's eternal
quest for an explanation of events.[47] The answer to Watt's
implicit question may lie in the mysterious figure of his boss,
Mr. Knott. A multiple pun, Knott's name could be meant to
imply his enigmatic nature (a *knot* that cannot be untied), his
negative approach to existence (Knott did *not* need anything),[48]
or the very absence of any existence (Knott = *naught*). Two
other characters also have punned-on names. The Lynch twins,[49]
Art and Con, together seem to suggest a "con" artist, and Mr.
Graves, though he paradoxically deals with gardens, is sexually
dead or impotent. In addition, the names of both Hunchy
Hackett and Sam suggest Beckett himself.

As in *Murphy*, disparaging remarks on Ireland are included.
Mr. Knott's linen is changed every St. Patrick's Day, and Watt's
unintelligible speech, suggestive of *Finnegans Wake* to at least
one critic,[50] is just "so much Irish" (*W*, p. 169) to Sam.

Beckett, like Joyce, is beginning to create a fictional world of
his own, in which characters from one book will reappear in
another. *More Pricks Than Kicks* exhibited this literary device,
and the trilogy will make even greater use of it. But Beckett
will go still further and approximate the technique of *Finnegans
Wake*, where all the characters merge into one another. Here
already there is a hint that Watt may be a reincarnation of
Murphy, for at one point we read of the "constellations which
he [Watt] had once known familiarly by name when he lay
dying in London" (*W*, p. 212). Murphy himself will be mentioned in *Mercier et Camier* (p. 137), as will a Mr. Gall (Lord
Gall?), Mr. Graves, and Watt himself. J. Mitchell Morse notes
this practice of Beckett's, and even makes the association with
Joyce's method. Beckett's creations, he writes,

> are indeed all one, but only as in *Finnegans Wake* Napoleon
> and the Duke of Wellington are one . . . [they] have so many
> habits, attitudes and afflictions in common that I suspect that
> we have to do with a series of metempsychoses [shades of Molly
> Bloom!] or eternal returns. Beckett having been when young
> a disciple of Joyce, this is not surprising.[51]

Creating his own fictional world, Beckett seems also to have made several allusions to Joyce's. The meeting of Arsene and Mr. Ash is a direct parody of Earwicker's confrontation with the Cad.[52] Ash, like Earwicker, has several layers of clothing on his person (though not seven, as does Joyce's hero), and gives his friend the time of day. In the *Wake*, HCE announces that it is 12:00 at the same time that the clock strikes. Mr. Ash tells Arsene it is "seventeen minutes past five exactly," but "a moment later Big Ben . . . struck six" (*W*, p. 46).

The differences in content are matched by the different styles in which the two episodes are related. Joyce's language is elaborate, making use of numerous amplifications and side comments, while Beckett's prose is already marked by its straightforward and concise character. In spite of the stylistic contrast, according to David Hayman, "the two writers have one thing in common besides their subject: Both work against the comic traditions they exploit, at once instilling values and deflating them."[53] Moreover, both

delight in constructing what might be called oxymoronic conceits on all levels of discourse, turning an apparently senseless figure of speech into a means of expressing otherwise inexpressible relationships, comically conveying through avoidance the interrelatedness of diametrically opposed positions.[54]

Finally, on the personal level, "Since the *Wake* in 1945 was a closed universe to all but a tiny elite, we may read [Beckett's] passage as an oblique and probably reflexive homage."[55]

Other passages make other suggestions. Watt has difficulty entering Mr. Knott's house, and must finally go through the back door, just as Bloom does in "Ithaca." Mr. Knott is addicted to "solitary dactylic ejaculations of extraordinary vigour, accompanied by spasms of the members. The chief of these were: Exelmans! Cavendish! Habbakuk! Ecchymose!" (*W*, p. 209). Legitimate as these names are,[56] one feels tempted to underline the initial letters, which are those of HCE reversed, plus an extra "E" (ricorso?).

Along with Stephen Dedalus, Watt will not touch water (*W*, p. 23) and, equally unhygienically, picks his nose (*W*, p. 39). His entry into the train station involves a fall and a rise (*W*, p. 25), much as does the *Wake* itself.

Even more fascinating, though speculative, are some possible allusions to Joyce himself. Traveling by train, Watt meets Mr. Spiro, the editor of *Crux*, a popular Catholic monthly. This magazine publishes prize competitions, such as anagrams on the fifteen letters of the Holy Family (Mary, Joseph, and Jesus). The winning entry was "Has J. Jurms a po? Yes" (*W*, p. 27). According to William York Tindall, "J. Jurms" could be a distortion of Joyce's own name; "po" might be an unfinished (chamber) pot,[57] perhaps Molly Bloom's, since her word, "Yes," is the answer to the question. The Galls, father and son, recall the blind piano tuner in *Ulysses*, but, Watt wonders, "were they not perhaps merely step-father and step-son" (*W*, p. 71)—like Bloom and Stephen, or, as some critics have suggested,[58] Joyce and Beckett themselves (both in a spiritual sense, that is).

Punning names aside, the chief stylistic influence of Joyce appears in *Watt*'s extensive catalogues and overly explicit language. The numerous lists, detailing the utterances of Watt's voices (*W*, p. 29), his ancestors (*W*, p. 46), Knott's clothes (*W*, p. 100) and footwear (*W*, p. 200), to name only a few, turn "the cataloguing process of *Ulysses* into a nightmare of pedantry."[59] The exhaustive descriptions, such as that of Watt's walk, derive, according to Hugh Kenner,[60] from Joyce's ultra-naturalistic style in the "Ithaca" chapter of *Ulysses*. Its extreme verbal detail surpassing the exactitudes of Zola, Joyce's language seems to be a satire on the notebook naturalism of Dreiser and Norris; Beckett's equally involved prose is, however, not a literary but a philosophic parody. Producing an inventory not of facts but of logical possibilities, he renders the subject matter trivial and the method of analysis absurd. And he does so in a style that complements his theme: the universe as a closed system. For, by examining a room or event, and explaining it in terms of all its possible arrangements of furniture or permutations of possible meanings, Beckett is creating his own closed system of language. As does Joyce, then, "he puts the closed form of his art to expressive use . . . but it remains a closed form. . . . It is closed because it depends on finite sets. . . ."[61] Murphy's biscuit-eating dilemma was the precursor of this technique; Molloy's sucking stones are its hilarious and ridiculous apogee.

Joyce found implicit significance and solace in his closed circles, contemplating a formal pattern that accounted for everything. For Beckett, as we have seen, the concept of the closed system implied not union but isolation, and in *Watt* he attacks Joyce's belief in it by demonstrating that such a system contains no meaning, that all it circumscribes is, in fact, *nothing*.

The technique is simple. By using finite sets, and by exploring all the permutations possible within that set, Beckett ends, not with having said anything *definitive* about the event or object in question, but merely by having said some (and in some simpler cases, all) of the things that *could* be said about it. In this respect Beckett's style differs from that of "Ithaca," where the reader does learn a host of minute but real facts. In *Watt*, though, we never learn exactly what the incident of the Galls signifies; we see only its possible meanings. As are all the events of the book, it is one of "great formal brilliance and indeterminable purport" (*W*, p. 74). And even knowing his eating and sleeping habits, how he puts on his clothes, what he wears, the duties of his servants, and the regimen of his household, *what* do we really know about Knott? Nothing. He is as much an unknown quantity at the end of Watt's stay as he was at the beginning. Moreover, there is now the suspicion that Knott is *not*: he is the nonexistent center of his circle, and of the book itself.

Before attempting to untie that Knott, first let us look at the significant circles of *Watt*. As in *Murphy*, life iself is circular. Detailing the progression of the seasons, Arsene begins and ends with "the cruellest month," April, the month both of Christ's rebirth and Beckett's nativity. For Arsene April is simply the signal for "the whole bloody business starting all over again"

(*W*, p. 47). Not only cyclical, life, as are Vico's history and Joyce's *Wake*, is repetitious, a predestined pursuit that never changes and cannot be changed by anything, not even knowledge:

> And if I could begin it all over again, knowing what I know now, the result would be the same. And if I could begin again a third time, knowing what I would know then, the result would be the same. And if I could begin it all over again a hundred times, knowing each time a little more than the time before, the result would always be the same, and the hundredth life as the first, and the hundred lives as one. (*W*, p. 47)

(Note how the syntax, repeated several times, conveys the circular monotony of life.) As does Eliot in "East Coker" Beckett knows that "the coming is in the shadow of the going and the going is in the shadow of the coming . . . the purpose that budding withers, that withering buds, whose blooming is a budding withering" (*W*, pp. 57–58).

The microcosm imitates the macrocosm: human events, like the plants, go round in circles. Eating is a mechanical process, an endlessly revolving sphere that propels itself onward without any hope of stopping. Arsene tells of a servant girl, Mary, whose diet consists in part of peppermints and onions, each food necessitating the other. Her hands move like

> piston rods. At the moment that the one hand presses, with open palm, between the indefatigable jaws, a cold potato, onion, tart or sandwich, the other darts into the pouch and there, unerringly, fastens on a sandwich, onion, tart or cold potato [note reversal of terms], as Mary wills. And the former on its way down to be filled meets the latter on its way up to be emptied. (*W*, p. 55) [62]

Human labor is circular and futile, a closed system that encloses nothing but meaninglessness. The porter in the train station spends his time wheeling milk cans back and forth, from one group to another. Watt's experience of life is similar to the porter's. Approaching Knott's house, he hears a threne or mixed choir. The number 52.28571428 is a surd representing the number of weeks in a year; the surd in the second verse, 51.1428571, is more puzzling and seems to be the result of merely dividing 360 by 7, as if to show the infinite nature of a circle (= 360 degrees). As surds, or irrational numbers that repeat their decimals *ad infinitum,* both figures represent an endless, circular continuity. In contrast to this circular progression that does not progress, is the linear descent of the four generations mentioned in the song. Sung by soprano, alto, tenor, and bass, the threne includes great granma Magrew, granma Magrew, mama Magrew, and Miss Magrew. Lest anyone should still miss the point, the "thanks" go from "blooming" to "drooping" to "withered" and "forgotten." It sounds indeed "like a funeral dirge that summarizes man's life or part of it."[63]

Threne is eventually followed by round, only this time the voices are those of frogs. "Krak! Krek! Krik!" they go, similarly to the sound of Stephen Dedalus's feet on Sandymount Strand: "Crush, crack, crick, crick."[64] But more significant than a possible reference to Joyce's *Ulysses* is the fact that it takes Beckett's frogs 360 intervals—the number of degrees in a circle—before they can sing simultaneously once more.

In Knott's service, Watt assumes the complete nature of experience that the circle's shape implies. It is inconceivable to him that he should remain on the ground floor for either less or more than one year's time:

> if it was less than one year, then there was want, seasons passing, or a season, or a month, or a week, or a day, wholly or in part, on which the light of Mr. Knott's service had not shone, nor its dark brooded. . . . But if it was more than one year, then there was surfeit, seasons passing, or a season, or a month, or a week, or a day, wholly or in part. (*W*, p. 132)

Watt soon learns the folly of his expectations, but "the severance of his relation to anything but the circle is total."[65]

Serving Knott, Watt serves in a closed system:

Watt had more and more the impression . . . that nothing could be added to Mr. Knott's establishment, and from it nothing taken away, but that as it was now, so it had been in the beginning, and so it would remain to the end. (*W*, p. 131)

This household, in constant flux, achieves eternal stasis: "nothing remained, and nothing came or went, because all was a coming and a going" (*W*, p. 132). His two servants are "for ever about Mr. Knott in tireless assiduity turning" (*W*, p. 61). Mr. Knott, for his part, sleeps in a round bed and rotates his position in it at the rate of one degree a night, thus accomplishing a complete circle in the space of one year, like the earth around the sun.

Knott is the center of the book, literally as well as figuratively. Circular in form, *Watt* begins and ends in summer. Moreover, in part 1 we see Watt entering a train station, and in part 4 we again observe him in a depot. Hunchy Hackett tells us he lent Watt five shillings to buy a boot, and in the last pages of the book we witness Knott putting on one boot, shoe, or slipper. Thus we are brought "in a full solipsistic circle" [66] back to Watt.

In between depots and boots we have the story of Watt at Knott's house. Yet this obviously spherical outline[67] of the book, surrounding Knott the way his servants do, is deceptive.[68] For, as the author-surrogate, Sam, tells us:

As Watt told the beginning of his story, not first but second, so not fourth, but third, now he told its end. Two, one, four, three, that was the order in which Watt told his story. (*W*, p. 215)

The two railroad parts (one and four in the book) are thus *one* continuous part of Watt's life, namely, his departure from Knott's house and his journey to the asylum and Sam. Chronologically, then, Watt's story ends with him out of the normal world, not traveling ahead to the farther end of the railway line, but walking backwards, through the hole of the fence, into his garden and toward his habitation in the asylum. Beckett is then fooling the reader into thinking that Watt, having learned something from his service to Knott, rejoins normal society at last. Most important, by distorting the chronology in order to place Knott at the center of his book, Beckett is telling the reader that it is a book about Knotting, that all anyone can ever speak of is nothing, and that all language and life are merely illusions covering the reality of nothingness.

One incident in Knott's house reveals the full extent of Beckett's negative views. Contemplating Erskine's picture, Watt sees a broken circle with a blue dot "in the eastern background" (*W*, p. 128). Although the picture gives the illusion of perspective and motion, that is to say, the circle and dot seem to be subject to time and space, the circle is really "in boundless space, in endless time" (*W*, p. 129). True to his analytical mind, Watt proceeds to enumerate the possible interpretations of this painting. The possibility that it is perhaps "a circle and a centre not its centre in search of a centre and its circle respectively" (*W*, p. 129) causes him to weep with unchecked tears. But, without crying, we can see a different, more symbolic meaning behind it. The circle could represent the circle of language and logic that collapses for Watt at Knott's house, collapses because it fails to grasp or envelop the meaning behind objects, events. This meaning is, figuratively speaking, the dot, or center of the circle, and it too is in search of something: a method by which it can be surrounded or understood. The break at the bottom of the circle is perhaps there because, as Watt remarks, "It is by the nadir that we come . . . and it is by the nadir that we go" (*W*, p. 130). But that break in the circumference also signifies the irremediable disjunction between meaning and means, between knowledge and man's ability to learn. For the dot, if it ever did occupy the center of the circle, has slipped out and now occupies a place eternally to right of it. Significantly, we are told that the circle does not turn but is static, and that there is only one correct position for the painting on the wall. There may, then, be a pattern operating in the universe, but it is destined to remain a hidden one, forever beyond man's reach.

Language, man's tool for dealing with the world, is, according to Beckett, inadequate and false in the sense that it does not discover the meaning behind external reality. Watt at first avoids the problem of finding such meaning by devoting himself to purely surface reality, ignoring irrational behavior such as that of the porter and Lady McCann. But once in Knott's house, this man of reason is confronted by irrationality, causing him to lose faith in and abandon the logical, if arbitrary, process of speech:

> it was in vain that Watt said Pot, pot. . . . For it was not a pot, the more he looked, the more he reflected, the more he felt sure of that, that is [sic] was not a pot at all. It resembled a pot, it was almost a pot, but it was not a pot of which one could say, Pot, pot, and be comforted. (*W*, p. 81)

Watt is no longer capable of turning "little by little, a disturbance into words," and the "pillow of old words" (*W*, p. 117) that had protected his head from the bed of reality has been removed. From not being able to name things, and so control them, Watt proceeds, or rather regresses, to an inability to compose sentences. Only "short and isolated phrases" (*W*, p. 119) can issue from his lips. Finally, he is reduced to treating language like any other closed set, hoping that by manipulating its members into the right order[69] he will be able to formulate the reality that eludes his expression. And so, speaking to Sam, he methodically inverts words, letters, and sentences in almost all possible permutations. In doing this, Watt is presumably still looking, not for *the* meaning, but for *a* meaning, although, by saying all that can be said of an object or event, Watt is implicitly hoping to trap the ultimate significance in a maze of possibilities.

There has been much speculation that Beckett, whose interest in philosophy did not end with Descartes,[70] has actually, in

Watt, written a fictional counterpart to Ludwig Wittgenstein's *Tractatus* and, indeed, the whole philosophical movement. of logical positivism. Jacqueline Hoefer, in an article on this theory, calls attention to a sentence from Arsene's "brief" speech: "Do not come down the ladder, Ifor, I haf taken it away" (*W*, p. 44). Wittgenstein, it seems, explained his ideas with a similar metaphor:

> My propositions are elucidatory in this way: he who understands me finally recognizes them as senseless, when he has climbed out through them, on them, over them. (*He must so to speak throw away the ladder, after he has climbed up on it.*)[71]

"Ifor," Miss Hoefer continues, is the logical construction "if . . . or" condensed into one word, and Beckett's use of "haf," German pronunciation of "have," also points to Wittgenstein. Of course, the real proof of any such theory lies not in its surface allusions but in its content, and here too the identification seems plausible. Wittgenstein equated words with thought. If there were no language or thought, then all would be undifferentiated, and so Nothing. There is either words or, on the other hand, silence: "*Wovon man nicht sprechen kann, darüber muss man schweigen.*"[72] This choice does run through *Watt*, and, to an ever greater extent, through the trilogy of novels Beckett wrote after the war. But, now that we have set up such a convincing ladder, we too are forced to throw it away. Beckett told critic John Fletcher in 1961 that the ladder is a reference to a Welsh joke, and confessed he had read Wittgenstein only "within the last two years."[73] Professor Joseph Bauke of Columbia's German Department has, I believe, found the solution to the puzzle. Fritz Mauthner, the philosopher whose works Beckett had read aloud to Joyce, wrote that, "If I wish to ascend in the critique of language, which is the most important business of thinking mankind, then I must destroy language behind me and in me from step to step, then *I must destroy every rung of the ladder once I step upon it*."[74] Gershon Weiler acknowledges that the

ladder image also occurs in Wittgenstein's *Tractatus,* but whether Mauthner took this metaphor from Wittgenstein is irrelevant.
What is now clear is that Beckett, in writing Arsene's speech,
must have had Mauthner, not Wittgenstein, at the back of his
mind. It is all the more significant, then, that it was Beckett
who informed Weiler of Joyce's ownership of the three-volume
Beiträge that "mysteriously disappeared [from Joyce's library]
after his death."[75]

Whatever the philosophical sources or implications of *Watt,*
it is certain that Beckett's attitude toward words is vastly different from Joyce's. Seeing them as demons of falsity, Beckett would
question the very foundation and raison d'être of literary art.
But where Beckett maligned speech, calling it false and traitorous
to any search for self or reality, Joyce worshiped the word. A
lapsed Catholic, Joyce nevertheless still believed that "in the
beginning was the Word," and, with Vico, that all language
originated from man's effort to arrive at the meaning of the
divine thunderclap. Beckett followed Joyce and Vico in tracing
language from gesture,[76] but the tendency of his works to silence
and mime suggests that he has found gesture to be more truthful,
less distorted than words. Joyce's high regard for human speech
is reflected in both his fictional and critical writings. In an early
essay, "The Study of Languages," Joyce states that "in the
history of words there is much that indicates the history of men,
and . . . we have a useful illustration of the effect of external
influences on the very words of a race."[77] Martha Clifford, in
Ulysses, equates "word" with "world"[78] and in *Finnegans Wake*
we read, "The war is in words and the wood is the world" (*FW*
98.34–35) . Later Shaun speaks of "silbils and wholly words" (*FW*
424.33) .

Unlike Yeats and Joyce, Beckett does not believe that "words
alone are certain good."[79] Richard Coe puts it succinctly:

> Like Joyce, he [Beckett] is intrigued by words, but whereas
> for the author of *Finnegans Wake,* language was an intimate
> part of the mystery of creation, for Beckett words are the chief
> ingredient of the art of failure; they form that impenetrable

barrier of language which forever keeps us from knowing who
we are, what we are.[80]

Harvey writes that "Beckett uses language but has no faith in
language,"[81] and Nathan Scott that Beckett's work is "a literature
uninformed by any faith in literature itself, and [there is] . . .
profound skepticism about the Word and about Mythos. . . ."[82]

The failure of language and logic for Watt implies the failure
of fiction and art for Beckett, a theme that will greatly concern
the author in his trilogy. It also suggests the failure of man to
know, to learn. For how else do we acquire knowledge if not
by speech and reason? "It becomes evident that for Beckett the
understanding of reality remains an impossibility. The Beckettian
hero is incapable of knowledge."[83] Even

> rational and sensible knowledge can lead only to solipsism.
> Hence the comic emphasis upon the circle, that perfect self-
> contained solipsistic symbol. But Watt's circle is broken. Even
> less than Murphy and Belacqua does Watt find solipsism
> possible.[84]

Unlike the metaphysical cosmos of the seventeenth century,
which was shattered by Galileo and modern science, Beckett's
circle is broken by the uncertain and irrational nature of the
world, before which reason and speech are helpless. Joyce's early
art is of surface clarity; people and objects in *Dubliners, Portrait,*
and *Ulysses* all have sharp outlines. Very rarely in these works
is there a question of what is happening or who is present. In
Finnegans Wake Joyce's actual content soon becomes evident.
Here the *difficulty* is all on the surface: deciphering the allusions
and references. Beckett's work is ambiguous in a more fundamental sense. In part this is due to his belief that "nothing is
known" (*W,* p. 15)—or can be—and in part to the fact that
Beckett's universe, unlike Joyce's, is not a contingent one. But
even given a certain amount of uncertainty in the world, Beckett
likes to add to it. The form of *Watt,* as we have seen, is deliberately achronological, and even the narrator, Sam, like all of
Beckett's subsequent narrators, is not to be trusted:

it is difficult for a man like Watt to tell a long story like Watt's without leaving out some things, and foisting in others. And this does not mean either that I [Sam] may not have left out some of the things that Watt told me, or foisted in others that Watt never told me. (*W*, p. 126)

If the story is questionable, the characters are physically vague, unrecognizable from a distance. Tetty Nixon, on first observing Watt, is not sure whether "it" is a man or woman, and Hunchy Hackett thinks that "it" could be "a parcel, a carpet for example, or a roll of tarpaulin, wrapped up in dark paper and tied about the middle with a cord" (*W*, p. 16). At the end of the novel the situation is reversed and Watt, walking toward the railway depot, sights a figure, "human apparently," although "Watt was unable to say whether this figure was that of a man, or that of a woman, or that of a priest, or that of a nun" (*W*, p. 225).

Time and space are also uncertain. Watt does not know how long he served on the ground floor, the first floor, or how long he stayed in Knott's house altogether (*W*, p. 138). The actual location of Knott's house, except for its proximity to a race course, is never revealed.

The ambiguity of space, time, and people plagues Beckett and his characters. To alleviate the pain of it, his heroes resort to considering everything as part of a series. Knott's servants, the Lynch twins and their dog, Erskine's picture, and even Knott himself[85] all belong to a progression of servants, dogs, pictures, and Knotts. Why a series? First, a series can comfort, as witness Leopold Bloom's smile upon thinking of the series of Molly's lovers:

each one who enters imagines himself to be the first to enter whereas he is always the last term of a preceding series even if the first term of a succeeding one, each imagining himself to be the first, last, only and alone, whereas he is neither first nor last nor only nor alone in a series originating in and repeated to infinity.[86]

If, in Joyce, a series comforts because it gives companionship, it also soothes the pain of uncertainty by placing a thing in relation to at least two others, the one before it and the one after it. This is not to say that a series is causal, that is governed by the law of cause and effect, so that each member necessitates the next one. On the contrary, to give only one of many examples in *Watt,* "Tom's two years on the first floor are not *because* of Dick's two years on the ground floor, or of Harry's coming then" (*W,* p. 134). Each element is independent of the others, and yet, paradoxically, there is a serial relationship between them all.

Raymond Federman even places Beckett's book in a series:

> Watt's futile quest remains forever part of an incomprehensible, universal series of quests which mathematically, geometrically, philosophically and artistically, can reduce, divide, or repeat themselves to infinity and absurdity.[87]

And it is comforting to the reader to realize that the series of Beckett's own works is still in the process of being produced.

Mercier et Camier (written 1945–46;
published in French in 1970)

Only recently published and translated from its original French, *Mercier et Camier*[88] is worth the reader's attention because of the light it sheds on Beckett's subsequent works and on the circular motif in particular.

The book consists of twelve chapters, with every third chapter being, in outline form, a summary of the previous two. Narrated in the third person, except for the beginning of chapter 4, which is told in the first person, the story concerns two friends, Mercier and Camier, who leave for the country and a journey of no apparent purpose. Whatever their quest, it is not achieved, for in the end they return to the still-unnamed city of their departure.

A journal novel that prefigures *Molloy* in its theme, *Mercier et Camier* also presents for the first time Beckett's characteristic clown couple. Until now we have had solitary heroes—Belacqua, Murphy, Watt—but Mercier and Camier, although a "pseudocouple," look forward to A and C, Vladimir and Estragon, Hamm and Clov, Winnie and Willy. Their conversations, stichomythic, repetitious, and trivial as they are, forecast the similar but far superior dialogue of *Waiting for Godot.*

To a certain extent, the novel is a satire on heroic quests. Beckett informs us at the start that the climate for their journey was always temperate, and that they did not suffer too much. Far from being an extraordinary feat of endurance, the journey of Mercier and Camier is distinguished only by its ordinariness. This fact is underlined by the beginning of the trip. After nearly missing each other, the two friends finally meet, only to be delayed by a sudden shower. While waiting for the rain to stop, they observe two dogs copulating, much as Molly Bloom observed a similar event from her hotel window. By the time the weather permits them to depart, the heroism of the journey has been significantly deflated and undercut. In the same manner Joyce undercut Homer's *Odyssey* by having his Ulysses, Bloom, experience such a static, seemingly uneventful day.

The book's epic façade is further mocked by Camier's identity as a private detective. His profession implies the bravery of a Sherlock Holmes, but Camier is always finding an excuse to terminate his quest and return home. Traveling at first by train, both he and Mercier symbolically sit with their backs to the engine.

Ulysses is, perhaps, the object of direct parody. There is a father-and-son recognition scene but, unlike "Ithaca," there is no communion, and Mercier drives his children away from him. Teresa, a bar-girl, refuses to pay M. Conaire, a customer, any marked attention. Lydia Douce and Mina Kennedy are equally cold to Lenehan and Bloom. There is a discussion on artificial insemination, perhaps a parody of the medical students' discussion of contraception in "The Oxen of the Sun" episode in *Ulysses.*

The real influence of Joyce, however, can be seen in the circular structure and imagery of the book. In the original French version, Camier says "J'ai le gland en feu, en effet. . . . **C'est** un cercle vicieux,"[89] and both he and Mercier are forever circling around the city, returning to it and Helen's place, a brothel. The impulse to retrace their steps is compulsive; before they allow themselves to rest, Mercier and Camier must tire themselves out, with only enough energy to take them back to the spot where they had originally decided to spend the night. At the same time, there is the same inner imperative to go on that Molloy, Malone, and the Unnamable will all experience: " 'What does it matter,' said Mercier, 'Where we are going? We are going, that's enough' " (M&C, p. 90) .

To understand this contrary desire for both motion and stasis it is necessary to go back to Beckett's remarks in his essay on Proust. Habit, Beckett writes, is a "great deadener" (*Proust,* p. 9) , paralyzing man's awareness of his situation and the world around him. For this reason Beckett is driven from it, as Mercier and Camier are impelled to leave the routine of the city. On the other hand, however, Beckett fears the suffering and direct confrontation with reality that are a result of the suspension of habit and "the free play of every faculty" (*P,* p. 9) . Boredom, the price of habit, is "the most tolerable . . . the most durable of human evils" (*P,* p. 10) . So too, Mercier and Camier, having left the city, find themselves possessed by a desire to return to its tedium. This constant tension between motion and stasis affects all Beckett's heroes, and yet, as forbidding as the extremes are, eternal flux is even more despicable because it is eternal loss: "our life a succession of Paradises successively denied, . . . the only true Paradise is the Paradise that has been lost" (*P,* p. 14) . For Joyce, flux, because it is the order of things, was the supreme good; for Beckett, flux is to be avoided for that very reason, because it partakes of habit: "considered as a progression, this endless series of renovations leaves us as indifferent as the heterogeneity of any one of its terms" (*P,* p. 16) . Beckett craved a stasis, a finality that the perpetual motion of Joyce's system could not provide, and that his own system, because it copied the closed circularity of Joyce's, could not satisfy.

Beckett's use of time in this novel also presents another contrast to Joyce's technique. With Joyce, Beckett views time as circular and static. "One does what one can, but one can nothing. Only squirm and wiggle, to end up in the evening where you were in the morning," says Mercier to Camier (*M&C*, p. 84). Moreover, rain falls at the end of the novel as it did at the beginning, preserving the illusion of an unchangeable world.

In Joyce, time is respected and appointments, for the most part, are kept. Although Joe Dillon fails to go to the Pigeon House, Corley meets his slavey, Lenehan meets Corley, Gallagher meets Little Chandler, and Boylan comes to see Molly at 4:00 P.M. as he had said he would. Beckett's works, on the other hand, display an amazing number of trysts that never take place. Belacqua never meets Winnie at the asylum gate, and Lucy fails to meet him in the park. Mercier and Camier miss each other for three-quarters of an hour, and, of course, Godot never shows up. The farcical efforts of Mercier and Camier to meet at 9:15 A.M. constitute a comedy of time in the best tradition of American slapstick. For forty-five minutes they each arrive either five minutes late or early, and when they finally meet, they argue over whose fault it all was.

Anticipating *Endgame* as well as *Godot,* Beckett treats time as a medium in which objects are lost, disappear, become quickly ruined. Bags, umbrellas, raincoats, and—shades of Belacqua—even a bicycle all show the ravages of time's cancerous action. The bicycle, in particular, will become a recurrent appendage of Beckett's bums, symbolic, according to Hugh Kenner,[90] of man's physical existence. Here it undergoes the same deterioration that the heroes of the trilogy will endure. Abandoned, after eight days its wheels are gone, its seat and reflector also missing.

But it is the *Godot*-like elements that are most significant, pointing the path Beckett's fiction will take. Unlike Joyce, who had a keen awareness of history and in whose works there is usually a past, present, and future, Beckett would reduce his closed system to a continuous present. The weather is "what it's always like" (*M&C*, p. 67), and the time is the continuous twilight hour of Vladimir and Estragon's vigil on a country road. Indeed, that play's theme is clearly enunciated by Mercier (like Vladimir, the more intellectual of the pair), who concludes that all that man can do to combat the pain of living is to wait for its end:

> Do you not inkle, like me, how you might adjust yourself to this preposterous penalty [i.e., existence] and placidly await the executioner. . . ? (*M&C*, p. 89)

This statement also shows how far Beckett has traveled since writing *More Pricks Than Kicks* (1934). In that work he openly espoused the Joycean universe of cyclical progress and constant motion (see the previous discussion of the story "Ding-Dong"). Here, however, the emphasis is already on stasis, on waiting, and the characteristic pessimism of Beckett, apparent even in such a comparatively crude book as *Mercier and Camier,* is in sharp contrast to Joyce's exuberant joy in the world. Demanding a finality that the closed but infinitely renewable universe of *Finnegans Wake* excludes, Beckett will now try to find a way out of that universe. Like the new scientists of the seventeenth century, who contested the then current metaphysical philosophy of macrocosm and microcosm that placed man and earth at the center of the spherical universe, Beckett will try to break the circle of Joyce's universe, to destroy the concept of a contingent world so that he may reach an ultimate point, invulnerable to the slings and arrows of outrageous physical fortune, immune to the degrading decay of time and space. *Molloy, Malone Dies,* and *The Unnamable,* the trilogy of novels that will be discussed in the next chapter, represent his first and, some think, Beckett's most brilliant attempt to break out of the Joycean trap.

4

The Voice of the Artist

Even Beckett's staunchest admirers must have been surprised
when, in 1951, *Molloy* was published. Written a decade after
Murphy (1938), *Molloy* was light-years away from the earlier
work in content, form, and style. Surprise probably turned to
consternation over *Malone meurt,* published the same year, and
by the time the third part of the trilogy, *L'Innomable,* was
issued in 1953, it was clear to friend and critic alike that Beckett's
fiction had taken a radically new, and at first somewhat incomprehensible, direction. Gone was the realistic city setting of
More Pricks Than Kicks and *Murphy*; Dublin was replaced by
an island that could be Ireland but that possessed French-named
streets and a bare, sinister no-man's landscape. Instead of the
alienated, eccentric, but relatively normal Murphy and Belacqua,
the reader was now presented with a series of beings, scarcely
recognizable as human, who became progressively less so from
book to book until, in the third and final novel, this literary
devolution culminated in a vegetablelike character named
Worm. Plot, too, underwent a deformation or decay. The still
traditional quest of *Molloy* soon gave way to the monologues or
logorrhea of Malone and the Unnamable. Indeed, the trilogy
seemed to turn inward, like a dragon eating his tail, feeding upon
itself and "spiralling down from all externals to an examination
of the internal silence that fills each individual being."[1] As in

Finnegans Wake, form and content were synonymous, integrated to a degree few writers had ever before achieved. Indeed, to apply his own words on Joyce, Beckett had not written about something, he had written that something itself.[2]

It was also apparent that the Joycean elements in Beckett's style had been almost entirely discarded. A few puns and possible references[3] to the Master could be discerned, but they are vestigial traits in a style that is now uniquely the author's own. It is a curious paradox that Beckett, having found his fictional voice at last, makes the search for one's voice or identity the major theme of the three novels.

Finally, and most obviously, Beckett had abandoned English and was now writing in French. Much speculation has since been expended on the reasons for such a linguistic volte-face, but even Beckett's own puzzling explanation sheds hardly any light on the matter. To Niklaus Gessner he replied that he had changed languages "parce qu'en français c'est plus facile d'écrire sans style."[4] Perhaps he meant that it was necessary to write in French in order to escape, not the discipline of style per se, but only the all-too-familiar limitations of the English syntax. Or, as William Y. Tindall has suggested,[5] Beckett may have wanted to get away from the richness of his native tongue, and so traded the extensive vocabulary of English for the simpler, but more precise, words of French, words that, in their relative newness to Beckett, gave him aesthetic distance as well, perhaps as a new way of seeing reality. Equally important, writing in French affirmed Beckett's exile from Ireland and his integration into the life and culture of his adopted country, France.[6] Such assimilation was never achieved—or indeed desired—by Joyce, but Beckett's literary gallicization may also represent a subconscious desire on his part to get out from under Joyce's shadow by turning away from the language of *Ulysses* and *Finnegans Wake.* Regarding the latter work as highly as he did, Beckett may have considered it the supreme achievement possible in English prose. Admiring Proust's novels, especially his treatment of time and memory, Beckett nevertheless evidently found the Frenchman's style less intimidating than Joyce's. There was, at any rate, room for experimentation.

In a sense, however, Beckett has not abandoned English at all. Aside from *Molloy,* which was translated with the assistance of Patrick Bowles, all the English editions of Beckett's novels and plays are the work of the author himself. Like Joyce, who could never read a galley or page proof without expanding the text, Beckett, though completely bilingual, cannot simply translate. A polished and polishing artist, he uses the English versions of his works as opportunities for slight but significant revision, pruning and shaping in seemingly minute ways so as to bring his compositions closer to that ideal concept of them which he alone possesses. As a result, in many cases, such as that of *Endgame,* the original French text is actually superseded by the later English translation. For this reason alone, the serious reader and critic of Beckett's work must be capable of reading him in both languages, savoring the immediacy of the French but carefully scrutinizing the English texts for a clearer, more refined statement of his artistic intention.

And yet the fact that Beckett chooses to compose *directly* in French is extremely important. Whether he feels himself inhibited by English or Joyce's achievement in it, it is as if Beckett *must* write his first draft in French before he is free to write the second, more definitive one, in English. Perhaps a question of psychological need, Beckett's bilingual artistry has, according to at least one critic, significant implications for all of contemporary literature. Along with the similar proficiency of Vladimir Nabokov and Jorge Luis Borges, it suggests to George Steiner

that the modernist movement can be seen as a strategy of permanent exile. The artist and the writer are incessant tourists window-shopping over the entire compass of available forms. The conditions of linguistic stability, of local, national self-consciousness in which literature flourished between the Renaissance and say, the nineteen-fifties are now under extreme stress. Faulkner and Dylan Thomas might one day be seen as among the last major "home-owners" of literature,

Joyce's employment at Berlitz and Nabokov's residence in a hotel may come to stand as signs for the age. *Increasingly, every act of communication between human beings seems an act of translation.*[7]

This last sentence of Steiner's statement represents an important idea of Beckett's own, one that, I believe, conditioned the development of his art away from that of Joyce. For, turning his back on Joyce's language for literary purposes, Beckett also turned away from the style and substance of his master's fiction. To understand just how and why this occurred, it is necessary first to explore the critical credo of both writers.

For Joyce, art was a divine calling, possessing the implicit value of religion and demanding the same dedication that the Church required of its priests.[8] Indeed, the very terms that Joyce uses in discussing the artist and his profession are religious ones. Stephen Dedalus, faced with a choice of vocations, chooses to be a "priest of eternal imagination, transmuting the daily bread of experience into the radiant body of everlasting life."[9] And although, at the end of chapter 4 of *A Portrait of the Artist as a Young Man,* he sees a young girl wading in the waters of Bull Island, it is Stephen who has been symbolically baptized into the religion of art and beauty. In *Ulysses* he recounts his literary effort, "The Parable of the Plums," and, with the aid of Leopold Bloom, transforms his Hamlet hat into that of a deacon. Both character and author derive their own critical theories from sacred texts. Stephen uses the aesthetic doctrine of St. Thomas Aquinas to define the beautiful and the threefold process of perceiving it (wholeness, harmony, and radiance). Joyce, in his turn, calls the revelation in each *Dubliners* story by a name originally applied to Jesus' spiritual manifestation to the Magi: epiphany. Finally, the artist, for both Joyce and Stephen, is analogous to God. A divine creator, he too "remains within or behind or beyond or above his handiwork, invisible, refined out of existence, indifferent, paring his fingernails."[10] On the human level the artist is a bardic voice, "the intense centre of the life of his age,"[11] capable of forging in his superior soul the uncreated conscience of his race.

Nothing could be more foreign to Beckett than this exalted portrait of the artist. For him, literature is a futile exercise and its practitioners, like the biblical builders who tried to erect a tower to heaven, doomed to failure: the result for both is sheer "babble." In the third of three dialogues with friend and philosopher Georges Duthuit, Beckett explicitly articulated this view. He praised Bram van Velde, a modern painter, for being "the first to admit that to be an artist is to fail, as no other dare fail, that failure is his world and the shrink from it desertion. . . ."[12] If Joyce believed that "all those who have written nobly have not written in vain,"[13] Beckett is certain that

> you would do better . . . to obliterate texts than to blacken margins, to fill in the holes of words till all is blank and flat and the whole ghastly business looks like what it is, senseless, speechless, issueless misery.[14]

If Joyce admired the artist to the point of worship, for Beckett and his characters he is only an object of pity and scorn. The heroes of the trilogy, artists all, continually mock and question their literary skill, demeaning both themselves and the endeavor they are engaged in. "But it is not at this late stage of my relation that I intend to give way to literature," sneers Moran (*Molloy*, p. 207) ; later he deprecatingly adds: "Sometimes you would think I'm writing for the public" (*Molloy*, p. 232).

Far from praising life as Joyce stipulated literature must do,[15] Beckett's writings seem to declare that human existence is continual degradation and physical horror. Literature, morever, only contributes to the "senseless, speechless, issueless misery." In *How It Is* (1961), Beckett's "I" practices a literal fiction of cruelty. Writing on Pim's back with his nails, he digs out the letters and responses until the human paper bleeds.

Why these tremendous differences in critical outlook? Why does one writer consider the artist a god and the other see him

only as a tortured creature, crawling through the mud of life
to inflict additional torture on a second human being? Most
important, why is art possible for Joyce and, although he continues to practice it, an inevitable failure for Beckett?

The answers to these questions, according to George Steiner,
lie in a recent but decisive development in the cultural history
of Western civilization: "the retreat from the word."[16] Until
the age of Milton[17] the Judeo-Christian world believed in,
indeed was founded on, the primacy of language. "In the beginning was the Word," decreed the disciple (John 1:1), and the
secular pursuits of society echoed this belief:

> Literature, philosophy, theology, law, the arts of history, are
> endeavors to enclose within the bounds of rational discourse
> the sum of human experience, its recorded past, its present
> condition and future expectations. . . . They bear solemn
> witness to the belief that all truth and realness . . . can be
> housed inside the walls of language.[18]

Modern literature testifies to the collapse of those walls, a
collapse that is due, in great part, to the rise of modern science
and mathematics. With the discovery of the laws of physics, the
formulation of analytical geometry and calculus, math and
science ceased to be descriptive, mere systems of notation. Instead, they became fantastically complex languages of their own,
languages that, unlike French, Italian, or Volapuck, are *increasingly untranslatable* or incomprehensible to the average
man. Moreover, the power of autonomous conception possessed
by the sciences is now considered the pathway to truth and
reality: math, not *Moby Dick,* will reveal the secrets of the
universe. Conversely, the sphere of language—the areas of meaning accessible to rational discussion—has diminished:

> The world of words has shrunk. One *cannot* talk of transfinite
> numbers except mathematically; one *should not,* suggests
> Wittgenstein, talk of ethics or aesthetics within the presently
> available categories of discourse. And it is . . . exceedingly
> difficult to speak meaningfully of a Jackson Pollock painting
> or a composition by Stockhausen.[19]

In the arts, too, avocal or alinguistic disciplines are thriving. Music and art are rivaling literature in popular interest; George Steiner believes that *"they are beginning to hold a place in literate society once firmly held by the word."*[20] And literature itself has responded by turning to silence. The extensive vocabulary of Shakespeare and of Milton is unknown to any save a few contemporary writers (Nabokov, for one). Rather,

> the writer of today tends to use far fewer and simpler words, both because mass culture has watered down the concept of literacy and because the sum of realities of which words can give a necessary and sufficient account has sharply diminished.[21]

Beckett's later novels and plays are a prime illustration of this linguistic fact. Reducing his vocabulary to a bare minimum of words and phrases that are repeated over and over again in a sort of endless and futile incantation, Beckett, like his artist-heroes, aspires to total silence. Working more and more with gesture rather than sound, stasis rather than movement, Beckett "is moving, with unflinching Irish logic, toward a form of drama in which a character, his feet trapped in concrete and his mouth gagged, will stare at the audience and say nothing."[22]

Whether or not it is due to a historical process such as Steiner describes, it is this loss of faith in language, this distrust of the word, that separates Beckett from Joyce. Loving the sound of all words,[23] just as the child in "The Sisters" was fascinated by "paralysis," "gnomon," and "simony," Joyce lovingly shaped them to catch the contours of all human experience. The first pages of *Portrait* brilliantly record the sensations of infancy; the last chapter of *Ulysses* unforgettably reproduces the thoughts of Molly Bloom, goddess of fertility and guilty of infidelity. *Finnegans Wake,* Joyce's ultimate literary achievement, is round, like the world itself. Multilingual, it is not so much a novel as "a thing of words."[24]

For Beckett the word is traitor rather than truth. "You either lie or hold your peace" (*Molloy*, p. 119), concludes Molloy. Indeed, for him as for Steiner, speech itself is, in a sense, no longer possible: "There is no communication because there are no vehicles of communication" (*Proust*, p. 47). The pathetic efforts of Watt to communicate with Sam, the tortuous inversions of language that he indulges in, prove one by one inadequate to convey the reality of experience. And because communication between human beings is impossible, literature itself is reduced to a monologue, to a solitary voice crying in the void, attempting to establish contact with the only thing it possibly can: itself.

Failure to communicate, or to believe in the possibility of doing so, entails alienation. Beckett's characters increasingly divorce themselves from all human society, seeking not the contact of others but the sealed room or jar that, symbolic of the womb, signifies a contraction or retreat into the self. On the other hand, Joyce's characters and his fiction, grounded in the word, soar ever upward and out. Like Stephen Dedalus's inscription on the flyleaf of his geography book, they expand to include Ireland (*Ulysses*) and all of history and the universe (*Finnegans Wake*). Bloom, Joyce's greatest fictional creation, was admired by the author for his well-rounded character. Son to Rudolph, husband to Molly, father to Milly, and friend to Stephen, he relates to all mankind, a model of *l'homme engagé*. Even greater, perhaps, than Bloom, is Dublin itself. A city, it was for Joyce, like all cities, a network of related people, a place where human contact was the norm.[25] (It is no accident that the central episode of *Ulysses*, "The Wandering Rocks," shows all the parts and people of the city colliding or relating and interrelating, like the well-meshed gears of Tom Rochford's machine.) *Finnegans Wake* extends this sense of human community to all time and all space: Earwicker is Everyman, Anna Livia Everywoman, the twins and Isabel Allchildren. Together they constitute a family, the microcosm of all relationships: social, political, economic, and historical. As Joyce exalts the family, so Beckett excoriates it. The Lynches in *Watt* constitute a hilarious but physically deformed and morally depraved collection of individuals. Incest is imminent in the Lambert household (*Malone Dies*) and, less crude but more common, Sapo's parents are a sharp satire of the typical middle-class bourgeois family, interested only in money, health, and a liberal profession for their son.

Moreover, Beckett's bums, ahistorical as well as antisocial, can only laugh at and despise contact with other human beings. Physical love, the ultimate possible closeness between people, is gradually reduced to a disgusting animal exercise, a futile and grotesque endeavor to break down the barrier of otherness. Mrs. Gorman and Watt, lacking both time and desire, can achieve only a hysterical series of physical postures. Ruth/Edith and Molloy, in the latter's words, "toiled and moiled until I discharged or gave up trying or was begged by her to stop. A mug's game in my opinion and tiring on top of that, in the long run" (*Molloy*, p. 76). Macmann, likewise, struggles "to bundle his sex into his partner's like a pillow into a pillow-slip, folding it in two and stuffing it in with his fingers" until "they finally succeeded, summoning to their aid all the resources of the skin, the mucous and the imagination, in striking from their dry and feeble clips a kind of sombre gratification" (*MD*, p. 89). This idyllic relationship, which produced if not children at least quatrains on "Hairy Mac and Sucky Moll" (*MD*, pp. 91–92), ends when Moll begins to give off an offensive smell, vomits at length, loses her hair, turns yellow, and finally dies. But perhaps the most pathetic attempt at sexual union occurs when Malone observes the couple across the way:

> in vain they clasp with the energy of despair, it is clear we have here two distinct and separate bodies, each enclosed within its own frontiers, and having no need of each other to come and go and sustain the flame of life, for each is well able to do so, independently of the other. Perhaps they are cold that they rub against each other so. . . . It is all very pretty and strange. . . . Ah how stupid I am, I see what it is, they must be loving each other, that must be how it is done. . . . Back and forth, back and forth, that must be wonderful. They seem to be in pain. (*MD*, p. 65)

At its best, love in Beckett is a memory of paradise lost, like

Nagg and Nell on Lake Como, Krapp and his girl in the punt, or the unfortunate Pam, late wife of Pim. At its worst it is, as we have seen, animallike and disgusting. Romantic love is savagely satirized, and woman herself is hated and rejected. Responsible for the original sin of birth,[26] which traps man in time, she is often, like Lousse, Moll, or the Unnamable's Madeleine, depicted as a jaileress.

Joyce's fiction embodies totally opposite ideas. His women, notably Molly Bloom and Anna Livia Plurabelle, are both earth mothers and agents of reconciliation. Molly is the means of uniting Stephen and Bloom. Anna Livia, as granny or Isis incarnate, picks up the pieces of Earwicker and puts her Humpty Dumpty back together again. Physical love is not a sin, but the supreme affirmation of life. Molly's yeses are sexual and, although they undoubtedly include adultery, signify her total acceptance of life. Anna Livia's return to her mad, "feary" father is also sexual, a primary symbol of renewal and rebirth that starts the whole "vicocycle" rolling again.

Alienated from his fellow humans, the Beckettian man is alienated as well from the external world. "I have no reason to be gladdened by the sun and I take good care not to be," says Molloy (Molloy, p. 39), and Malone admits that "a mere local phenomenon is something I would not have noticed" (MD, p. 61). Objects, too, suffer from Beckett's lack of faith in language. As Watt painfully discovered, there is no connection between a thing and the word used to denote it: "there could be no things but nameless things no names but thingless names" (Molloy, p. 41). The number of objects in the Beckett world— the sticks, bicycles, crutches, pencils, sacks, and can openers that accompany his characters on their futile quests—have little implicit meaning. Divorced from the words that are the only source of significance in this world, their chief purpose is to dwindle and disappear, thus helping "to restore silence" (Molloy, p. 16).[27]

Joyce's universe, in contrast to Beckett's, is one in which objects proliferate, multiplying their meanings as they continually appear and reappear. From Stephen's glasses to Buck Mulligan's shaving bowl and mirror, they are, like the trees in Baudelaire's forest, symbols of a deeper reality, one that character and reader alike must unravel. "Signatures of all things I am here to read,"[28] announces Stephen. "No symbols where none intended" (*Watt*, p. 254) is Beckett's reply.

Alienation from the world and aversion to human contact are not the only consequences of this retreat from the word. Speech, a necessity because it is the only road to silence, must be wrenched by man out of the void that surrounds him. The work of art is similarly "neither created nor chosen, but discovered, uncovered, excavated, preexisting within the artist" (*Proust*, p. 64), who then becomes an artisan: "The duty and task of a writer . . . are those of a translator" (*Proust*, p. 64). Art, "an act of communication between human beings," is itself an act of (self) translation. In this sense, then, even the French editions of Beckett's works are somehow not in their original language. Beckett himself is highly aware of this. The trilogy is a spiral descent into human consciousness, an attempt to penetrate the veils of personality and art and arrive at the original voice, the true author: the self. Moran may be the author of Molloy,[29] but Malone seems to have created them both, as well as all of Beckett's previous fictions (*MD*, p. 63). Finally, the Unnamable seems to be the true author of all, the fixed center of the fictions that, like planets around the sun, revolve endlessly about him. But, far from being the final box in the Chinese puzzle, the Unnamable only points to a whole new nest of them. Doubting his own existence, he is conscious of an anonymous "they," voices that have tricked him into believing that it is he who speaks. Beckett wrote in his essay on Proust,

> the only fertile research is excavatory, immersive, a contraction of the spirit, a descent. The artist is active but negatively, shrinking from the nullity of extracircumferential phenomena, drawn into the core of the eddy. (*Proust*, p. 48)

If this is true, if this is the direction art must take, then the descent is an endless one, the eddy an eternally revolving current that sucks the seeker ever downward to a bottomless sea.

Given this concept of art as a translation, always at least one remove from the true self, it is no wonder that two of Beckett's works take the form of a long citation. *How It Is* begins: "how it was *I quote* before Pim with Pim after Pim how it is three parts *I say it as I hear it*," and ends, ". . . that is how it was *end of quotation* after Pim how it is."[30] Similarly, *Texts for Nothing* concludes, ". . . *it* says, *it* murmurs."[31] In both cases the speaker, by attributing fiction to another, is denying authorship and confessing his failure to find his identity, to reach his Self. We are left, as in the beginning, with the ever-elusive self and its voice. In between, to borrow some of Joyce's words, lies "the ginnandgo gap,"[32] the untraversable silence that cannot be negotiated or negated.

Different attitudes toward art and the word result in different methods of composition. Joyce's fictional characterizations are constructed and achieve universality from the principle of the many. That is, through analogy, myth, and allegory, he inflates his heroes until they are all men and Everyman. Stephen Dedalus, by parallel and analogy,[33] is his namesake, the fabulous artificer, as well as Napoleon, Parnell, the Count of Monte Cristo, Byron, Dante, Lucifer, and Jesus. Bloom, through the magic of myth, is Ulysses, completing a twentieth-century odyssey. And Earwicker, thanks to the literary device of allegory, is everyone from Adam to Wellington. Beckett's method of characterization is just the opposite. Isolating his heroes from past and present alike, he strips them too of clothing, limbs, and desires, until they are just Man in the abstract, crawling through the primeval mud that is life. Thus, where Joyce enlarges, Beckett reduces; where Joyce exalts man to heroic proportions, Beckett degrades him to animal nakedness. As critic Krystyna Stamirowska has observed: "The logical development in method from Joyce to Beckett is the development from HCE to the Unnamable, from variability and plurability to monotony and singleness."[34] Or, as David Hayman sees it, because of "his very refusal to compete with Joyce . . . the narrative tradition which Joyce so brilliantly projected into outer space, Beckett has pulled back to the pole of negative capability by a parallel process of attentuation and mockery."[35]

The problem of the author's relationship to his fictions also provoked similar and yet different responses from the two writers. Although in *Portrait* Joyce presents the artist as a detached God, standing "within or behind or beyond or above his handiwork, invisible, refined out of existence, indifferent, paring his fingernails,"[36] this is not true of his own relationship to his works. On the contrary, Joyce is everywhere in his books. Always writing about himself, his family, his country, Joyce used both character and plot for self-expression. As John Gross notes: "His books derive their power from the intensity of his obsessions and the energy with which he tried to master them. They are acts of concealment and exposure, of revenge and reconciliation, of self-purgation and self-definition."[37] *Dubliners* represents a series of possible selves, people Joyce might have become had he not left Ireland. Stephen Dedalus, in both *Portrait* and *Ulysses,* holds many of the same opinions, especially in art, that Joyce did, while Leopold Bloom, in his moral position and identity as a family man, represents still another facet of the author's personality. In *Finnegans Wake* everything and everyone merges, including Joyce and his characters.

Beckett the author also merges with his fictions; however, there is an important difference. Joyce is capable of distancing himself through irony from even such an autobiographical character as Stephen. Beckett, on the other hand, seems always to be losing his identity in that of his characters, and, indeed, as author, *despairs* of ever being able to decisively separate himself from them.

Finally, as consciously as Beckett had at first imitated Joyce's style, he now seemingly set out to develop an antithetical way of handling words. The sparkling, pun-infested prose of *Murphy* and *More Pricks Than Kicks* soon gives way to a steel-hard style whose humor is more bitter and biting. Some puns persist, but they are rare and are confined, for the most part, to character names. Molloy suggests moly, and Lousse is somewhat of a loose woman. As Sophie Loy, she is a combination of wisdom (sophia) and law (*loi* is French for "law"). Gaber's name means to mock or ridicule in Old French; Youdi could mean "you die" or "you-id." Obidil is an anagram of "libido," and Saposcat unites wisdom with dung.[38] Aside from these name puns, there are a few sexual ones. "Condom is on the Baise" (*Molloy*, p. 193), and Moran sends his son to buy a bicycle in Hole. Of the man whom he kills in the forest, Moran says, "If I could have seen his arse, I do not doubt I should have found it on a par with the whole" (*Molloy*, p. 206).

In general, however, Beckett's style is now marked by its extreme plainness and absence of rhetoric. The prose is sharp and lucid, almost unbelievably so. "Compared with the work of James Joyce, for example, *Molloy* is a revelation of the power which may reside in simplicity,"[39] commented one critic. Indeed, Beckett's sweet new style is a fulfillment of what he himself had written fifteen years ago: "The artistic tendency is not expansive, but a contraction. And art is the apotheosis of solitude" (*Proust*, p. 47). Reducing the number of characters and objects in his works, Beckett also reduced the number of words, repeating certain phrases until they acquired the force of motifs, as the "Sweets of Sin" passages in *Ulysses*. Speaking of Joyce, it is important to note that *his* artistic tendency *was* one of (verbal) expansion. Using the economic device of the pun, he attempted to make each word carry as many meanings as it might: "So you need hardly spell me how every word will be bound over to carry three score and ten toptypsical readings throughout the book of Doublends Jined. . . ."[40]

The third characteristic of Beckett's language, after verbal simplicity and repetition, is its particular rhythm. Malone describes it perfectly when he comments: "But my notes have a curious tendency . . . to annihilate all they purport to record" (*MD*, p. 88). For, instead of, as Joyce did, logically building on what he has said before, Beckett denies in the second breath what he had affirmed with the first. "In fact the monologue goes around in circles . . . going back is designed to erase: words are killed with words, which in turn need words to kill them."[41] An excellent example of this style can be found in Beckett's *Texts for Nothing,* a work that, in many ways, anticipates his last novel, *How It Is*:

> It's not true, yes it's true, it's true and it's not true, there is silence and there is not silence, there is no one, and there is someone, nothing prevents anything. (*STFN*, p. 139)

A style of constant creation and destruction, it finds its parallel in a form that is also self-annihilating. Jacques Moran ends his report (and the novel) by repeating—and repudiating—its opening lines:

> Then I went back into the house and wrote, It is midnight, The rain is beating on the windows. It was not midnight. It was not raining. (*Molloy,* p. 241)

So too, at the end of *How It Is,* Beckett negates the entire intricate schema he has erected:

> all these calculations yes explanations yes the whole story from beginning to end yes completely false, yes
>
> that wasn't how it was no not at all no. . . . (*CC,* p. 144)[42]

As Patrick Bowles observed of *Molloy*:

> the form is destroying itself, in the process of working itself out, playing itself out, as if joined to the imagination were a destructive, critical eye trying to get closer to experience, by divesting this of its familiar formal clothing, only to invest it with another, which in turn must undergo destruction and replacement.[43]

For the replacement is there. Spiraling down to almost nothingness, Beckett's work still retains the basic circular shape he inherited from Joyce. Molloy's section ends with its beginning: he is about to be taken to his mother's room where he will

start to write the words we have just read. Moran's final sentences
do lead us back to his first paragraph. The Unnamable declares
his intention to go on (asking the same questions with which
he "started" speaking), and *How It Is* ends with the words of
its title (in French this is a double pun, since "comment c'est"
is a homonym for "commencer," to begin). Paradoxically, then,
Beckett's style, far from Joyce's, is yet the very verbal equivalent
of the Viconian-*Finnegans Wake* philosophy: Words are written
only to be denied and then reaffirmed. Form is erected only to
be toppled and then rebuilt. Beckett's prose since the trilogy
possesses, in fact, the same characteristics of Joyce's fiction that
he himself observed:

> This inner elemental vitality and corruption of expression
> imparts a furious restlessness to the form, which is admirably
> suited to the purgatorial aspect of the work. There is an
> endless verbal germination, maturation, putrefaction, the cy-
> clic dynamism of the intermediate.[44]

> Mr. Joyce's [work] is spherical and excludes culmination . . .
> movement is non-directional—or multi-directional, and a step
> forward is, by definition, a step back. . . . There is a continual
> purgatorial progress at work, in the sense that the vicious
> circle of humanity is being achieved. . . . And no more than
> this: neither prize nor penalty, simply a series of stimulants
> to enable the kitten to catch its tail.[45]

From the very beginning of his writing career, then, "Beckett
saw in the Joycean purgatory the conditions of his own world
[and style]—no ascent and no ideal vegetation."[46]

The previous discussion of Beckett's aesthetic views, his new
concept of characterization, form, and style, although long and
somewhat involved, was necessary in order to understand the
great trilogy of novels that burst upon the literary scene twenty
years ago. By showing how his prose both rejected and reflected
Joyce's own I am also suggesting that Beckett's artistic development after Joyce's death—the gradual discovery of his own
literary identity—did not constitute a complete retreat from his

friend's influence. Rather, the new ideas and style had to be resolved within the Joycean framework that his fiction already possessed. This made, in effect, for a Joycean tension between opposites that is in large part responsible for the powerful impact made by *Molloy, Malone Dies* and *The Unnamable.* For, balancing the Beckettian impulse toward physical stasis and immobility is the Joycean thrust toward motion: "I can't go on, you must go on . . . I'll go on" says the Unnamable.[47] And Molloy "would have had the feeling, if [he] had stayed in the forest, of going against an imperative" (*Molloy,* p. 116). Opposing the pressure toward silence is the necessity for speech. Words are false, treacherous; "saying is inventing" (*Molloy,* p. 41). And yet, distortive as it is, language is man's only source of or means to knowledge: "All I know is what the words know . . ." (*Molloy,* p. 41). Finally, even if both Beckett and his artist heroes believe that art is doomed to fail, they are nevertheless compelled to keep on writing, to continue creating:

> Not to want to say, not to know what you want to say, not to be able to say what you think you want to say, and never to stop saying, or hardly ever, that is the thing to keep in mind, even in the heat of composition. (*Molloy,* p. 36)

This oscillation between two poles can be seen symbolically in the rivalry between circle and spiral. At first Beckett enthusiastically accepted the Joycean dictum of a circular universe that contained everything within it.[48] But then, realizing that self-containment was also self-confinement, he began to rebel. The final scene of *Murphy,* in which Mr. Kelly tries to fly his kite to the point of the circle's circumference, where seen and unseen meet, presented the conflict in terms of circle and line. Watt, accepting the idea of the universe as a closed system, tried—and failed—to find meaning within its circular walls. Likewise, Mercier and Camier tried to leave the city, but succeeded only in circling back to it. Now, Beckett tries to evade the repetitious tangle of the circle of time by spiraling down and out of it. By gradually dismembering his heroes until they can no longer move, by constricting the space they occupy to a jar, a single room, by reducing the number of objects until only a handful are left, Beckett hopes to ease them into blissful nonexistence. Going round in circles, he thus tries to make each circle successively smaller until, he hopes, he will succeed in entering the center: the void of eternal silence, nothingness—and peace. Beckett's quest will fail, but his fiction will not. Poised on a fulcrum of contradictory drives, "constantly on the brink of crumbling into nonsense, into self-negation,"[49] it will survive by sustaining the precarious balance, by not giving an inch either to the left or to the right, but by conveying, in a supple, perfectly suited prose, the frantic struggle for stasis and silence.

"The Expelled"; "The Calmative"; "The End"; Premier amour (1945)

The four short stories that Beckett wrote in 1945[50] belong to an intermediate period of his artistic development. Their style anticipates the trilogy, but the theme and much of the imagery is strongly Joycean. To critic Raymond Federman they represent "the transition from the formal intellectualism and social satire of the English fiction to the more intense existential concern of the French trilogy and plays."[51] The characters still inhabit a recognizable world, but they are increasingly alienated from society. Traditional approaches to them and to their situations are cracking: the narrator is beginning to criticize his subjects, but is careful to keep them within normal social and physical bounds. There is a gradual movement from the city to the countryside, a migration that, to Federman, signifies a retreat from rationality to absurdity, from civilization to an animal existence. A halfway house to the almost nonexistent landscape of the trilogy, the city of the *nouvelles* is, unlike the Dublin and London of *Murphy,* anonymous, with few identifying sites beyond those that could be found in any city: a cathedral, a park, a zoo. Entered by Shepherd's Gate, it is partly symbolic and partly surreal. The citizens have no real identity or personality of their own; they *are* what they *do:* cabman, policeman, public speaker. Most important, all the stories follow a fixed pattern; all the characters can be plotted on a Joycean circle that goes from birth to death, from death to birth.

In "The Expelled," the rounded, unbroken nature of life is quickly established. Faced with the problem of counting the steps to his door, the narrator is hopelessly puzzled: "I did not know where to begin nor where to end" (*STFN*, p. 9). After being evicted from his room and thrown down the steps by unnamed people, he muses:

> In what had just happened to me there was nothing in the least memorable. It was neither the cradle nor the grave of anything whatever. Or rather it resembled so many other cradles, so many other graves, that I'm lost. (*STFN*, pp. 11–12)

If the above passage presents the Joycean[52] poles of the story —cradle and grave—the narrator's fall seems to bear a direct relation to that of Tom Kernan in the *Dubliners* story "Grace." Both stories begin with a fall, and both Tom and the nameless narrator of "The Expelled" remain motionless while their hats come sailing down after them. Here the hat even "rotat[ed] as it came" (*STFN*, p. 10).[53] Fall, as Joyce well knew, implies rise or (re)birth, and Beckett will make the same connection.

Remaining motionless on the sidewalk, the narrator takes up a foetal position and reminisces about his father's taking him for his first hat. Hobbling off in a gait similar to Watt's, the narrator is stopped by a policeman for not walking on the sidewalk.[54] While they are arguing, a funeral procession passes: as both Dylan Thomas and Joyce knew, birth leads to death, womb to tomb. Walking on, the narrator hails a cab and asks to be taken to the zoo; he later changes his mind and confides that he is searching for a room (read *womb*). The cabman gives up a three o'clock appointment (at a funeral!) and tries to help him in his search. By the end of the day, however, they have had no success and it seems to the narrator that all they did was circle around the cabman's own lodging (*STFN*, p. 23). Still wishing to help, the cabman offers his stable as shelter for the night.

After spending many hours there, curled up in the cab in a foetal position, the narrator, in an obvious birth parody, leaves by the cab window:

> I went out head first, my hands were flat on the ground of the yard while my legs were still thrashing to get clear of the frame. (*STFN*, p. 24)

Freed at last, he walks toward the now rising sun, planning to follow it until he is "down among the dead" (*STFN*, p. 25). Beckett's pessimism cannot permit him to end on an image of renewal: for him, fall leads inevitably to death.

George Steiner notes that "Joyce is very much with us, Irish ballad, end of winter's day, horse cab and all, in 'The Expelled'. . . ."[55] The second story, "The Calmative," is more Beckettian, but the atmosphere and at least one episode in it recall *Dubliners* and *Finnegans Wake*. Seemingly written from beyond the grave, the story is a man's journey of old age toward death. Beginning with the line, "I don't know when I died" (*STFN*, p. 27), it concludes with the narrator, like Gabriel Conroy, deciding that "it's west I must go" (*STFN*, p. 46). Significantly, however, the sky is cloudy, and the stars that he would steer himself by are indistinguishable. Death, possible for Murphy and Belacqua Shuah, is now denied the Beckett hero: he must suffer an eternal dying without end.

The title refers to the story itself as well as to the phial the narrator receives from a man in exchange for a kiss. Literature, helping to pass the time, is a sedative: "So I'll tell myself a story, I'll try and tell myself another story, to try and calm myself" (*STFN*, p. 27). It is also a means of ironic and questionable resurrection.[56] The narrator wonders whether "in this story I have come back to life, after my death?" (*STFN*, p. 27).

Other Joycean touches include mention of a character, "Joe Breem, or Breen" (*STFN*, p. 30), Breen suggesting Dennis Breen of *Ulysses*. More pointed than this is another version of Earwicker's encounter with the Cad. Asking a passerby for directions to Shepherd's Gate, the narrator also asks for "the right

time for mercy's sake!" (*STFN*, p. 39). He is told "a time that
explained nothing" (*STFN*, p. 40) and, after leaving the man,
he thinks that "in a moment all will be said, all to do again"
(*STFN*, p. 44). This last comment, Joycean as it is, has implications for literature. Dying and ceasing to write or speak are
both impossible for the Beckett hero. There will always be
another story.

For this reason, the title of "The End" is an ironic one.
True, it does begin with a birth scene and seemingly ends with
the narrator's suicide by drowning. But the very existence of the
story denies the implication of the conclusion, and the last
sentence calls the whole fiction itself into question: "The
memory came faint and cold of the story I might have told,
a story in the likeness of my life, I mean *without the courage
to end* or the strength to go on" (*STFN*, p. 72; italics mine).

Premier amour is similar to "The Expelled" in theme and
imagery. Here, however, the cradle-grave progression is reversed.
Beginning with the death of the narrator's father and his own
"marriage" (the two are specifically linked in his own mind), the
story ends with the birth of the narrator's child and his self-
expulsion from the apartment. The four events together, occur-
ring in one year that stretches from December to December,
constitute a life cycle, one that, it is implied, will be repeated
from generation to generation *ad infinitum*.

As in "The Calmative" and "The End," death is a desired
state, a goal that will release the sufferer from the prison of time
and life. The narrator's love of cemeteries and his prematurely
composed epitaph illustrate the Beckett hero's longing for the
silence of the grave:

> Ci-gît qui y échappa tant
> Qu'il n'en échappe que maintenant.
> (*PA*, p. 10)

Sexual love is not, as in Joyce, a means of renewal, but rather
an unconscious act, accomplished in the night, that leaves the
narrator no memory of it in the morning. Love as an emotion is

highly fickle. The narrator's love for Lulu, the girl who seduces
him and bears his child, disappears as soon as it is returned.
And:

> Ce qu'on appelle l'amour c'est l'exil, avec de temps en temps
> une carte postale du pays. (*PA*, p. 22)

Exiled from love and life, from *ami* and *amour*, the Beckett
hero is ready to undertake the last lonely journey: the quest for
the self.

The Trilogy: *Molloy; Malone Dies* (1951);
The Unnamable (1953)

In his three strange and wonderful books, *Molloy, Malone
Dies,* and *The Unnamable,* Beckett brilliantly combines two
themes and, by so doing, discovers a new ground for his fiction,
one that is large enough to accommodate the Joycean elements
and even integrate them with the purely individual aspects of
his own emerging literary personality.

The first theme, explored by Joyce in all his works, is that of
art. *Finnegans Wake,* a four-sided wheel, revolves endlessly
about itself. It is its own true subject, as witness the chapter on
the Letter. Moreover, form and content have been merged until
style *is* substance, and substance style. Joyce, as Beckett perceptively remarked, is not writing about something, he is writing
that something itself. And, in another sense, the same can be
said of Beckett's own achievement. Sitting in a room, writing,
he writes not about the war, love, or his childhood, but about
the artistic experience per se: the act of sitting in a room and
writing. Language, as in the case of *Finnegans Wake,* becomes
entirely self-referential. Each word is about itself at the moment
of being written, and the novels together are an "épopée du
langage, une aventure de mots."[57] "Literature has reached a
point at which it is looking over its own shoulders,"[58] says
Wellershoff, a view that is also held by Robinson:

> the writer who has abandoned literature yet who is compelled
> to write by a force he doesn't understand, sits in a room and

writes three novels that are, in themselves, a commentary on the fictional imagination and the techniques which this author has forsaken.[59]

The second theme, more Beckett than Joyce, also reflects inward and upon itself. Considered as a single book, the three novels can be seen, on three separate levels, as an increasingly intensive search for the self: the true Being that, according to Sartre and the existentialists, is a timeless, spaceless, motionless void—a non-Being.[60] *Molloy,* the first attempt at self-discovery, involves a double quest. Molloy is searching for his mother, who is literally the source of his being and therefore symbolic of his true Self. Moran, in pursuing Molloy, is also seeking his inner identity, the violent hidden side of his nature that is the very antithesis of his outwardly calm, bourgeois appearance. Like Molloy, who finds not his mother but only her room, Moran is only partially successful. Unable to confront his self, he does succeed in approaching it by coming to resemble it more and more. Both Moran and Molloy, it should be noted, externalize the Self by visualizing it as another person. Both, moreover, are artists operating under the guise of fictional characters.

Malone Dies transfers the quest to a more aesthetic and, at the same time, more interior ground. In this book the artist stands naked before us. Alternating fragments of fiction with snatches of autobiography, Malone searches for his true identity in both—and again the result is failure. As with two parallel lines or the wheels of Moran's bicycle, Malone and his stories begin and end simultaneously; but they never cross, they never merge to reveal the Self that informs both creator and creation.

Retreating one step further into the maze, we encounter the Unnamable, a seemingly irreducible being that is somehow still not the Self. Realizing the futility of seeking the self through others—whether real people or fictional characters—the Unnamable renounces the mask of artist (it was he who created Malone, who was in turn responsible for all of Beckett's fiction) and resolves to speak of the self directly. Admirable as it is, his intention proves impossible to accomplish, for he too is just another mask, another creation of the self. Reduced to an immobile torso in a jar, the Unnamable is nonetheless a concrete, finite entity—and as such he cannot comprehend the infinite, noncorporeal Self. Substance is alien to the void; Watt-ness cannot apprehend the nature of Knott-ing.[61]

The two themes—art and the search for the self—are indissolubly connected: it is through art, or the telling of stories, that the speaker (artist or storyteller) seeks his identity. Creating characters, he hopes, in doing so, to trap his self in one of them. But if art is the medium of the quest, it is also the inevitable reason for its failure. Creations of the self, the fictional characters cannot *be* the self, and far from bringing the narrator-hero closer to it, they only separate him even further from his goal: "I am neither, I needn't say, Murphy, nor Watt, nor Mercier, nor . . . any of the others" (*Unn,* p. 53), and "there might be a hundred of us and still we'd lack the hundred and first, we'll always be short of me" (*Unn,* p. 72).[62] Indeed, they generate confusion rather than clarity. Imperceptibly merging into one another—Moran into Molloy, Sapo into Basil, Macmann into Mahood, Mahood into Worm—they cannot even retain their own separate (fictional) identities. Worse still, the narrator-hero begins to coalesce with his own creations, and "more and more, this becomes the dominant comic, ironic theme—that creation and creator are indistinguishable, inseparable, irreconcilable."[63] The Unnamable speculates whether he is Mahood, "or is one to postulate a tertius gaudens . . . responsible. . . ?" (*Unn,* p. 71).

The true significance of the conjunction of the two themes now emerges. Not only is it a question of the narrator's seeking his true self, but of the

> author agonizing with himself about the nature of *his* own identity, how far he is the creator of his own characters, something other than himself. The artist-God is no longer paring indifferent fingernails, He is chewing them and in the center of his book.[64]

To determine their identity aside from that of their works,

all Beckett's artist-heroes are, in the very moment of composition, engaged in trying to kill their own creations, end their own fictions, so as to arrive at the reality of the Self: "I shall try and make a little creature, to hold in my arms, a little creature in my image. . . . And seeing what a poor thing I have made, or how like myself, I shall eat it" (*MD*, p. 52). Molloy attacks the charcoal-burner in the forest, and the man Moran kills strangely resembles him: "same little abortive moustache, same little ferrety eyes, same paraphimosis of the nose, and a thin red mouth" (*Molloy*, p. 206). Malone not only kills off Macmann, but three of his (and Beckett's) previous fictional creations as well. The asylum inmates who go on Lady Pedal's excursion include "a young man, dead young, seated in an old rocking chair" (*MD*, p. 112)—undoubtedly Murphy. A second is notable for "his stiffness and his air of perpetually looking for something while at the same time wondering what that something could possibly be" (*MD*, p. 113)—a very good description of Watt. The third, like Mercier, is small and thin, carries a cloak and umbrella, and has a "fine head of white flossy hair" (*MD*, pp. 113–14).

The Unnamable disavows all his fictions by refusing to use the grammatical sign of such literary personae, the deceptive first-person pronoun: "I shall not say I again, ever again, it's too farcical" (*Unn*, p. 94). Finally, behind all the artist-heroes, there is the trilogy's author, Beckett himself. Each narrator, then—Molloy, Moran, Malone, and the Unnamable—"is a fiction, a creature who depends for his existence upon artifice,"[65] and their attempts to annihilate their creations reflect Beckett's own vain efforts to cease writing.

Aside from this confusing and diversionary nature of fictional characters, writing itself is an untrustworthy means of seeking out the self. The narrator, as all Beckett's artist-heroes are quick to point out, is totally unreliable. Molloy, after describing the scene where A and C approach each other, is careful to admit he may be inventing, embellishing, or "perhaps confusing several different occasions, and different times" (*Molloy*, p. 17).

Malone specifically mocks the Joycean concept of the author as an omniscient god. Although Saposcat is his creation, Malone confesses that he does not know Sapo's Christian name or why he was expelled from school. Both Molloy and Malone are, in fact, representatives of Wayne Booth's "self-conscious narrator" who "intrudes into his novel to comment on himself as writer, and on his book, not simply as a series of events with moral implications, but as a created literary product."[66]

> "Well, well, I didn't think I knew this story so well" (*Molloy*, p. 78).
> "This is awful" (*MD*, p. 14).
> "Soon it will be better, soon things will be better" (*MD*, p. 15).

At times the novels take on the appearance of a first-draft version, with outline and corrections incorporated into the text. Molloy notes that "this should all be rewritten in the pluperfect" (*Molloy*, p. 20). Malone sketches the end of his story: "Visit various remarks, Macmann continued, agony recalled, Macmann continued, then mixture of Macmann and agony as long as possible" (*MD*, p. 99). And the Unnamable specifies style and substance for his recitation: "The whole to be tossed off with bravura. Then notes from day to day, until I collapse" (*Unn*, p. 90).

All this has the effect of weakening the credibility of the story, undermining the authority of the artist. Because we see how the trick is done, how the ventriloquist moves the lips of the dummy,[67] art is revealed as illusion, the artist as a cheap magician dazzling the audience with his sleight of hand. For this reason and because fiction, composed of the lies we call words, is false at its core, it cannot be trusted to undertake the arduous and difficult search for the self. Art is, as Beckett told Georges Duthuit, doomed to failure. Why then go on writing? Why create endless lies if one knows that they are lies and that "there's nothing to be got, there was never anything to be got from those stories" (*Unn*, p. 130)? Because one must, because the will to create is an inner imperative the artist cannot ignore:

Malone: "I did not want to write, but I had to resign myself
   to it in the end" (*MD*, p. 32).
Unnamable: "I am obliged to speak. I shall never be silent,
   never" (*Unn*, p. 4).

Because language is all we have and "there is no use indicting
words, they are no shoddier than what they peddle" (*MD*, p. 19).
Because, finally, art, a man-made thing, can—however imperfectly
and temporarily—bestow on life the shape and significance it
lacks:

> Not that for a moment Watt supposed that he had penetrated
> the forces at play, in this particular instance, or even perceived
> the forms that they upheaved, or obtained the least useful
> information concerning himself, or Mr. Knott, for he did not.
> But he had turned, little by little, a disturbance into words, he
> had made a pillow of old words, for a head. (*W*, p. 117)

> All I know is what the words know, and the dead things, and
> that makes a handsome little sum, with a beginning a middle
> and an end as in the well-built phrase and the long sonata
> of the dead. (*Molloy*, p. 41)

Art then, for Beckett, although he never admits it, is man's
only hope of ordering the chaos of the universe, of breaking out
of the circular trap of time by creating a linear progression:
"a handsome little sum, with a beginning a middle and an end."
Necessary as beginning and middle are, it is ending, however,
that is of supreme importance to Beckett. A final act, it gives
a finite shape and significance to all that preceded it. Writing
is a selective process, so that the writer may one day cease to
write at all: "For if you set out to mention everything you
would never be done, and that's what counts, to be done, have
done" (*Molloy*, p. 55), "for it's the end gives meaning to words"
(*STFN*, p. 111). Silence, the only proof of having completed
one's pensum, is the goal of speech.

"The End," Endgame, Krapp's Last Tape—Beckett's titles tes-
tify to his artistic aim and progress toward it. And yet, as we

have seen, neither Beckett nor his narrator-heroes can end. His
work must remain true to his unrelenting, uncompromising
vision of existence—a world without an end:

> I listen and the voice is of a world collapsing endlessly, a
> frozen world . . . down towards an end it seems can never
> come. For what possible end to these wastes where true light
> never was, nor any upright thing, nor any true foundation,
> but only these leaning things, forever lapsing and crumbling
> away, beneath a sky without memory of morning or hope
> of night. . . . Yes, a world at an end, in spite of appearances,
> its end brought it forth, ending it began, is it clear enough.
> (*Molloy*, p. 53)

Forever ending, never finished, this is the fate of Beckett's
artist-heroes. Born into the suffering of eternal time, they can
decay but not die. Yearning for silence, they are obliged to
speak; straining toward stasis, they must remain in motion. The
novels too, as we have seen, experience the same inability to
resolve themselves, either by reaching the bedrock of the self
or by dwindling into nothingness. If Beckett succeeds in burning
everything down to *Embers*, the next step is only to *Comment
c'est* (and "commencer"). And yet, deprived of the possibility
of ending, of shaping itself into a neat compact package, Beckett's
fiction is nevertheless not without form. Unable, like Joyce's
books, to celebrate or illustrate the principles of order and harmony, Beckett's writings focus on chaos and acquire shape by
finding a form for the formless.[68] Speaking to Tom Driver,
Beckett emphasized that such a form meant not excluding "the
mess," but including it:

> This form will be of such a type that it admits the chaos and
> does not try to say that the chaos is really something else.
> The form and the chaos remain separate. . . . To find a form
> that accommodates the mess, that is the task of the artist now.[69]

Beckett's early novels—*Murphy* and *Watt*—sought to avoid the
chaos by affirming some supreme principle of organization, the
mind or language itself. But, unable to enter the completely

sealed sanctuary of the mind except through death, unable to find implicit meaning in language or any closed system, Beckett was at last forced to acknowledge the existence of an irrational element in the universe, what he calls "the mess." From this moment on, his art changed direction, away from the logos of word and world, toward the chaos of language and the failure of art:

> I began again. But little by little with a different aim, no longer in order to succeed, but in order to fail. Nuance. What I sought, when I struggled out of my hold, then aloft through the stinging air towards an inaccessible boon, was the rapture of vertigo, the letting go, the fall, the gulf, the relapse to darkness, to nothingness. (*MD,* p. 19)

In his later novels—the trilogy and *How It Is*—Beckett acknowledges the new task of the artist by creating "a literature which is open on all sides to the irreconcilables of the void."[70] These works find a form for chaos by failing in their own search for pattern and order. Molloy cannot, no matter how hard he tries, distribute his sixteen sucking stones equally among his four pockets so as to suck them all in turn—until he sacrifices "the principle of trim" (*Molloy,* p. 96). Settling for an unequal allotment of the stones, he assures that all sixteen will be sucked once before any one is sucked twice. But the element of hazard or chaos still remains: he cannot hope to duplicate the *order* of sucking:

> But that was a drawback I could not avoid . . . in the cycles taken together utter confusion was bound to reign. (*Molloy,* p. 98)

In *Malone Dies,* Mrs. Lambert, we are told, "could have gone on sorting her lentils all night and never achieved her purpose, which was to free them from all admixture" (*MD,* p. 39). The Unnamable can neither trap his self in a fictional creation nor talk directly of it by ceasing to create. Caught on the horns of a seemingly logical dilemma, he discovers that there is no logical way out of it. The "I" of *How It Is* creates a complex, intricately ordered cosmos, only, in the end, to yield to the chaos it conceals by destroying it as utterly false. Stylistically, Beckett, as I have tried to show, incorporates chaos by organizing his prose according to this same pattern of affirmation and denial.

Beckett's ultimate form for chaos is, significantly, one that Joyce (again, among many authors) used—that of Purgatory. The world of the trilogy is truly a state of limbo existence:[71] Molloy's island home is symbolically "suspended between the mountains and the sea" (*Molloy*, p. 20); his favorite time of day is "that golden moment" of twilight, when "the forenoon's toil [has] ended, the afternoon's [is yet] to come" (*Molloy*, p. 27). The atmosphere surrounding Malone and the Unnamable is neither dark nor light but the in-between shade of gray.

Nearly dead in body but alive in the mind, denied either the mobility of life or the complete rigidity of death, the trilogy's artist-heroes are exiled from others and from themselves, caught between the external and the internal:

> Perhaps that's what I feel, an outside and an inside and me in the middle, perhaps that's what I am, the thing that divides the world in two, on the one side the outside, on the other the inside, that can be as thin as foil, I'm neither one side nor the other, I'm in the the middle, I'm the partition . . . I'm the tympanum, on the one hand the mind, on the other the world, I don't belong to either. (*Unn*, p. 134)

Experiencing a metaphysical as well as physical limbo, Beckett's characters, like Dante's Belacqua, are trapped in a life that has been lived but not ended:

> My life, my life, now I speak of it as something over, now as of a joke which still goes on, and it is neither, for at the same time it is over and it goes on and is there any tense for that? (*Molloy*, p. 47)

Indeed, there is no proper tense for Beckett's three novels. Contrary to Molloy's beliefs, neither the "pluperfect" (*Molloy*, p.

20) nor the "mythological present" (*Molloy,* p. 34) is appropriate. Eternally suspended in space, the Beckett hero is also suspended in time, condemned

> to wander the last of the living in the depths of an instant without bounds where the light never changes and wrecks look all alike. (*MD,* pp. 59–60)

Any motion is, like that of *Finnegans Wake,* circular. Trying to keep on a straight line and so leave the town he is in, Molloy finds he has instead "described a good quarter of a circle" (*Molloy,* p. 87) ; he attributes his movements "to the buckled wheel that carried [him] in unforseeable jerks, from fatigue to rest and inversely" (*Molloy,* p. 88). Macmann, in the forest with rain pelting down, discovers he is "advancing with regularity, and even a certain rapidity, along the arc of a gigantic circle" (*MD,* p. 74). The Unnamable, who likes to think of himself "fixed and at the centre of this place" (*Unn,* p. 9), tells how, as Mahood, he had "already advanced a good ten paces . . . not in a straight line . . . but in a sharp curve which, if I continued to follow it, seemed likely to restore me to my point of departure" (*Unn,* p. 39). Before, he had seen two shapes and thought: "their path too must be a curve" (*Unn,* p. 11).

The form of Beckett's fiction duplicates the movements of its protagonists by means of a circular chronology. We have already seen how each of the two parts of *Molloy* leads back to its own beginning. A different kind of circularity is present in *Malone Dies.* Opening with Malone's announcement that he will die in April or May, the novel's closing episode with Macmann specifically occurs on Easter weekend, most probably a year later. Scattered references to the seasons accord with such a time scheme. Mr. Lambert slaughters his pig in December, at Christmas time; Malone loses his pencil and finds it at "high summer" (*MD,* p. 84) ; and Macmann's journeys seem to take place in autumn (*MD,* p. 58). Finally, Malone records that he has reached "what is called the month of May" (*MD,* p. 60). The

Unnamable has no such circular chronology, but its hero is himself "a big talking ball. . . . I always knew I was round, solid and round . . ." (*Unn,* p. 24), who dreams of having "some little job," like that of continually filling and emptying the same water vessels (*Unn,* pp. 154–55). His dilemma is also expressed in circular imagery: "I have no voice and I must speak, that is all I know, it is round that I must revolve" (*Unn,* p. 26). Finally, life for the Unnamable is represented by the same cyclical jingle that Vladimir sings in *Waiting for Godot*:

> A dog crawled into the kitchen and stole a crust of bread, then cook up with I've forgotten what and walloped him till he was dead, second verse, Then all the dogs came crawling and dug the dog a tomb and wrote upon the tombstone for dogs and bitches to come, third verse as the first, fourth, as the second, fifth, as the third. . . . (*Unn,* p. 128)

Obsessed with birth and death, the trilogy heroes join womb to tomb. They imagine themselves born—but into death, not life: "The feet are clear already of the great cunt of existence. . . . My head will be the last to die" (*MD,* p. 283). Moll, dying, exhibits symptoms of pregnancy, and the Unnamable's gradual recession into his womblike jar seems to resemble a backwards birth.

And yet, Beckett's purgatory is decidedly different from Joyce's, and in ways that once again suggest these authors' separate approaches to life and art. *Finnegans Wake* is, as Beckett claimed, purgatorial in the sense of continual circular motion and the "absolute absence of the Absolute."[72] But there is no sense, as there is in Beckett's world, of being *trapped* in time or a permanent state of being. The vicocycle runs *through* history, not outside it; all centuries and eras are incorporated into the schema of Divine, Heroic, and Human ages. Moreover, if Beckett's trilogy tends to greater and greater stasis, Joyce's "farraginous chronicle" seeks only its own perpetual motion. And where Beckett's heroes are caught between life and death, unable to get born or to die (*MD,* pp. 51–52), Joyce's are continually achieving both—going from birth to death to rebirth.

In terms of tone, too, the two purgatories radically diverge. Joyce is joyous, celebrating Finnegan's fall because he knows he will rise (wake) again. Sin, a serious thing, causes concern but even greater comedy. In general, *Ulysses* and *Finnegans Wake,* despite their themes of guilt and pride, are "genial books. . . . Reappearing in art, the horrors of life have become elements in a joyous, impersonal structure. The dominant tone of Joyce's great harmonies of sound and rhythm is one of brightness and gaiety."[73]

Beckett's tone, on the other hand, is grim. The unknown sins of his artist-heroes have condemned them to a purgatory as vicious and unrelenting as Dante's hell, to a life of eternal suffering that leads to no expiation because it is itself a new sin:

> And without knowing exactly what his sin was he felt full well that living was not a sufficient atonement for it or that this atonement was in itself a sin, calling for more atonement, and so on, as if there could be anything but life, for the living. (*MD,* p. 67)

Finally, the Joycean universe, although in constant flux, is easy to grasp because, despite some inexplicable elements, it is essentially an ordered, rational world. Once the fundamentals are understood—the Viconian structure, Bruno's conflict of opposites, the allegorical identities of the characters themselves—once these are mastered and the reader is familiar with certain basic motifs, all the rest—although admittedly difficult to decipher —follows logically and inevitably. The center of Beckett's world, however, is no such nub of reason or formal arrangement.[74] Chaos is his world's core, doubt its dominant principle. Where Joyce's cosmos is a set of interrelations, Beckett's remains unconnected, uncoordinated. Even the law of cause and effect does not operate, and Malone laughs at the idea that "there existed a relationship between that which suffers and that which causes to suffer" (*MD,* p. 69) . Suspended in space and time, the artist-heroes are all in mental limbo as well. Molloy has no idea how he got to his mother's room ("Perhaps in an ambulance," *Molloy,* p. 7) , or the reason for his journey in the first place. Knowing that he does not work for money, he yet is ignorant of just what he *does* write for. How much time he spent with Lousse, whether she was man or woman (*Molloy*, p. 75), these matters too are outside his field of knowledge. Finally, he is uncertain of his own identity: "And even my sense of identity was wrapped in namelessness often hard to penetrate . . ." (*Molloy*, p. 41).

Moran is, at first, the very model of confident certitude. Full of belief in religious communion and rational common sense, he begins to experience doubt as he is exposed to the vague, irrational Molloy. No sooner does he give his son instructions on what to pack than he wonders whether they were the correct instructions. Uncertain whether he should take his autocycle on the assignment, he is soon unable to tell if it is always the same knee that hurts him. By the time he crawls home he is a broken man, doubting the organization to which he belongs, the existence of its head, Youdi, and even that of God himself. His new Lord's Prayer begins: "Our Father who are no more in heaven than on earth or in hell, I neither want nor desire that thy name be hallowed . . ." (*Molloy*, p. 229). Moran has, in effect, repudiated the entire religious, rural, and rational basis of his existence.

Malone, like Molloy, is unsure how he came to occupy his room. He does not know what floor it is on, or whether it is night or day. He thinks that he may have died, but he is not certain: "But have I not perhaps just passed away?" (*MD*, p. 79). The Unnamable begins with questions about space, time, and person ("Where now? Who now? When now?" p. 3), and ends by doubting whether it is he who speaks, whether, in fact, he exists at all.

Uncertainty and horror of time's trap drive the Beckett hero to escape from his purgatorial confinement. To Joyce the circle was a symbol of unity and order, self-containing and self-fulfilling. Beckett, however, saw no such harmony in the sphere(s)—only eternal confusion and chaos. Seeking the stasis of silence and selfhood, he tries to break Joyce's circle, to bend it into a finite line that, he hopes, will take him to a final resting place, a point of no departure or return. Thus, Molloy, lost in the forest, does his best to go in a circle, "hoping in this way to go in a straight line" (*Molloy*, p. 115). But linear progression is impossible because ending is itself impossible. The universe *is* circular, as Molloy learns, and "the most you can hope is to be a little less, in the end, the creature you were in the beginning, and the middle" (*Molloy*, p. 42). And yet the Joycean circle is, in a sense, broken—not into a line, however, but a spiral; approaching his family in the windowless rotunda, Mahood finds himself "embroiled in a kind of inverted spiral . . . the coils of which, instead of widening more and more, grew narrower and narrower and finally . . . would come to an end for lack of room" (*Unn*, p. 39).[75] The Unnamable was "under the impression I spent my life in spirals round the earth" (*Unn*, p. 54). But the inverted spiral—a perfect image for the trilogy itself—[76] is, like the circle, an inescapable snare. Its coils may decrease in diameter, but they will never disappear altogether. Fleeing the continuous cycles of Joyce's wheel, Beckett found only the endless whorls of his own horrendous helix. Retreating from *Finnegans Wake* and an art of infinite expansion, Beckett contracted content and form only to realize that they too could be *infinitely* contracted. Literature, even literature about nothingness, was limitless. Critic Vivian Mercier put it in mathematical terms:

> The Unnamable's interior monologue may go on to infinity, for all we know. If it were to, we might describe this novel as a curve having one of its axes as an asymptote. In other words, as y (the length of the novel) approached infinity, x (the content of the novel) would approach nearer and nearer to zero. Content zero, length infinity—these are the mathematical limits of the novel.[77]

Writing the trilogy, then, Beckett realized that Joyce was partly right: there is a circular course to existence, and that course is infinite (and infinitely cyclical). Unable, however, as Joyce was, to accept the infinitude as a positive good, or the word

as a divine instrument capable of dealing truthfully with the
world, Beckett was propelled in another artistic direction. Dis-
trusting language, he would move toward silence; rejecting the
ordered plenitude of life, he would try to deal with the chaos
and nothingness that he believed were the ultimate reality. The
structure of his work, however, would remain Joycean—cyclical
and purgatorial. Realizing that he could only bend, not break
Joyce's circle, Beckett accepts it as the framework of his own
fiction. Turning now to the medium of drama, he will turn
the circle his way—not to show its fullness, but to reveal the
futility and emptiness at the center of its smooth circumference.

5

"Me to Play"

"In my beginning is my end. . . . In my end is my beginning,"[1] said T. S. Eliot, and Beckett, after a decade of denying it and trying to break the Joycean circle of existence, finally came to acknowledge the inescapable truth.[2] Turning to the theater, he fashioned plays spherical in shape, well-rounded tragicomedies that, like *Endgame,* indeed end where they began, or go on to begin all over again, like the punningly titled *Play*.

Completely Beckettian in voice and point of view, the plays nevertheless exhibit the chief characteristics of Joyce's purgatorial fiction.[3] As in the trilogy, ending is impossible; only stasis can be achieved: Godot will never come, Hamm does not die, and Clov cannot leave. Fighting against this fate of always becoming and never being, Beckett's characters search for a finite, final moment in the eternity of time, but their quest is continually mocked and defeated by the infinite nature of their own dramatic vehicles: the circular, cyclical form of the plays resists their efforts and denies even the idea of linear progress.

Time itself exists but, because no real movement within it is possible, it does not really pass. "Was," "is," and "shall be" all coalesce into one static state, an interminable and limbolike present that has no memory of the past nor hope of a future. Existing in a closed world that is as much an inferno as a purgatory, all Beckett's characters are eternal Belacquas, but, unlike

Dante's sinner, they must wait *forever,* without any prospect of ultimate salvation, condemned to "wander the last of the living in the depths of an instant without bounds" (*MD,* p. 59). In *Waiting for Godot,* it is always evening, before sunset and moonrise; Clov, asked the time by Hamm, replies, "The same as usual" (*E,* p. 4), and he later informs his blind master that it is neither dark nor light outside, but gray, or "light black. From pole to pole" (*E,* p. 32). With each play the atmosphere becomes more sinister: Winnie spends her "happy days" under a broiling sun that she calls "hellish light,"[4] Krapp continually moves from light to dark and back again, and the man and two women of *Play* are plunged in total darkness except for the penetrating circle of light that, like a grand inquisitor, compels them, in turn and yet independently of each other, to speak.

Accompanying the temporal limbo is a physical stasis that gradually but relentlessly increases. Gogo and Didi are rooted to a single spot, a country road with a tree, and Hamm is blind, paralyzed, and confined to his chair. In *All That Fall,* many of the characters maintain a precarious but static state of health. Christy's wife is "No better" and "No worse,"[5] Mr. Tyler is "half alive" (*ATF,* p. 41), and the little girl in Mrs. Rooney's story is dying although "she had never been really born!" (*ATF,* p. 84). In *Happy Days,* Winnie is buried in a pile of sand, first up to her waist, but then up to her neck, leaving her only the movement of her eyes. Finally, in *Play,* all three characters are stuck, like the Unnamable, in jars; their heads cannot move and they are able to speak only when the light shines upon their faces.

Paralyzed, immobilized, forced to remain stationary, Beckett's characters must remain passive as well. Unable to act, they are capable only of a purgatorial nonaction: waiting, waiting for the end they know will never come, for the salvation that may or may not exist. Unlike Joyce's characters, who do act, and in acting fulfill themselves, Beckett's must remain still, in constant hope of being acted upon, in eternal expectation of being fulfilled. Vladimir and Estragon wait for Godot, Hamm waits for something to take its course; Winnie, literally buried in the sands of time, waits for "the happy day . . . when flesh melts at so many degrees and the night of the moon has so many hundred hours" (*HD*, p. 18). Even the characters of *Play* are waiting for something: "All this, when will all this have been . . . just play?"[6]

To while away the endless hours, to make the time pass as quickly as possible, Beckett's heroes become artists, that is, they tell stories. No longer the medium for a penetrating search into the Self, literature becomes an innocuous pastime, an existential "filler." Thus, Nagg tells about the Englishman and his incompetent tailor, Maddy Rooney relates a story told to her by a psychiatrist, and Winnie tells about Mildred, a child of four or five who bears a strong resemblance to Winnie herself.[7] Krapp, of course, is both narrator and audience to the story of his life.

By making waiting, in a sense, the subject of his plays, Beckett is writing about life per se, life minus the traumatic events, the emotional or spiritual crises that are usually the focus of novels or plays. Aside from this effort to reproduce the fundamental texture of life, the sheer living of it, Beckett's plays, by concerning themselves with such integral but intangible human experiences as waiting and ending, also attempt to discover their own texture, their own theatrical form. Made conscious of what it is to be an audience, to sit in a theater and wait for and watch a play, the Beckett playgoer is also made aware of what a play actually is. Alain Robbe-Grillet, in discussing *Waiting for Godot*, explains the revolutionary purpose and effect of Beckett's tragicomedy:

We suddenly realize, as we look at them [Didi and Gogo], the main function of theatre, which is to show what the fact of *being there* consists in. For this is what we have never seen on the stage before, or not with the same clarity, not with so few concessions and so much force. A character in a play usually does no more than *play a part*, as all those about us do who are trying to shirk their own existence. But in Beckett's play it is as if the two tramps were on the stage without a part to play.[8]

Hugh Kenner makes a similar observation:

> If the seeming improvisation of the tramps denies theatricality, it affirms at the same time quintessential theater, postulating nothing but what we can see on stage: a place and men present in it, doing what they are doing.[9]

Stripping his characters down to their irreducible humanity and mortality, Beckett also reduces the theater to its pure naked essence. His plays become, in a Platonic sense, the very Idea of a play—people on a stage conscious that they are people on a stage:

> Vladimir: We'll come back to-morrow.
> Estragon: And then the day after to-morrow.[10]

Form, in the Platonic sense of Idea, is all; content becomes minimal: two tramps on a road, a woman buried in sand, a man listening to himself on a tape-recorder. The shape, the structure, is what matters, and so Beckett's most recent works are plays not for the theater but for radio. Creations of pure sound and silence, they do not use the basic elements of any play; they *are* those elements. If *Godot* and *Endgame* did away with dramatic action for the sake of drama and situation per se, then *Krapp's Last Tape, Cascando,* and *Words and Music*—not to mention Beckett's brief and shockingly misproduced contribution to Kenneth Tynan's *Oh! Calcutta*—have abolished even that for speech itself. In these most recent literary efforts, everything— style, characterization, content—becomes form and the plays themselves become an abstract symbol or embodiment of what Beckett is trying to convey. "For if an art form can use the fact and nature of its own being for part of its statement, what is implied is that in the form itself there exists potential statement."[11] As do the novels, the plays seek silence in language and significance in their own structure.

The stress on form over content, on shape over substance, is an emphasis that Beckett himself is conscious of and has acknowledged:

I take no sides. I am interested in the shape of ideas. There is a wonderful sentence in Augustine: "Do not despair; one of the thieves was saved. Do not presume; one of the thieves was damned." That sentence has a wonderful shape. It is the shape that matters.[12]

Here Beckett differs significantly from Joyce, who primarily pursued not form but style. Exploring the ultimate refinements of verbal articulation, Joyce's concern was for the words. Form or structure he regarded merely as a (necessary) scaffolding, the skeleton that he would flesh out with language and languages. And Joyce's structures, the forms of his fictions are, indeed, far from original. For *Portrait* he borrowed the *Bildungsroman*; for *Ulysses*, a Greek myth; for *Finnegans Wake*, the historical theories of Giambattista Vico. Once given the organizing principle, Joyce's interest—and his reader's—is centered on what he does with it, how he develops the material from form to fictional art. For, despite Beckett's encomium, there is a sense in which Joyce's form is not its content; a slight, barely visible seam shows where the author of *Finnegans Wake* masterfully joined the two. Beckett's forms, however, although they owe a great deal to Joyce, are discovered in the process of writing itself. All grow out of and into the works, until there is no distinction whatsoever between shape and substance, between form and content. Indeed, if Joyce tended to merge form and content into pure style, Beckett seems to transform all aspects of literature into form. The plays themselves become almost an abstract, a symbolic shape that incarnates the very thought and intent of their author.

Beckett takes stylization to the utmost limit; all matter is dissolved in form. . . . Even speech is deprived of its function as a medium of communication, being reduced to a formal element, like structure or atmosphere.[13]

Waiting for Godot (1952)

Perhaps the greatest of Beckett's plays, the most masterly fusion of content, character, and style into form, is *Waiting for*

Godot. Written before *The Unnamable, Godot* was predicted by Malone, who told of "the hour when nothing more can happen and nobody can come and all is ended but the waiting that knows itself in vain" (*MD,* p. 68). Estragon echoes this sentiment in almost the same words: "Nothing happens, nobody comes, nobody goes, it's awful" (*WFG,* p. 27b).

Awfully funny and poignant perhaps, but not awful. Beckett's play, his most famous one, is also his nearly perfect expression of man's purgatorial existence: endless cycles of time during which one can do nothing but wait, in fear and uncertainty, for Godot, for an end to the "senseless, speechless, issueless misery" (*Molloy,* p. 16), for nothing. The title's emphasis, then, is not on the noun, the unknown deity (?) who never comes, but on the participle, "waiting," the only act possible in a universe where nothing is ever truly lost or gained, only recycled.

As in *Murphy* and *Finnegans Wake,* existence is a closed system: "The tears of the world are a constant quantity. For each one who begins to weep somewhere else another stops. The same is true of the laugh," reports Pozzo (*WFG,* p. 22a). Time itself has achieved the stasis of a closed system, repeating itself *ad infinitum,* so that the two acts of *Waiting for Godot* take place, in a sense, on the same day (as evidenced by the fact that sunset and moonrise occur simultaneously in both). This, in turn, is only part of a larger, endlessly repeated pattern, the cosmic rhythm of light and dark:

> Estragon: But night doesn't fall.
> Vladimir: It'll fall all of a sudden, like yesterday.
> Estragon: Then it'll be night.
> Vladimir: And we can go.
> Estragon: Then it'll be day again. (*WFG,* p. 46a)

Although it brilliantly contains a circular, cyclical world, the real genius of *Waiting for Godot* is that the play itself—its *form* and movement—"is circular, like a worn-out wheel of fortune at a deserted fairground, mysteriously turning."[14] Indeed, "the idea of refrain, or repetition, is seen in several details, and it is the focal point of the entire structure, for the 'dramaturgy' of the play is cyclical."[15] For, with the exception of a few changes, act 2 precisely duplicates the content and structure of act 1; together they give the impression of infinite repetition, of a "closed circular plot from which no exit is possible."[16] In both acts Vladimir and Estragon embrace, then discuss Estragon's boots and whether they should part or hang themselves. In both Vladimir gives Estragon something to eat, Pozzo and Lucky arrive and leave, and a boy appears to say that Godot will not come that night "but surely tomorrow" (*WFG*, p. 33b). Finally, both acts end with the identical dialogue and stage direction:

Vladimir: Well? Shall we go?
Estragon: Yes, let's go.
    (*They do not move*)   (*WFG*, p. 60b)[17]

According to critic Colin Duckworth, the

sameness of the end of each act stresses the circularity of the whole structure; the return to symmetry leaves us with an overall impression of the monotony and futility of the eternally repeated ritual enacted on that deserted road.[18]

It also reinforces "the perfect circularity of time. Nothing ever finishes, and everything begins again."[19]

Circularity excludes the possibility of ever ending, and any end, therefore, is illusory and arbitrary. Even the play itself never really terminates, but is performed again the following night, as Gogo and Didi themselves realize:

Vladimir: We'll come back to-morrow.
Estragon: And then the day after to-morrow.
Vladimir: Possibly.
Estragon: And so on. (*WFG*, p. 10b)

The theater itself is thus a closed system: "There's no way out" (*WFG*, p. 47b), as Vladimir discovers when he tries to leave. Rather, any end or exit is blocked, and the heroes of the plays are fixed in the perpetual cycle where each night begins and continues to the moment where the last night stopped. They are condemned to pause forever in the stasis where the curtain leaves them, eternally approaching and never entering the future beyond. . . . What they seek to complete is the arbitrary series begun by birth, to reach that end where time is no more and where their present unreality is changed into the certainty of their own identity or existence.[20]

The principle of circular repetition upon which the play is built extends internally to the stage directions and dialogue. Estragon, at the beginning of act 1, repeatedly tries to take off his boot; Vladimir, at the beginning of act 2, "comes and goes" and "halts" three times (*WFG*, p. 37a). Constantly "looking round" (*WFG*, pp. 10b, 11a, 24a), Vladimir is always peering into his hat, shaking it, and putting it back on again. Lucky alternately picks up and puts down his bag and basket, steps forward and back, when he hastens to obey the commands of Pozzo (*WFG*, pp. 16b–17a), who lights, extinguishes, and relights his pipe (*WFG*, pp. 18a, 19a, 19b, 20b). In a pantomime reminiscent of both vaudeville and Joyce's Mutt and Jute, Didi, Gogo, and Lucky frantically exchange their hats through a series of thirty-three separate stage directions (*WFG*, pp. 46a–b). Robinson comments that "in the plays the ceaseless linguistic permutations of the novels [and of Joyce] are replaced by equally pedantic and mechanical physical permutations."[21]

Dialogue proves to be even more repetitious and circular than physical gestures. The conversations of Didi and Gogo possess a litanylike structure, with constant verbal repetition and recurrence of phrases and motifs such as "Nothing to be done" (*WFG*, pp. 7a, 8b, 14b), "It's inevitable" (*WFG*, p. 17b three times), and "You want to get rid of him" (*WFG*, p. 21a five times). In many such "canters" Estragon and Vladimir change places, each asking or declaring what the other had just a few moments before:

Vladimir: It hurts?
Estragon: (*angrily*). Hurts! He wants to know if it hurts?

Vladimir: (*angrily*). No one ever suffers but you. I don't count.
I'd like to hear what you'd say if you had what I
have.
Estragon: It hurts?
Vladimir: (*angrily*). Hurts! He wants to know if it hurts.
(*WFG*, p. 7b.

Conversation to both is a "ball" that has to be "return[ed]"
(*WFG*, p. 9a), another game to pass the time until Godot comes.
But, at their best, the short, stichomythic speeches of Didi and
Gogo are a lilting counterpoint, poetic as well as musical:

Estragon: All the dead voices.
Vladimir: They make a noise like wings.
Estragon: Like leaves.
Vladimir: Like sand.
Estragon: Like leaves. . . .

Vladimir: Rather they whisper.
Estragon: They rustle.
Vladimir: They murmur.
Estragon: They rustle. . . .

Vladimir: They make a noise like feathers.
Estragon: Like leaves.
Vladimir: Like ashes.
Estragon: Like leaves. (*WFG*, p. 41b)

Circling around itself, the play always returns to this central
refrain:

Estragon: Let's go.
Vladimir: We can't.
Estragon: Why not?
Vladimir: We're waiting for Godot.
Estragon: Ah! (*WFG*, pp. 10a, 31b, 44a, 46b, 50a, 54a)

Two single speeches exemplify this extraordinary ability of
the dialogue to turn back on itself. Lucky's monologue in act
1, seemingly sheer gibberish, establishes the pitiful mortality of
man and his works. Uttered in pseudo-scientific and philosophical
jargon, it gives the impression of a record stuck in a single

groove. The phrases "quaquaquaqua," "for reasons unknown but time will tell," and "it is established beyond all doubt," recur constantly, and the whole tour de force finally culminates in lines whose repeated echoes of "stone" and "skull" evoke the image of the graveyard that is every man's end:

> the skull fading fading fading . . . the flames the tears the stones so blue so calm alas alas on the skull the skull the skull the skull . . . the labors abandoned left unfinished graver still abode of stones in a word I resume alas alas abandoned unfinished the skull the skull . . . the skull alas the stones . . . the stones . . . unfinished. (WFG, p. 29b)

Death imagery also pervades Vladimir's second-act song, a round about a dog whose life and epitaph are synonymous, which is capable of infinite expansion (or rather, regression). Circular in structure, repetitious in vocabulary, the song is a symbol of the play itself, a "closed plot from which there is no exit."

Death imagery combined with that of birth makes another round, the Joycean one of life itself:

> one day we were born, one day we shall die, the same day, the same second, is that not enough for you. . . . They give birth astride of a grave, the light gleams an instant, then it's night once more. (WFG, p. 57b)

Vladimir continues the mixed metaphor even more poignantly:

> Astride of a grave and a difficult birth. Down in the hole, lingeringly, the gravedigger puts on the forceps. (WFG, p. 58a)

Speaking of Joyce, several critics have seen covert references to the author of *Finnegans Wake* in Beckett's play. More apocryphal than accurate, their theories seem to reflect their own ingenuity, not Beckett's genius. Murray Schumach, in an article in the *New York Times Magazine,* quotes Bert Lahr as saying, "we have to remember that Beckett was a disciple of Joyce and that Joyce hated England. Beckett meant Pozzo to be England,

and Lucky to be Ireland."[22] If this suggestion was made with tongue in cheek, Lionel Abel's is much more seriously offered. The master-slave relationship of Pozzo and Lucky, he claims, represents the earlier friendship of Joyce and Beckett. Colin Duckworth cogently protests—if such a protest is at all necessary —that Pozzo is not literary and, anyway, Joyce never made Beckett perform (write) on demand. Abel goes on to state that Lucky's monologue is nothing but a parody of Joyce's style; Duckworth again demurs, and Martin Esslin adds that "It is, if anything a parody of philosophical jargon and scientific doubletalk—the very opposite of what either Joyce or Beckett ever wanted to achieve in their writing."[23]

While Abel is certainly wrong, it should be noted that Didi and Gogo, like the Dubliners in the "Cyclops" episode of *Ulysses*, discuss the erection of a hanged man. Lucky, like Joyce before him (and Beckett elsewhere), does make scatological puns. The "Acacacademy of Anthropopopometry" (*WFG*, p. 28b) recalls Molloy's "Duchess of Caca" (*Molloy*, p. 22), Joyce's verbal playfulness in general, and perhaps Molly Bloom's chamber pot in particular.

These examples aside, Richard Francis is correct in calling the style of *Godot* "a Joycean game of cross-reference and allusion,"[24] and some of the allusions may be to Joyce's own works. Estragon asks the Boy what time it is (*WFG*, p. 32b), perhaps another parody of Earwicker and the Cad. Even more pointedly, in act 2 Estragon tells Vladimir to "look at the little cloud" (*WFG*, p. 54a). The student of Joyce will immediately think of the *Dubliners* story of the same name. Finally, at the end of the play Estragon's trousers fall down, recalling the incident of Buckley and the Russian general. Critic Hugh Kenner certainly had this source in mind when he wrote: "The student of *Finnegans Wake* will identify this mishap as the play's epiphany."[25]

Should any or all of these suggestions prove false, it is nonetheless true that "the play as a whole radiates the same kind of patient, mocking Pyrrhonism as *Finnegans Wake*. . . ."[26] Jeremy Beckett agrees:

There is too that wry humor and acute sense of the absurd—
not untinged by personal animosities—that links him [Beckett]
to Joyce and the traditions of Irish writing that run back to
Swift himself.[27]

An even more pervasive influence of Joyce and *Finnegans
Wake* in particular can be seen in *Waiting for Godot's* careful
balancing of opposites. The overwhelming tendency to circular
movement is countered if not conquered by an effort at linear
progression. "Against the monotony of the circle is set the fearful descending line that ends in the grave."[28]

Minute as they are, certain significant changes do occur in
act 2. The tree has sprouted leaves, Pozzo is blind, Lucky dumb,
and Vladimir has no more carrots, only turnips and a radish.
Except for the tree, we seem to have reached a further state of
disintegration; but neither the promise of rebirth nor the ad-
vance toward complete decay is fulfilled. Godot, the hoped-for
culmination of Gogo and Didi's waiting, is symbolic of a goal
that is never attained, an end that is never (and never can be)
reached. Once again, the tension between form and content only
proves that the circle cannot be broken.

Godot, like the trilogy, balances the conflicting poles of stasis
and motion, mind and body, time and place. Nothing if not
economical in his use of material, Beckett encompasses all three
sets of opposites in only four characters. Gogo and Didi, rooted
to a single spot and a specific time of day, are symbolic of the
Beckett hero's enforced immobility and stasis. Pozzo and Lucky,
arriving only to depart (and rearrive), represent the contradictory urge to eternal motion. Unfettered by even temporal bonds,
they are scornful of time's tyranny: "Have you not done tor-
menting me with your accursed time! It's abominable!" (*WFG,*
p. 57b).

Distinct individuals, Gogo and Didi are also two complementary halves of a single personality. Vladimir is man's mental
aspect, Estragon his physical body. If Vladimir's mouth smells,
Estragon's feet stink; if Vladimir continually plays with his
hat, Estragon is always trying to take off his boots. Both wish to

see Lucky perform, but Vladimir wants him to think and Estragon wants him to dance. Separate beings, Vladimir and Estragon are tied together as surely as if they were connected by rope, as Pozzo and Lucky in fact are. The latter pair, of course, represent another dual relationship, that of master to slave, exploiter to exploited, Cain to Abel (*WFG*, p. 53b). Together, the two couples are indeed "all humanity" (*WFG*, p. 54a), or as Didi puts it: "at this place, at this moment of time, all mankind is us, whether we like it or not" (*WFG*, p. 51a).

Beckett himself is aware of this delicate balancing of opposites in character, theme, and structure. Pozzo's right lung is good, but his left one is bad (*WFG*, p. 27a), and Beckett told English reviewer Harold Hobson that "one of Estragon's feet is blessed, and the other is damned. The boot won't go on the foot that is damned; and it will go on the foot that is not."[29]

Circular in shape, *Waiting for Godot* revolves on a double axis of hope and uncertainty. The doubts of the trilogy's heroes, greatly magnified, assault the four characters of the play. Unsure whether they are in the right place (*WFG*, p. 10a), Didi and Gogo are uncertain as well of the time of their appointment:

Estragon: You're sure it was this evening?
Vladimir: What?
Estragon: That we were to wait.
Vladimir: He said Saturday. (*Pause.*) I think . . .
Estragon: . . . But what Saturday? And is it Saturday? Is it not rather Sunday? . . . Or Monday? . . . Or Friday? (*WFG*, pp. 10b–11a)

Names are ambiguous[30] and open to question. "Pozzo" is confused with the similar-sounding Godot, Bozzo, and Gozzo (*WFG*, p. 15b); at one point he is called both "Cain" and "Abel." Estragon states that his name is Adam (*WFG*, p. 25a), and Pozzo thinks Godot may be "Godin" or "Godet" (*WFG*, p. 19b).

Doubt and uncertainty, like the snow in "The Dead," are general over Beckett's theatrical universe. Is it the "same lot" (*WFG*, p. 7a) that beats Estragon every night? Is the fourth evangelist the correct one? Is the tree a willow? or a bush? or a shrub? (*WFG*, p. 10a). Are Didi and Gogo tied to Godot? (*WFG*, p. 14b). Does Pozzo smoke a briar, dudeen, or Kapp and Peterson? (*WFG*, p. 23b). Does he carry a spray, vaporizer, or pulverizer? Are Estragon's boots gray, brown, or green? Is it sunset or sunrise? Is Pozzo Godot? "Nothing is certain" (*WFG*, p. 10b), and though we strongly suspect that Godot will never come, even that belief is not by any means a justifiable one. Indeed, all doubt and insecurity are balanced by a single hope—that Godot will come tomorrow—and a single fact: they must keep on waiting:

Estragon: And if he doesn't come
Vladimir: We'll come back to-morrow.
Estragon: And then the day after to-morrow.
Vladimir: Possibly.
Estragon: And so on.
Vladimir: The point is—
Estragon: Until he comes. (*WFG*, p. 10b)

Vladimir: . . . What are we doing here, *that* is the question. And we are blessed, in this, that we happen to know the answer. Yes, in this immense confusion one thing alone is clear. We are waiting for Godot to come—

                                    .   .   .
Vladimir: Or for night to fall. . . . We have kept our appointment and that's an end to that. (*WFG*, p. 51b)

Structurally, the play contains its own opposites of form and shape. Within its circular movement there is both expansion and contraction. Spare (but not sparse) and economical in his technique, Beckett has contracted the infinite circles of Joyce into two. Two acts, representing two essentially identical days, are all that is necessary to convey the thought and feeling of endless, senseless repetition. Place, too, is reduced to a minimum —an ordinary country road—and we have already seen how much Beckett compresses into four characters.

At the same time, there is expansion. The two days of the

play are an intensive examination of those "depths of an instant without bounds" (*MD*, p. 233) in which Malone felt himself trapped. Seconds, minutes, hours, excruciatingly magnified under Beckett's theatrical telescope of a play, all pass painfully for both character and audience alike. Waiting, living, passing the time—these are the true subjects of Beckett's play, and in order for us to see them, not as a part of daily routine, but as the routine iself, the author has had, in the words of Estragon, to "Expand! Expand" (*WFG*, p. 55b).

Finally, *Waiting for Godot* balances the opposites of art and artifice. A play, it is aware, as are all of Beckett's works, of its own theatrical illusion. Far from pretending that their stage has four walls, Gogo and Didi are highly conscious of the audience watching them. "Inspiring prospects" (*WFG*, p. 10a) is Estragon's comment on the playgoers. Vladimir, not so polite, perhaps voices the secret hostility of many an author when he turns toward the auditorium and says, "that bog . . ." (*WFG*, p. 10b). Estragon, like an usher, directs Vladimir to the men's room: "End of the corridor, on the left," while Vladimir appropriately responds, "Keep my seat" (*WFG*, p. 23b). Aware that he and Vladimir are actors uttering lines, Estragon comments directorially on their delivery: "That wasn't such a bad little canter" (*WFG*, p. 42a), and on the play itself:

Vladimir: Charming evening we're having.
Estragon: Unforgettable.
Vladimir: And it's not over.
Estragon: Apparently not.
Vladimir: It is only beginning. (*WFG*, pp. 23a–b)

Estragon: I find this really most extraordinarily interesting. (*WFG*, p. 9a)

Vladimir: . . . Some diversion. (*WFG*, p. 56a)

Moreover, all the characters perform their own play-within-a-play. Vladimir tells his story of the two thieves, Estragon tries to reveal his dreams, Lucky is made to perform (dance and think) on cue, and Pozzo, the most obvious thespian of all, delivers a speech on night that is alternately "lyrical" and "prosaic" (*WFG*, p. 25a).

And yet, despite the fact that we are constantly reminded of its make-believe and man-made nature, *Waiting for Godot* is as real as life itself to us. We believe in Gogo and Didi's anguish and their joys, their failures and their triumphs, but most of all we believe in their waiting, especially when it appears futile, senseless, and without hope. Life may repeat itself, and repeatedly disappoint the liver, but, like Molloy, Gogo, and Didi, we feel the moral imperative to go on living, waiting, hoping if not believing that one day the suffering will end and Godot (God, salvation, death, peace, or what-you-will) be there at last.

Endgame (1957)

The note of Joycean optimism that Beckett sounded in *Waiting for Godot* is greatly diminished—and, some would say, entirely eliminated—in his second play, *Endgame*. Once again the action is nonaction—waiting—but now the anticipation is not for salvation, a new life free of misery, but for an end to all existence, and to time as well. The scene is similar to that in a fall-out shelter after a nuclear holocaust. Hamm is confined to a single room and Clov can go only as far as the kitchen. Possibly father and son, they may be, as Lionel Abel has suggested, surrogate figures for Joyce and Beckett themselves. Blind Hamm, Abel avers, represents the ocularly troubled author of *Finnegans Wake,* while Clov is the young disciple made to serve an egotistical, tyrannical master. (This relationship is duplicated in the partnership of Lucky and Pozzo.) Such an exclusive reading of the play, highly hypothetical as it is, only serves to reduce Beckett's work to a narrow and insignificant level. At the same time, however, Beckett does seem to be mocking Joyce by creating a play around a situation directly opposite to that of *Ulysses.*

In Joyce's book, a father (Bloom) finds a surrogate son (Stephen), but in Beckett's play a foster son (Clov) repeatedly tries to leave his foster father.

Many of Beckett's previous writings incorporated the theme of friendship between two men, a theme that often seems to have a direct bearing on Beckett's own relationship with Joyce. Mercier and Camier were the author's first "pseudocouple," and in *Watt* the hero talks to his friend *Sam* in language that more than one critic has identified as noticeably Joycean. Even in *Waiting for Godot,* Estragon's attempts to tell Vladimir his dreams recall the dream-book of *Finnegans Wake,* and Vladimir's attention to his hat coincides with the importance headwear has in *Ulysses.* The friendship motif reaches a climax in a little-known work by Beckett. "Assez," a short story published in French in 1966, recounts the course of the narrator's close but brief relationship with an unnamed friend. Concluding as mysteriously as it had begun, the friendship is over, but not before we learn that the other was a tall man, bent over, and not accustomed to much talking. The two men shared an interest in mathematics (cf. Beckett and Joyce's mutual interest in numerology), and the narrator reveals that "contrairement à ce que je m'étais longtemps plu à imaginer il n'était pas aveugle."[31] Whether or not Beckett intended it, the description bears a remarkable resemblance to Joyce. And aside from friendship, the constant father-son relationships in Beckett's works recall Joyce's own obsession with this theme. Jacques Moran and his son, Hamm and Clov, and Henry Bolton and his father all betray Beckett's persistent interest in the parent-offspring relationship.

Another important aspect of both Joyce and Beckett's fiction, one that is especially visible in *Endgame,* is the religious imagery both authors habitually employ. Here, however, the differences in purpose and technique are greater than the similarities. Joyce alludes to Christian theology in a traditional way; if he himself no longer believed in Catholic dogma, he nonetheless admired and respected it as a universally accepted truth and principle of order. Using religion to give his characters a heroic and biblical dimension—Bloom "is" Moses, Molly "is" Mary, and Stephen "is" Jesus—Joyce also used it to give his novels classic shape. *Ulysses* has a trinitarian form of sorts: part 1 deals with the son, part 2 with the father, and part 3 is the word made flesh: Molly Bloom. Earwicker's fall and rise parallel the Nazarene's own crucifixion and resurrection two thousand years ago.

Beckett, on the other hand, although also a former believer, is not so benevolent or respectful toward religion as Joyce was. All his biblical allusions seem, in the words of Ruby Cohn, to be "mocking echoes, probably because Christianity (like love, another major Beckett target) seemed to promise so much to man."[32] According to George Fraser, "If Beckett is an atheist, his atheism springs from the scar left by a Christian belief once deeply felt, in which one has a grudge against God even for not existing."[33] Beckett does, in fact, seem to create God-like figures— Mr. Knott, Youdi, Godot—only to demonstrate how impotent and unfeeling they are.[34] The jokes against religious dogma are even more vicious. In the French edition of *Molloy,* A and B are referred to by the hero as "mes deux larrons." In *Malone Dies,* Macmann's aged lover, Moll, wears earrings that depict the crucifixion of the two thieves. A third crucifixion—of Christ—is elaborately carved on her tooth—a literal and grotesque sort of eucharist. Godot's name, if it is a diminutive French form for God (analogous to *Charlot* for Charles), does seem a somewhat irreverent way of referring to the deity. Furthermore, *Endgame* presents a reverse parody of the opening chapter of Genesis. Clov looks out on the world, sees "nothing," and calls it "good" (*E,* p. 78). Hamm himself is probably a parody of Jesus. The opening words of the play—"It is finished"—are those of Christ on the cross, and Hamm, like the Nazarene before him, calls out "Father father" (*E,* p. 84) and covers his face with a handkerchief that has the imprint of his features—a veronica. Sheets and napkins are used as shrouds, and the hammer-nail overtones of all the characters' names could also be intended as allusions to the crucifixion. Turning to the Old Testament, Beckett's central character also could be one of Noah's three sons; indeed, Clov, looking out of the window at one point, thinks the earth has been flooded.

Other allusions enrich the parody. Hamm's story takes place on Christmas Eve, and there is a reference to the manna that fell from heaven for the Israelites in the desert. On page 12, Hamm hints at Daniel's successful deciphering of the handwriting on the wall of King Belshazzar's palace: "Mene, mene?" The kitchen, which we never see, has equal dimensions (10'x10'x10'), and, according to the Book of Revelation, so does the New Jerusalem. If all this were not enough, the original French version of the play contained even more pointed suggestions that the home of Hamm and Clov is an ironical, perverse Eden. Hearing that Clov has sighted a boy outside, Hamm comments, "la pierre levée," an allusion to Christ's resurrection; he assumes that the child is looking at the house "avec les yeux de Moïse mourant." Clov, however, reveals that, like Buddha, he is merely contemplating his navel.

Considering *Endgame* in the light of Beckett's previous works, we see that it contains many of his usual themes and motifs, elements that link it to Joyce's fiction as well. Again there is the awareness on the part of the characters that they are involved in a theatrical experience, a play:

Hamm: . . . Did anyone ever have pity on me?
Clov: What? . . .
Hamm: An aside, ape! Did you never hear an aside before? (*E*, p. 77)
Hamm: I'm warming up for my last soliloquy.
Hamm: More complications! . . . Not an underplot, I trust. (*E*, p. 78)
Clov: This is what we call making an exit. (*E*, p. 81)
Clov: . . . (. . . *picks up the telescope, turns it on the auditorium.*)
I see . . . a multitude . . . in transports . . . of joy. (*E*, p. 29)
Clov: What is there to keep me here?
Hamm: The dialogue. (*E*, p. 58)

Again, too, the time and place are those of purgatory. Situated between earth and sea, the room constitutes a no-man's-land, a metaphorical limbo where things are over but not yet finished. The time is that eternal present which we encountered in both the trilogy and *Godot*. "What time is it," Hamm asks Clov. "The same as usual," is the reply (*E*, p. 4). Suffused in a consistent gray light, the stage is in the eternal twilight of *Waiting for Godot*, the time when it is no longer day and not yet night:

Hamm: Is it light?
Clov: It isn't dark. (*E*, p. 63)

There is a sense of the past, but it is isolated from the present. Yesterday is "that bloody awful day, long ago, before this bloody awful day" (*E*, pp. 43–44). Each day resembles the one before it, and yet, unlike Joyce's recycling world, there is no continuity between days. Just because Nell scratched Nagg yesterday does not mean that she will do so today, or, conversely, just because Clov oiled the castors of Hamm's chair yesterday does not mean that he should not oil them again today. Even if the past was pleasant—Nell's memories of Lake Como, for instance—the present is painful and seemingly eternal. Future time in Beckett's world is a state that can be postulated but never achieved. That is, "The future event cannot be focussed, its implications cannot be seized, until it is definitely situated and a date assigned to it" (*Proust*, p. 6). Thus, we wait for Godot to come "tomorrow," but he never does. Future time is imagined, never realized. As Hamm says, "Moments for nothing, now as always, time was never and time is over" (*E*, p. 83).

Ending is still an impossible task for the Beckett hero. Decay and deterioration constantly occur; in *Endgame* we learn that the Beckettian universe has been stripped of almost all its objects. There are no more bicycle wheels, sugar plums, coffins, navigators, pap, Turkish Delight. Even Hamm's painkiller is no longer available. And yet, life itself is not extinguished. Although blind and paralyzed, Hamm lingers on. Clov's eyes and legs are bad, Nagg and Nell have lost their sight and seem closer to death than to life, but a flea is found by Clov and there is the horrifying possibility that everything may regenerate and the world be full of painful plenitude once again. "Finished, it's finished, nearly finished" (*E*, p. 1), says Clov at the beginning of the play, and the operative word is *nearly*. Seemingly winding down to total nothingness, Hamm, Clov and their world somehow never end, nor do we have the impression that they ever will. Even words cannot cease. Built on a limited vocabulary of phrases and motifs that occur and recur, Beckett's play is an endgame of language, a record stuck in its final grooves, going round and round in a series of endless verbal repetitions: "It's finished," "What's happening?" "Something is taking its course," "Is it time for my painkiller?"

Using the Greek philosopher Zeno, Beckett tries to suggest why there can never be an end to things. Just as Zeno's paradoxes point to the existence of irrational numbers, numbers whose valuation could only be approached, never definitely ascertained, so too Beckett's plays reveal an irrational element in life, the "mess" that prevents an orderly progression to a final end. Time, like Zeno's millet grains, patters down ceaselessly, "and all life long you wait for that to mount up to a life" (*E*, p. 70). But it doesn't mount, and it doesn't amount. Rather,

> it piles up all about you, instant on instant, on all sides, deeper and deeper, thicker and thicker, your time, others' time, the time of the ancient dead and the dead unborn, why it buries you grain by grain, neither dead nor alive, with no memory of anything, no hope of anything, no knowledge of anything. (*Unn*, p. 143)

Whereas for Joyce time destroyed only to recreate, for Beckett time is an eternal gravedigger, burying alive the ever-decaying corpse of life. In *Happy Days* we see this metaphor given concrete form. Winnie is literally interred alive in the sands of time. Act 1 sees her buried to her waist, act 2 up to the neck. Presumably in act 3 she would be completely submerged, but one has the feeling that there still will be many many happy days just like these two for her.

So too for *Endgame*. At game's end, Hamm, the red king, sits paralyzed on his thronelike chair, unable to move from his "square." Clov, the white knight, and the two white pawns, Nagg and Nell, hold him in a sort of checkmate that is really a stalemate. This endgame of chess will never end, and Clov will remain motionless in the doorway until the following night, when Hamm will uncover his face and the duel start all over again.

"The end is in the beginning and yet you go on" (*E*, p. 69) says Hamm, and so it is with Beckett. From the interminable chess game of *Murphy*, to this perpetual *Endgame*, Beckett has come full circle. Discarding the initial stylistic influence of Joyce, he has, after much resistance, accepted the idea of the universe as a closed cyclical system. Unlike Joyce, however, who viewed the eternal round of life as a blessing and guarantee of immortality, Beckett sees the endless circles of existence as purgatorial imprisonment, a temporal trap that prevents man from reaching the ultimate finality of the self. A modern-day Tithonus, Beckett is unable to see the meaning of life apart from its end. Rebelling against a reality that is never resolved or regenerated, simply perpetuated, and striving for an art that is founded not on the word but on wordlessness, Beckett moves toward nothingness and the unsurpassable eloquence of complete silence. His contribution to Kenneth Tynan's *Oh! Calcutta*, consists of symmetrical intervals of sound and silence. A recent short story, translated by Beckett and published in the *Evergreen Review*,[35] is significantly titled "Lessness," perhaps an oblique admission on Beckett's part that art cannot achieve, only approximate, the void. Equally important, the word *endlessness* is frequently repeated. Together, the two words—*lessness* and *endlessness*—represent the dilemma confronting Beckett and his fiction. Faced with what is for him a meaningless and meaninglessly eternal plenitude, Beckett has retreated toward nothingness. Both the tension and poignancy of his work derive from the fact that, unable to accept one absolute, he is equally incapable of achieving the other. And so, rejecting Joyce's views and methods, Beckett has, paradoxically, reaffirmed them and his writings have become more than ever like those of his friend and fellow author. As is *Finnegans Wake*, Beckett's novels and plays are built on a conflict of opposites—all versus nothing, continuing versus ending, words versus silence, circle versus line—that both complement and perpetuate each other. Trying to end, Beckett must go on; urged toward silence, he must utilize words to reach it. Beckett's very effort to cease creating, then, is virtual assurance that he will continue to create. For, in his own words, "The search for the means to put an end to things, an end to speech, is what enables the discourse to continue" (*Unn*, p. 299).

Searching for silence and finality, Beckett is seeking an answer to the problems posed by Joyce's works: the primacy of the word and the circular pattern of the world. Forced to employ language and to reaffirm the cyclical nature of existence, Beckett has been unable decisively to refute the linguistic and philosophical theories underlying *Ulysses* and *Finnegans Wake*. But there is no question that the silent debate with Joyce's ideas that pervades Beckett's stories, poems, novels, and plays has deepened his art, just as the friendship with his fellow exile enriched his personal life.[36]

Appendix A: Beckett and Irish Literature

Beckett's relationship to older Irish literary traditions is strongly suggested at the same time that it is extremely difficult to document. As Vivian Mercier puts it in his invaluable book, *The Irish Comic Tradition*:

> We have the peculiar case here of an Anglo-Irishman who, like Swift, seems to fit comfortably into the Gaelic tradition yet has almost no conscious awareness of what that tradition is. Beckett might be described as *in* the Gaelic tradition but not of it.[1]

Beckett, like Joyce, draws on one of the richest veins in the tradition of Irish humor, that of wit, satire, and parody. All three depend on language, with wit being most closely connected to the form of wordplay that Joyce elevated into an art: the pun. It was the Joycean pun that Beckett exploited so heavily at the beginning of his career, but satire and parody also received his attention, as the stories "A Wet Night" and "What a Misfortune" in particular demonstrate (see chap. 2 above for a fuller discussion of these early works).

Beckett soon virtually abandoned this particular Joycean comic technique. However, the style of his work since *Watt* increasingly depends on the very source of Irish humor and, indeed, of all humor. For where wit, satire, and parody depend on language, the origins of humor, according to Mercier, are "preverbal,"[2] that is to say, they antedate speech. It is the effort to return to this preverbal humor, to the humor of silence, that marks much of Beckett's recent work, especially the mimes *Act Without Words I* and *II* and *The Lost Ones.*

A third link with the older Irish literary tradition, and one that requires more extensive discussion, involves the Swiftian overtones in Beckett's prose. Along with Swift, Beckett feels a fundamental disgust for the physical. Sex is a grotesque act that affords little or no pleasure, but degrades the participants by betraying them into ridiculous postures and statements (see chap. 4). Reproduction is an even greater horror, prolonging as it does the misery of human existence through yet another generation. In *Endgame,* Clov destroys a rat and flea because each might find a mate and start the whole evolutionary process all over. The one grace that Molloy finds in his mother is that she did all she could not to have him, and, when that failed, she at least did not compound the error by having another child. In *All That Fall,* Mr. Rooney confesses to the wish of "nip[ping] some young doom in the bud"[3] and, indeed, might have pushed a child off the train he was riding. This grotesque humor not only ties Beckett to Swift, but also, according to Mercier, to the larger Gaelic tradition that debunks the view of sex and reproduction as sacred and sees them as repellent and macabre. Tracing this tradition back to the sheela-na-gig, or ancient Irish stone carving of a grotesque female figure, Mercier sees in the statue's skull-like face, huge scowling mouth, skeletal ribs but grossly enlarged genitalia, an archetypal symbol of the Irish attitude that sex implies death and vice versa.[4] Beckett's own fictional creations, particularly Macmann's Moll, who deteriorates physically as soon as her affair with Macmann is consummated, are virtual incarnations of the sheela-na-gig, although Mercier admits that there is no evidence whatsoever that Beckett was aware of the carvings.

While Joyce apparently was also oblivious to the existence of the sheela-na-gig, an examination of his works indicates that he too absorbed some of the traditional Gaelic revulsion against the body and its functions. Frightened by Father Arnall's sermon and fearful for his soul, Stephen Dedalus, in chapter 3 of *A*

Portrait of the Artist as a Young Man, develops a visceral reaction against both his sinful behavior and the physical self that practiced it. After dreaming of evil, dung-covered, goatlike creatures, symbolic of his lechery, Stephen purges himself physically by vomiting, but still despises his body, especially his sexual organ:

> What a horrible thing! Who made it to be like that, a bestial part of the body able to understand bestially and desire bestially? Was that then he or an inhuman thing moved by a lower soul? His soul sickened at the thought of a torpid snaky life feeding itself out of the tender marrow of his life and fattening upon the slime of lust.[5]

After confessing his sins to a priest, he embarks on a carefully regimented spiritual existence that includes systematic mortification of the senses. Although Stephen eventually rejects the spiritual life in favor of the artistic one, his ascetic attitude remains more or less intact, his body as well as his mind devoted to art. In *Ulysses* he is portrayed as a bloodless prig, whose opening chapters are significantly devoid of any corresponding physical organ in Joyce's schema, and who refuses the opulent curves of Molly Bloom when they are symbolically offered to him by her husband. Moreover, he sees the world in the light of the grave: the living corpse of the old milkwoman, the dead cancer-ridden body of his mother, the drowned bodies of the man Mulligan saved and of Lycidas, the grandmother buried by the fox. All is mortal, and Stephen is repelled by mortality, by even his own mother's "weak blood and wheysour milk."[6]

Bloom himself often exhibits a similar disgust at man's physical habits. In the "Lestrygonians" chapter, hungry as Bloom is, the sight of people eating revolts him, and he has to leave Burton's restaurant for Davy Byrnes's pub. Man's sexual appetite is equally abhorrent to Bloom. It can be a selfish one that condemns women like Mrs. Purefoy to a "life with hard labour,"[7] placing her continually in the throes of childbirth. Vivian Mercier also sees Bloom's fantasized pregnancy in the "Circe" episode as grotesque sexual humor of the type inherent in the Irish tradition established with the sheela-na-gig.[8] Finally, even Molly occasionally considers the male physique grotesque:

> compared with what a man looks like with his two bags full and his other thing hanging down out of him or sticking up at you like a hatrack no wonder they hide it with a cabbage-leaf.[9]

This anti-physical strain in Joyce's writings might have been a source for Beckett's own disgust of the body and its regenerative powers.

And yet, to leave the impression that Joyce seriously found sex and physical life repellent would be to distort the meaning of his work. In *Portrait* Stephen's ascetic behavior is implicitly criticized. An extreme, it is as wrong as the excessive sensuality he previously indulged in. The decision to reject the priesthood and embrace art is not so much a rejection of the spiritual for the aesthetic as it is an acceptance of a way of life that is both spiritual and physical. Stephen is called to art by his sight of the girl wading in the waters off Bull Island. Dressed in blue like the Virgin Mary, she nonetheless has bared "thighs, fuller and softhued as ivory." Spiritual and sensual at the same time, she is "touched with the wonder of *mortal* beauty,"[10] and it is on this worldly loveliness that Stephen's new religion of art will, hopefully, base itself. Asceticism and hedonism were the two extremes, the two purging fires the young artist had to pass through before arriving at the "holy silence of his ecstasy."[11]

In the same way, it is not eating and sex per se that disgust Bloom, but only extreme, excessive indulgence in them: the animallike gorging of lunchtime diners and the lust-inspired lovemaking of a Blazes Boylan.[12] Indeed, Bloom is equally repelled by the other extreme: denial of the flesh. He even defends prostitution against the sexless spirituality and exaggerated purity of Bella Cohen turned coy nymph: "If there were only ethereal where would you all be, postulants and novices?"[13] And although she can, like Swift, disparage man's sexual organs, Molly's jaundiced opinions in no way alter her enjoyment of sex. Indeed, her famous "Yes" that ends the book is as much an affirmation of the physical (sexual) side of life as it is an acceptance of Bloom's proposal. No less a critic than Richard Ellmann believes that Joyce placed sexual love above all other kinds of love.[14]

In citing these proofs of *Ulysses*'s—and Joyce's—fundamentally positive attitude to sex I do not mean to suggest that Joyce has written a gushing, Whitmanesque paean of praise to the body. On the contrary, as I have tried to show above, Joyce was certainly conscious of the grotesque nature of the physical. However, these repellent aspects are included because they constitute a normal part of man's total attitude toward sex, just as defecation, urination, and menstruation—all of which the book mentions in detail—are a normal part of man's (and woman's) total physical existence. Far from worshipfully adoring the body, Joyce simply acknowledges and accepts it in all its variety, in its ridiculous aspects as well as in its sublimer moments. The same cannot be said of Beckett, whose greater revulsion for the physical marks him as a truer follower of the Irish tradition inherent in the sheela-na-gig.

Appendix B: Joyce and the Jews

Despite Joyce's favorable treatment of Henry Sinclair, many readers have detected anti-Semitic overtones in *Ulysses*. The most frequently cited proof is the "Hades" references to Reuben J. Dodd, a Dublin solicitor and money-lender. However, a careful reading of the passage (pp. 93–95) reveals that the negative remarks are all based on Dodd's profession and character, not his religion. Simon Dedalus's hostility is the natural animosity of a debtor toward a creditor (as did Joyce's own father, Stephen's owed money to Dodd), and the ready concurrence of Jack Power and Martin Cunningham is easily attributed to the fact that they too have borrowed from Dodd. " 'We have all been there,' Martin Cunningham said broadly."[1] An additional cause of Simon Dedalus's hatred—and the main factor in both Joyce's and Bloom's disapproval of Dodd—is the latter's treatment of his son. In real life the younger Dodd, disappointed in love, tried to commit suicide by throwing himself into the Liffey. He was rescued by a poor dockworker and fellow Jew, Moses Golden, who, as a result, was hospitalized for weeks with pulmonary trouble. Suffering financially from her husband's disability, Mrs. Golden visited Dodd Sr., who told her that Golden should have minded his own business but finally condescended to give her 2s. 6d., or half a crown. Such behavior—and Bloom's reference to the incident shows that it was well known to Power and Cunningham if not to Simon Dedalus—is reason enough for the scorn heaped on Dodd.

Ultimately, however, for Joyce, Dodd's sin was not that of

the usurer extracting money from his victims (there is, indeed, no evidence whatsoever that he charged unlawful or immoral rates of interest), but that of the father denying his son, one of the central themes of *Ulysses*. (It is interesting that their denial of Christ is the one thing Joyce did hold against the Jews.[2]) Bloom, who has been brooding on little Rudy's death is, of course, extremely sensitive to Dodd's callousness. And even Simon Dedalus, who from Bloom's point of view does not recognize the worth of *his* son either, is also properly offended: " 'For God's sake!' Mr. Dedalus exclaimed in fright. 'Is he dead?' "[3] Moreover, if Dedalus's remark that Dodd paid "one and eight-pence too much" is derogatory, so is the opinion of the Dublin newspaper, *The Irish Worker*, which concluded its leading article on the event thus: "Mr. Dodd thinks his son is worth half-a-crown. We wouldn't give that amount for a whole family of Dodds."[4] Clearly, both remarks reflect a disapproval that has nothing to do with racism but is rather a reaction to an individual. Joyce himself was remarkably free of anti-Semitism, even going so far as to ridicule those who were not, such as Mr. Deasy in the "Nestor" chapter. Indeed, he proudly saw crucial similarities between the Jews and the Irish: both were outsiders in European culture, isolated, and looked down upon. Both were good family men, valuing close personal ties. On a personal level, Joyce, like Bloom, felt an outcast in his own country, betrayed by his friends as Leopold is cuckolded by Molly. For these reasons and many more, Bloom emerges as one of the most sympathetic portraits of the Jew in Western literature. And *Ulysses*, even in its minor characters such as Reuben J. Dodd, supports Joyce's statement that "I have written with the greatest sympathy about he Jews."[5]

Notes

Preface

1. Among them Hugh Kenner in his *Flaubert, Joyce and Beckett: The Stoic Comedians* (Boston: Beacon Press, 1962), William York Tindall in his pamphlets *Beckett's Bums* (privately printed) and *Samuel Beckett* (New York: Columbia University Press, 1964), and Francis Warner in *Theatre and Nationalism in Twentieth-Century Ireland* (Toronto: University of Toronto, 1972).

2. Colin Wilson, *The Strength to Dream: Literature and the Imagination* (Boston: Houghton, Mifflin, 1962), p. 89.

3. Christopher Ricks, "The Roots of Samuel Beckett," *The Listener* 72 (17 December 1964): 964.

4. V. S. Pritchett, "An Irish Oblomov," *New Statesman*, n.s. 59 (2 April 1960): 489.

5. Lionel Abel, "Samuel Beckett and James Joyce in *Endgame*," in *Metatheatre* (New York: Hill and Wang, 1963), p. 139.

6. Samuel Beckett in a letter to Sighle Kennedy dated "Paris 14. 6. 67" and reproduced in *Murphy's Bed: A Study of Real Sources and Surreal Associations in Samuel Beckett's First Novel* (Lewisburg, Pa.: Bucknell University Press, 1971), p. 300.

7. Northrop Frye, "The Nightmare Life in Death," *Hudson Review*, 13 (Autumn 1960): 442.

8. David Hayman, "A Meeting in the Park and a Meeting on the Bridge: Joyce and Beckett," *James Joyce Quarterly* 8 (Summer 1971): 375.

9. Maria Jolas, "A Bloomlein for Sam," in *Beckett at 60: A Festschrift* (London: Calder and Boyars, 1967), p. 16.

10. A. J. Leventhal, "The Beckett Hero," in Martin Esslin, ed., *Samuel Beckett: A Collection of Critical Essays* (Englewood Cliffs, N.J.: Prentice-Hall, 1965). p. 47.

11. J. Mitchell Morse, "The Choreography of the New Novel," *Hudson Review* 3 (Autumn 1963): 396–419.

12. Laurent Le Sage, *The French New Novel: An Introduction and a Sampler* (University Park, Pa.: Pennsylvania State University Press, 1962), p. 47.

13. Martin Esslin, "Samuel Beckett," in *The Novelist as Philosopher*, ed. John Cruikshank (London: Oxford University Press, 1962), p. 129.

14. Ruby Cohn, "Joyce and Beckett, Irish Cosmopolitans," *James Joyce Quarterly* 8 (Summer 1971): 390.

15. Francis Warner, "The Absence of Nationalism in the Work of Samuel Beckett," *Theatre and Nationalism in Twentieth-Century Ireland* (Toronto: University of Toronto, 1972), p. 180.

16. J. Mitchell Morse, "The Ideal Core of the Onion: Samuel Beckett's Criticism," *French Review* 38 (October 1964): 24.

17. Ihab Hassan, *The Literature of Silence: Henry Miller and Samuel Beckett* (New York: Alfred A. Knopf, 1967), p. 115. The fact that Beckett began where Joyce left off has also been noted by Francis Warner ("Absence of Nationalism," p. 181).

18. George Steiner, "Of Nuance and Scruple," *New Yorker* 44 (27 April 1968): 164.

19. To say that Beckett was influenced by Joyce is not to claim that his work is identical to Joyce's. According to Maria Jolas "there's a fundamental difference. Joyce could still say yes, whereas Sam's answer is definitely no" ("A Bloomlein," p. 16). Allan Brick is of the opinion that "Samuel Beckett takes Joyce's world view and removes all possibility for consoling illusions" ("The Madman in His Cell: Joyce, Beckett, Nabokov and the Stereotypes," *Massachusetts Review* 1 [Fall 1959]: 45), and J. Mitchell Morse maintains that in contrast to Joyce's concrete language, Beckett's is "almost entirely abstract and subjective. Whereas Joyce has each character speak in an individually characteristic idiom, and even describes them all in a highly mannered abstract style, and with exceptions even has them talk in that style" ("Ideal Core of the Onion," p. 25). These differences, as well as many others, will be discussed at greater length in the pages that follow.

Chapter 1 Friendship

1. James Joyce, *A Portrait of the Artist as a Young Man*, ed. Chester G. Anderson (New York: The Viking Press, Inc., 1968), p. 253. All future references are to this edition.

2. Ibid.

3. James Joyce, *Ulysses* (New York: Random House, 1961), p. 42. All future references are to this edition. Interestingly enough, Adrienne Monnier has remarked that at that time "Beckett looked to us like a

new Stephen Dedalus . . . striding all by himself along the Strand"
(Gisele Freund and V. B. Carleton, *James Joyce in Paris: His Final
Years* [New York: Harcourt, Brace and World, 1965], p. 56.

4. *Public Schools Yearbook* 1927 (London, 1928), pp. 134–35.

5. Ernest Hemingway, *A Moveable Feast* (New York: Charles
Scribner's Sons, 1964).

6. Lawrence Harvey, *Samuel Beckett: Poet and Critic* (Princeton,
N.J.: Princeton University Press, 1970), p. 199.

7. Samuel Putnam, *Paris Was Our Mistress* (New York: The Viking
Press, 1947), p. 74.

8. Ibid., p. 137.

9. Ibid., p. 138.

10. Hemingway, *Moveable Feast*, p. 20.

11. Putnam, *Paris Was Our Mistress*, p. 136.

12. Abraham Lincoln Gillespie, a protégé of Eugene Jolas, separated
from his wife, Molly, after being published in *transition* because he
no longer considered her his intellectual equal (ibid., p. 224).

13. Ibid., p. 221.

14. Ibid., p. 5.

15. Ibid., p. 7. America's commercialism and anti-artistic atmosphere
were probably more in the minds of her writers than in the air of her
cities. Malcolm Cowley, in *Exile's Return*, admits as much when he
recounts how his stay in Europe altered his attitude toward his country
until he came to believe that it was not so much "the dragon of
American industry" that "blotted out the sky" for American artists as
those artists' own unfounded "inferiority complex" about America. Her
literature was suffering, not from any real ignorance or inattention on
the part of the public, but from the literati's mistaken belief that
Europe and European art were indisputably superior. (Malcolm Cowley, *Exile's Return: A Literary Odyssey of the 1920's* [New York: The
Viking Press, 1969], pp. 106–7).

16. Eugene Jolas, "Revolt Against the Philistine," *transition* 6
(September 1927) : 176.

17. Eugene Jolas, "Super-Occident," *transition* 15 (February 1929):
15.

18. Ibid.

19. "We are for an anarchic *state of mind* primarily" (*transition*
9 [December 1927]: 167). (Italics mine.)

20. Eugene Jolas, "Literature and the New Man," *transition* 19–20
(June 1930): 15.

21. Eugene Jolas, "Preface," *transition* 21 (March 1932) : 284.

22. "Suggestions for a New Magic" (editorial), *transition* 3 (June
1927): 178.

23. Ibid., p. 179.

24. Ibid., *transition* 16–17 (June 1929) : 13.

25. "Suggestions for a New Magic" (editorial), *transition* 3 (June 1927) : 179.

26. Hans Arp, et al., "Poetry is Vertical," *transition* 21 (March 1932) : 148–49.

27. Putnam, *Paris Was Our Mistress*, p. 97.

28. A suggestion made to me by George Reavey, poet and translator of Russian verse, whom McGreevy introduced to Beckett. Reavey later published *Echo's Bones* on his Europa Press.

29. Richard Ellmann, *James Joyce* (New York: Oxford University Press, 1965), p. 104.

30. By an interesting coincidence, Beckett, like Joyce, first earned his living as a language instructor.

31. Jerry Tallmer, "A Nobel Prize Is . . . Waiting for Beckett," *The New York Post*, 1 November 1969, p. 22.

32. Joyce, *Portrait*, p. 244.

33. Tom Driver, "Beckett by the Madeleine," *Columbia University Forum* 4 (Summer 1961) : 24.

34. Ellmann, *James Joyce*, pp. 628–29.

35. Ibid., p. 629.

36. Ibid., p. 131.

37. Ibid., pp. 628–29.

38. Stuart Gilbert, ed., *Letters of James Joyce*, 3 vols. (New York: The Viking Press, 1966), 1: 283.

39. The other was probably Thomas McGreevy.

40. Gilbert, ed., *Letters*, 1: 283.

41. Samuel Beckett, "Dante . . . Bruno. Vico . . Joyce," *transition* 16–17 (June 1929) : 244.

42. Ibid., p. 246.

43. The technique was sophisticated, but the result was, like the aim of Jolas, to recapture the concise simplicity of primitive speech. Thus Beckett was right in saying that "Mr. Joyce has desophisticated language" (ibid., p. 249).

44. The slightly revised text in *Exagmination* . . . (Paris: Shakespeare and Co., 1929) at this point inserts the phrase, "It is that something itself" (p. 14).

45. Beckett, *transition*, "Dante . . . Bruno," p. 248.

46. Jolas, "A Bloomlein," p. 45.

47. Gilbert, ed., *Letters*, 1: 280.

48. Ibid., p. 281. I have not been able to locate the review in question, nor is it mentioned by Federman and Fletcher in their bibliography.

49. Ibid., p. 283.

50. Ibid. The twelve customers at Earwicker's pub are numerically suggestive of Joyce's disciples—and Christ's! Joyce included his "twelve Marshals" in *Finnegans Wake* on p. 284: "Imagine the twelve deaferended dumbbawls of the whowl abovebeugled to be the contonuation through regeneration of the urutteration of the word in pregross."

51. Especially since Beckett was interested in philosophy per se. Witness his later poem "Whoroscope" and his Master's Essay on Descartes.

52. Ellmann, *James Joyce*, p. 645.

53. The original appointment to the Ecole Normale Supérieure was part of an exchange program conducted between that school and Trinity.

54. Ellmann, *James Joyce*, p. 506.

55. Ibid., p. 645.

56. Ibid., p. 646.

57. Ibid., p. 726.

58. Beckett, in an interview with Israel Shenker of the *New York Times*, stressed this point: "I was never Joyce's secretary, but, like all his friends, I helped him. He was greatly handicapped because of his eyes. I did odd jobs for him, marking passages for him or reading to him. But I never wrote any of his letters" (Israel Shenker, "Moody Man of Letters," *New York Times*, 6 May 1956, § 2, p. 1).

59. Ellmann, *James Joyce*, p. 662. There has been much effort and speculation devoted to finding the passage. Nathan Halper, in *A Wake Newslitter* (n.s. [June 1966], pp. 55–56) reports that he was unable to do so, but suggests that Joyce either (a) eventually transformed the phrase into "come into" (*FW* 243.01, 253.17, 446.34, 529.17) or "Come-Inn" (512.34); (b) used the sound that caused it ("Knock knock" appears on 330.30); or (c) as Clive Hart suggested, "having made a good story of it to Beckett, quietly expunged it later." J. S. Atherton thinks the phrase may have been changed to a single word, "comma" (*A Wake Newslitter*, n.s. [October 1966], p. 109). But the most recent suggestion is the best, for it not only confirms the incident but includes Joyce's reply to Beckett as well. Leo Knuth convincingly cites the phrase "Comme bien" (420.12–13) and notes that, aside from being a phonetic approximation of French *combien*, it also is very close to the Dutch *kom binnen* (imperative singular) or *komt binnen* (imperative plural): "come in." Moreover, Knuth continues, "at 420.11–12 we read: 'let it stayne!' (Dutch *staan*, German *stehen*, 'stand')" (*A Wake Newslitter*, n.s. [December 1970], p. 96). This seems to me to be the answer to the riddle.

60. As John Joyce told it, Buckley, an Irish soldier in the British army during the Crimean War, confronts the Russian general on the field of battle. Aiming at his enemy, Buckley is prevented from shooting by the general's imposing epaulettes and military decorations. Nerving himself a second time to execute the general and his duty, Buckley is again stopped, this time by the general's common humanity. For, heeding the call of nature, the general has lowered his pants and proceeds to defecate in front of his captor. Buckley is paralyzed by the Russian's helpless posture—until the general wipes himself with a piece of turf. Disgusted, Buckley at last pulls the trigger.

61. Ellmann, *James Joyce*, p. 411.

62. James Joyce, *Finnegans Wake* (New York: The Viking Press, 1966), p. 353. All references to the *Wake* are to this Compass Edition, and are cited as *FW*.

63. Italics mine. Note the echo of "Beckett" in "berbecked."

64. *FW* 49. 21–22. Perhaps Beckett remembered this passage when he named the blind hero of his play *Endgame*.

65. *FW* 112. 3–6. Note again the pun on Beckett's name (italics mine). The many references to Saint Thomas A'Beckett would also include Sam.

66. *FW* 408. 22–24.

67. Ibid., 467. 18–32 (italics mine).

68. Patricia Hutchins, *James Joyce's World* (London: Methuen & Co., Ltd., 1957), p. 169. The card is interesting for another reason. Its formal salutation and close support Rayner Heppenstall's statement in *The Fourfold Tradition* (Norfolk, Conn.: New Directions, 1961), p. 138, that "to the end of their relationship Joyce and Samuel Beckett solemnly continued to address each other as 'Mr. Joyce' and 'Mr. Beckett.'" Ellmann reports (presumably from Beckett) that, although Joyce enjoyed Beckett's company, he nevertheless kept him at a distance (*James Joyce*, p. 661).

69. Ellmann, *James Joyce*, p. 661. Beckett read Fritz Mauthner's *Beiträge zu Einer Kritik der Sprache*, a book that advanced the nominalist view of language in which Joyce was interested, and that Beckett would attack in *Watt* and subsequent works.

70. A. J. Leventhal, a close friend of Beckett's who knew Joyce as well, has remarked that Beckett's "silences in company were as marked as James Joyce's" (in *Festschrift*, p. 10).

71. Ellmann, *James Joyce*, p. 661.

72. Alec Reid writes: ". . . the silences are as important as the sounds, and the sounds as important as the meaning. Beckett will speak of leading up to a pause and going away from it as others might of a rhetorical climax or even a physical action. The pauses are always

shown on the printed text, of which they form an integral part no less than the words surrounding them" (*All I Can Manage, More Than I Could: An Approach to the Plays of Samuel Beckett* [Chester Springs, Pa.: Dufour Editions, 1968], p. 29).

73. Joyce once asked Beckett if anyone in Dublin was reading *Ulysses*, then remarked: "I may have oversystematized *Ulysses*" (Ellmann, *James Joyce*, p. 715).

74. Ellmann, *James Joyce*, p. 715. This association of intellectuals and turnips may have remained with Beckett. In *Waiting for Godot*, Vladimir's pockets are filled with turnips, but Estragon, the more physical of the pair, prefers carrots or radishes.

75. Ibid., p. 625.

76. Ibid.

77. Ibid., p. 662.

78. According to Peggy Guggenheim, Beckett confessed that he had no feelings, that he was emotionally "dead" and so could not fall in love with Lucia (Marguerite Guggenheim, *Out of This Century: The Informal Memoirs of Peggy Guggenheim* [New York: Dial Press, 1946], p. 205).

79. Guggenheim, *Out of This Century*, p. 205. Beckett felt guilty about this and later told Peggy Guggenheim that he "had caused her [Lucia] great unhappiness" (ibid, p. 194).

80. Jane Lidderdale and Mary Nicholson, *Dear Miss Weaver: Harriet Shaw Weaver 1876–1961* (New York: The Viking Press, Inc., 1970), p. 312.

81. Ellmann, *James Joyce*, pp. 662–63.

82. Ibid., p. 663.

83. Gabriel d'Aubarède, interview with SB in *Les Nouvelles Littéraires*, 16 February 1961, p. 7.

84. Letter from Patric Farrell to Barbara Gluck, dated July 1970.

85. Samuel Beckett, "Home Olga," *Contempo* (Chapel Hill, N.C.) 3 (15 February 1934): 3.

86. Harvey, *Samuel Beckett*, p. 296n.

87. Adaline Glasheen, "Home Olga," *A Wake Newslitter*, n.s. 3, no. 2 (April 1966): 31 n. 87.

88. Harvey, *Samuel Beckett*, p. 297n.

89. Joyce, *Ulysses*, p. 3.

90. Lawrence Harvey points out that the bird imagery of the line suggests Dedalus, the bird man, and, indeed, all the birds of *Portrait* (*Samuel Beckett*, p. 297n).

91. Joyce, *Ulysses*, p. 15. Harvey also cites as perhaps relevant a then current Irish joke: "Take a tip from me—as the Jew said to the Rabbi" (*Samuel Beckett*, p. 297n).

92. Although he has written directly only on *Finnegans Wake*, Beckett seems to have read all of Joyce's works. "Dante . . . Bruno. Vico . . Joyce" contains references to both *Portrait* and the lesser-known "The Day of the Rabblement." *More Pricks Than Kicks* has several allusions to *Ulysses*.

93. James Joyce, *Chamber Music*, in *The Portable James Joyce*, edited and with an introduction and notes by Harry Levin (New York: The Viking Press, 1967), p. 634. Beckett would also use this word in *Waiting For Godot*, Complete Works Edition (New York: Grove Press, 1970).

94. Ruby Cohn, *Samuel Beckett: The Comic Gamut* (New Brunswick, N.J.: Rutgers University Press, 1962), p. 235.

95. Harvey, *Samuel Beckett*, p. 297n.

96. Harvey concludes that Beckett portrays himself as "an ungrateful lamb who has decided to leave the flock" (ibid., p. 298n), but I find no evidence for such a reading. Rather, Beckett seems to declare his devotion to Joyce. Ellmann has a slightly different interpretation of the poem, also one that I fail to agree with. It is here given in full: "If Joyce had any hope in his exile that the Irish would renounce Catholicism, the national malady, he, untouched by it, might be able to yield to his comic spirit. His books are full of natural love and silence, in man and woman, and in their portrayer (Joyce), expressed in a *dolce stil nuovo*, and also full of faith and cunning. When he says goodbye he winks because what was shall be again, a point unknown to Homer, but demonstrated by Joyce because he himself is a kind of Christ (another word-man) returned to life: hail and alas!" (Ellmann, *James Joyce*, pp. 714–15).

97. Joyce, *Letters*, 1: 323.

98. *Contempo* 3 (15 February 1934): 3.

99. Harvey, *Samuel Beckett*, p. 296.

100. Ibid., pp. 257–58.

101. Beckett visited the cities of "Lubeck, Luneberg, Brunswick, Leipzig, Halle, Naumberg, Weimar, Wurzburg, Nuremberg, Regensburg . . . lingering especially at Hanover, Munich, Berlin, and Dresden" (ibid., p. 170). George Reavey has kindly permitted me to examine his correspondence with Beckett during these years, and together we have been able to piece together a more exact chronology: By 13 November 1936 Beckett was in Hamburg; he reached Berlin on 20 December and stayed there until 14 January when he left for Dresden. He remained in Dresden well into February (at least till 15 February) and went on to Munich. By 13 April 1937 (his thirty-first birthday) he was back at his home in Clare Street, Dublin.

102. Ibid., p. 183. A passage in *More Pricks Than Kicks* is also

strangely prophetic: "The Wanderjahre were a sleep and a forgetting, the proud dead point. You came back wise and staked your beat in some sheltered place, pennies trickled in, you were looked up to in a tenement" (p. 48).

103. Samuel Beckett, "Gnome," *Dublin Magazine* 4, no. 3 (July–September 1934): 8. Harvey makes a similar comment: "Beckett's travels had no specific goal. Having sacrificed the long years of scholastic preparation by abandoning an academic career, uncertain of the future, he roamed partly to escape into another linguistic cosmos . . . partly to follow his love of art wherever it might lead him" *Samuel Beckett*, p. 171).

104. Joyce also knew of this habit and referred to it in a letter of 15 January 1935 (James Joyce, *Letters*, 1: 356).

105. Guggenheim, *Out of this Century*, p. 194.

106. Guggenheim, *Confessions*, p. 50.

107. Guggenheim, *Out of this Century*, p. 195.

108. Ibid., p. 199.

109. The London *Times*, 2 April 1937, p. 6.

110. Oliver St. John Gogarty, *As I Was Going Down Sackville Street* (Dublin: Rich and Cowan, 1937), p. 65.

111. Ibid., p. 71.

112. Fitzgerald then asked Beckett what that made him to Sinclair, and Beckett condescendingly replied he would "leave it to Counsel to work out the relationship." Fitzgerald countered with a reversal of the *Hamlet* line: "A little more kind than kin" (Ulick O'Connor, *The Times I've Seen: Oliver St. John Gogarty—A Biography* [New York: Ivan Obolensky, Inc., 1963], p. 324). The entire trial was punctuated by such acrimonious repartee.

113. Fitzgerald spoke French fluently but deliberately mispronounced Proust's name, hoping that Beckett would not miss the chance to correct him, thus making an unfavorable impression on the jury. Beckett, unfortunately, fell into the trap (O'Connor, *The Times I've Seen*, p. 325).

114. O'Connor, *The Times I've Seen*, p. 323.

115. Ibid., p. 328.

116. Wood's boast that one of Dublin's "great traditions . . . is that it has never persecuted the Jews" (ibid., p. 323) recalls Mr. Deasy's remark to Stephen in *Ulysses*: "Ireland, they say, has the honour of being the only country which never persecuted the jews" (*Ulysses*, p. 36).

117. O'Connor, *The Times I've Seen*, p. 329.

118. Richard Ellmann, ed., *Letters of James Joyce* (New York: The Viking Press, 1966), 2: 194. Padraic Colum also reports that he intro-

duced the Sinclairs to Joyce, who at one time tried to interest them in financing a new daily afternoon paper that he would edit along Continental lines (Padraic and Mary Colum, *Our Friend James Joyce* [Gloucester, Mass.: Peter Smith, 1968], p. 38).

119. Joyce, *Ulysses*, p. 164, 1.5. See Appendix B, Joyce and the Jews, below.

120. Ellmann, *Letters*, 3: 411 n. 5.

121. Heppenstall, *The Fourfold Tradition*, p. 256.

122. Letter from SB to George Reavey, dated 1 January 1938 and written from the hospital. Mr. Reavey thinks he may have given Beckett the idea of seeking Joyce's aid.

123. James Knowlson, *Samuel Beckett*, catalogue of an exhibition held at Reading University Library, May to July 1971 (London: Turret Books, 1971), p. 29.

124. Ellmann, *James Joyce*, p. 714.

125. Guggenheim, *Confessions*, pp. 50–51.

126. Constantine Curran, *James Joyce Remembered* (New York and London: Oxford University Press, 1968), pp. 90–91.

127. Ellmann, *James Joyce*, p. 722.

128. Ibid., p. 734.

129. Ibid., p. 741.

130. Ibid.

131. Maria Jolas, "A Bloomlein," p. 15.

132. Ellmann, *James Joyce*, p. 744.

133. Ellmann, ed., *Letters*, 3: 483.

134. Beckett was born on Good Friday, 13 April 1906.

135. Letter from Robert Kastor to Barbara Gluck, 7 November 1970.

136. Alan Simpson, *Beckett and Behan and a Theatre in Dublin* (London: Routledge & Kegan Paul, 1962), p. 67.

Chapter 2 Apprenticeship: 1929–34

1. Samuel Beckett, *Proust*, Collected Works Edition (New York: Grove Press, Inc., 1970). The inexpensive paperback edition has the same pagination. All future references are included parenthetically in the text after the identifying initial *P*.

2. Joyce, *FW*, 4.15.

3. Compare this wording to that of the Verticalist Manifesto that Beckett signed two years later: "the final disintegration of the 'I'. . . ."

4. Frederick J. Hoffmann, *Samuel Beckett: The Language of Self* (New York: E. P. Dutton & Co., 1964), p. 82.

5. Joyce, *FW*, 614.27

6. In May 1921 Joyce attended a supper party for Stravinsky and Diaghilev at the Paris home of Mr. and Mrs. Sydney Schiff. Proust was there and Joyce was introduced to him. He reported the conversation to Frank Budgen: "Our talk consisted solely of the word 'No.' Proust asked me if I knew the duc de so-and-so. I said, 'No.' Our hostess asked Proust if he had read such and such a piece of *Ulysses*. Proust said, 'No.' And so on." (Frank Budgen, *Further Recollections of James Joyce* [London: Shenval Press, 1955], pp. 10–11).

7. Leventhal, "The Thirties," in *Festschrift*, p. 8. The pun is that, from pronunciation, the motto can also be understood as "and the mud *is* the world" (italics mine). Leopardi's intention was "the mud and the world."

8. Samuel Beckett, *Molloy*, Collected Works Edition (New York: Grove Press, Inc., 1970), p. 22. Here the reference is to a "Countess Caca."

9. Ellmann, *James Joyce*, p. 499: Joyce "said only that it was a queer title for a book which contained neither crime nor punishment."

10. Cohn, *Samuel Beckett*, p. 12.

11. The poem can be found in Samuel Beckett's volume of verse, *Poems in English*, Collected Works Edition (New York: Grove Press, Inc., 1970), pp. 11–17, Copyright © 1961 by Samuel Beckett. Line references are included parenthetically in the text.

12. Leventhal, "The Thirties," in *Festschrift*, p. 9.

13. Professor Tindall has pointed out to me that one of the myriad names of Anna Livia Plurabelle's "untitled mamafesta" (*FW* 104.4) is "How to Pull a Good Horuscoup when Oldsire is Dead to the World" (*FW* 105.28–29). Joyce's pun, more myth-minded than Beckett's, includes a reference to Horus, Isis, and Osiris. The title of Beckett's poem, however, in a fashion anticipates Murphy, whose astrological forecast, obtained by a prostitute, is literally a "whoroscope."

14. Hoffman, *Samuel Beckett*, p. 87.

15. John Fletcher, "The Private Pain and the Whey of Words," in *Samuel Beckett: A Collection of Critical Essays*, ed. Martin Esslin (Englewood Cliffs, N.J.: Prentice-Hall, Inc., 1965), p. 25.

16. Cohn, *Samuel Beckett*, p. 14.

17. For instance, when Bloom sees John Howard Parnell, the Chief's brother, go by, he thinks, "Poached eyes on ghost" (*Ulysses*, p. 165). The entire chapter, following a peristaltic movement, goes from mouth to anus, and Beckett's poem traces a similar downward line, from the height of Descartes's confidence to his final helpless pleading against being bled: "Oh Weulles [the Dutch physician attending Descartes] spare the blood of a Frank . . ." (l. 94).

18. Harvey, *Samuel Beckett*, p. 22n.

19. A letter by Descartes, quoted in ibid., p. 22.

20. Included in *Poems in English*.

21. Compare the image of Eveline as a caged animal at the end of the story of that name in *Dubliners*.

22. Joyce, *FW* 3.2–3.

23. Harvey, *Samuel Beckett*, p. 136.

24. Joyce, *Dubliners*, p. 208.

25. Joyce, *Portrait*, p. 253.

26. Joyce, *Ulysses*, p. 377.

27. Ibid., p. 783. As Professor Tindall has remarked, the number eight on its side is the symbol for infinity, and Molly has infinite riches for both reader and Bloom, who is, as Joyce himself pointed out to Frank Budgen, an "all-round" character.

28. Joyce, *Letters*, 1: 251.

29. Harvey, *Samuel Beckett*, p. 79.

30. Ibid., p. 139.

31. Ibid., p. 143n.

32. In *A Portrait of the Artist as a Young Man*, the school pudding is known as "dog-in-the-blanket" (*Portrait*, p. 8), while the Black Mass scene in the "Circe" episode of *Ulysses* contains the backward statement "Htengier Tnetopinmo *Dog* Drol eht rof, Aiulella!" (*Ulysses*, p. 599; italics mine).

33. Samuel Beckett, "Text," *The New Review* (April 1932), p. 57.

34. Samuel Beckett, "Sedendo et Quiescendo," *transition* 21 (March 1932): 13–20.

35. Joyce also parodies the lines in *FW* 135.6–7: "washes his fleet in annacrwatter; whou missed a porter. . . ."

36. Michael Robinson in *The Long Sonata of the Dead: A Study of Samuel Beckett* (New York: Grove Press, Inc., 1969), p. 75, writes: "The Dublin background of *More Pricks Than Kicks* is carefully documented after the manner of *Ulysses*: the street names, the Liffey, Trinity College and the statue of Thomas Moore, combine to present the busy city landscape against which Belacqua is drawn." *More Pricks Than Kicks* is hereafter referred to as *MPTK*.

37. Hoffman, *Samuel Beckett*, p. 101.

38. The story is structured on certain pairs of opposites—life and death, mercy and justice—and much of the language cuts both ways. Evening off the "end" of bread on a newspaper picture of the "face" of McCabe (Cain + Abel), the assassin, Belacqua forecasts the beheading of the murderer that is scheduled to take place the next morning. His attitude toward the toast also encompasses two extremes: "He had his cheek against the soft of the bread, it was spongy

and warm, alive. But he would very soon take that plush feel off it, by God but he would very quickly take that fat white look off its face" (*MPTK*, p. 11). And, indeed, Belacqua does toast it to a "dead end" (*MPTK*, p. 12).

39. Other religious references occur throughout the story. The grocer makes a "wild crucified gesture of supplication" (p. 14), and Belacqua, calling the lobster a fish, reflects that "fish had been good enough for Jesus Christ, Son of God, Saviour" (pp. 19–20). Finally, the lobster is "exposed cruciform" (p. 21) to Belacqua and his aunt.

40. As early as this story we learn that a Beckett hero "scoffed at the idea of a sequitur from his body to his mind" (*MPTK*, p. 29).

41. It is with such stasis that Belacqua's desire for perpetual motion must be contrasted.

42. There is also the blind paralytic who, in his wheelchair (two circles), always returns to the same spot each day to beg.

43. Cohn, *Samuel Beckett*, p. 33.

44. Joyce, *Ulysses*, p. 498.

45. Joyce uses this expression in a letter to Louis Gillet (Joyce, *Letters*, 1: 401), and, as Professor Tindall informed me, in the *Wake* itself: "sursumcordial" (*FW* 581.13).

46. Note the reversal of Leopold's situation with Molly.

47. Music is a recurrent motif of the story. Belacqua spies on, and is beaten by, a "Tanzherr."

48. William Wordsworth, "A Slumber Did My Spirit Seal," in *William Wordsworth: Selected Poetry*, ed. and intro. Mark Van Doren (New York: Random House, Inc., 1950), p. 158.

49. G. C. Barnard, *Samuel Beckett: A New Approach* (New York: Dodd, Mead & Company, Inc., 1970).

50. Note Ruby Tough's name and her nether lip, "where she could persuade no bee to sting her any more" (*MPTK*, p. 91). Also "The Smeraldina's Billet Doux" discussed below.

51. In *Murphy's Bed: A Study of Real Sources and Sur-real Associations in Samuel Beckett's First Novel*, Sighle Kennedy recalls Beckett's description of time as a "cancer" (*Proust*, p. 7), and wonders whether this was the tumor on Belacqua's neck (p. 42). I wonder whether Beckett was thinking of Eliot's "patient etherised upon a table" (T. S. Eliot, *The Complete Poems and Plays: 1909–1950* [New York: Harcourt, Brace & Co., 1952], p. 3), or perhaps of John Millington Synge's two operations (1897, 1907) for cancerous tumors on the back of his neck.

Chapter 3 The Joycean Shadow: Murphy, Watt, Mercier et Camier

1. Samuel Beckett, *Murphy*, Collected Works Edition (New York: Grove Press, Inc., 1970), p. 1. First published 1938. All further references are to this edition, included parenthetically in the text after the identifying initial *M*.

2. Joyce, *Ulysses*, p. 622.

3. Ibid., p. 660.

4. Ibid., p. 674.

5. Letter from A. J. Leventhal to Barbara Gluck, 16 July 1970. It should be noted that "Austin" also suggests the poet Austin Clarke.

6. Ellmann, *James Joyce*, p. 714.

7. *transition* 3 (May 1927) : 106.

8. *transition* 8 (November 1927) : 25.

9. See Ruby Cohn's chapter on *Murphy* in her *Samuel Beckett: The Comic Gamut*.

10. "Joyce's influence was still strong when [Beckett] wrote *Murphy* and his admiration for *Ulysses* and *Work in Progress* as it then was, perhaps encouraged him in a cavalier but learned use of language" (Robinson, *The Long Sonata*, p. 96). Georges Bataille is of the same opinion: "Il s'en faut d'ailleurs que l'évidente influence de Joyce sur Beckett donne la clé de ce [roman]. Tout au plus l'intérêt prêté aux possibilités échevelées données dans le libre jeu—malgré tout volontaire, malgré tout concerté, mais violent—du langage rapproche-t-il les deux écrivains" ("Le Silence de Molloy," *Critique* 7 (15 May 1951) : 389).

11. Consider the preponderance of riddles in Joyce's works: Athy's on his name in *Portrait*, Stephen's on the fox and Lenehan's on opera in *Ulysses*, Shem's and the Prankquean's in *Finnegans Wake*.

12. Murphy's eccentricities in dress and deed contrast strikingly with the conventional aspects of the book. Like Belacqua Shuah, he is an alienated man who has been out of tune with "normal" life since his birth: ". . . of all the millions of little larynges cursing in unison at that particular moment, the infant Murphy's alone was off the note. To go back no further than the vagitus" (*M*, p. 71).

13. Raymond Federman, *Journey to Chaos: Samuel Beckett's Early Fiction* (Berkeley and Los Angeles: University of California Press, 1965), p. 60.

14. Robinson, *The Long Sonata*, p. 90.

15. *James Joyce: The Critical Writings*, ed. Ellsworth Mason and Richard Ellman (New York: The Viking Press, Inc., 1959), p. 153.

16. Joyce, *Stephen Hero*, p. 33. Padraic Colum writes: "It is from the time of this departure from Dublin in 1912 that the word 'exile' in the sense of 'banishment,' 'proscription,' comes to be used by Joyce as something that evokes all one's spiritual powers and by doing so leads to creativeness" (*Our Friend James Joyce*, p. 68).

17. Joyce, *Critical Writings*, p. 171.

18. Ellmann, *James Joyce*, p. 114.

19. Israel Shenker, "Moody Man of Letters," New York *Times,* 6 May 1956, § 2, p. 1.

20. Ibid.

21. Joyce, *Ulysses*, p. 579.

22. " 'Dear old indelible Dublin,' said the coroner" (*M*, p. 267).

23. Quoted in Cohn, *The Comic Gamut*, p. 60 (italics mine). Cohn also cites a similar instance of translation: "Les termes du passage ci-dessus furent choisis avec soin, loin de la rédaction en anglo-irlandais, afin de corrompre le lecteur cultivé."

24. Ibid.

25. The question of Bloom's final relationship with Molly is almost as problematic and controversial as that of her "union" with Stephen. Edmund Wilson believed that the Blooms resumed sexual intercourse (*Axel's Castle: A Study in the Imaginative Literature of 1870 to 1930* [New York: Charles Scribner's Sons, 1931], p. 202), but William Empson foresees only another affair for Molly, this time with Stephen. In Richard Ellmann's opinion, such speculation is simply "a nineteenth-century parlour game" (*Ulysses on the Liffey* [New York: Oxford University Press, 1972], p. 160).

26. Joyce, *Ulysses*, p. 678.

27. Ibid., p. 55.

28. Ibid., p. 6.

29. Ibid., p. 37.

30. Ibid.

31. Ellmann, *Ulysses on the Liffey*, p. 75.

32. Joyce, *Ulysses*, p. 656.

33. Ibid., p. 614.

34. A. Walton Litz, "Ithaca," in *James Joyce's Ulysses: Critical Essays*, ed. Clive Hart and David Hayman (Berkeley: University of California Press, 1974), p. 401.

35. Joyce, *Ulysses*, p. 703.

36. Budgen, *James Joyce*, p. 59.

37. S. L. Goldberg, *The Classical Temper: A Study of James Joyce's Ulysses* (New York: Barnes and Noble, 1961), p. 169.

38. H. Frew Waidner, III, "*Ulysses* by Way of *Culture and Anarchy*," in *Approaches to Ulysses: Ten Essays*, ed. Thomas F. Staley and Bernard Benstock (Pittsburgh: University of Pittsburgh Press, 1970), p. 182.

39. It is true that many writers, both ancient and modern, have used the circle as structure and motif for their fictions. Beckett, a widely read and learned man, could have been influenced by any or all of them; however, his close relationship with Joyce and the espe-

cially close reading he gave to Joyce's works make it highly probable that Joyce was his particular influence.

40. W. Y. Tindall, *James Joyce: His Way of Interpreting the Modern World* (New York: Charles Scribner's Sons, 1950), p. 69.

41. Miss Dwyer is "the one closed figure in the waste without form, and void!" (*M*, p. 5).

42. Wylie, as time ("while-y"), and Neary, as space ("near-y"), could be an allusion to the time-space conflict that runs throughout *Finnegans Wake* (Shem and Shaun, Prof. Jones). Murphy, like Belacqua Shuah, resolves the conflict by avoiding, through death, both terms of the dispute. He is the last of Beckett's characters to be allowed to do so.

43. Joyce, *Ulysses*, p. 164.

44. Stephen Dedalus and the newspapermen head for this bar at the end of the "Aeolus" episode in *Ulysses*.

45. Murphy's death appears to be the result of an accident. Someone put on the gas from the w.c.; it ignited with the candle and caused an explosion. But in chapter 12 we learn that Murphy left a note detailing his requests for burial (cremation). Whether or not Beckett intended it as such, the situation remains ambiguous.

46. Samuel Beckett, *Watt*, Complete Works Edition (New York: Grove Press, Inc., 1970). Further references are to this edition, included parenthetically in the text after the identifying initial *W*.

47. Jacqueline Hoefer, in "Watt," *Samuel Beckett: A Collection of Critical Essays,* ed. Martin Esslin (Englewood Cliffs, N.J.: Prentice-Hall, Inc., 1965), suggests that Watt really asks "how?" things occur, not what occurs.

48. "except, one, not to need, and, two, a witness to his not needing" (*W*, p. 202).

49. Note the recurrence of twins in Joyce: the Caffrey boys in *Ulysses*, Shem and Shaun in the *Wake*. Beckett has Bim and Bom, Art and Con.

50. Thomas W. Lombardi, "Who Tells Who *Watt*," *Chelsea* (June 1968), p. 179n: "Beckett may be thinking of *Finnegans Wake* and the early days he spent with Joyce."

51. J. Mitchell Morse, "The Contemplative Life According to Samuel Beckett," *Hudson Review* 15 (Winter 1962–63): 514–15.

52. I am indebted to Professor Tindall for pointing this out to me.

53. David Hayman, "A Meeting in the Park and a Meeting on the Bridge: Joyce and Beckett," *James Joyce Quarterly* 8 (Summer 1971): 379.

54. Ibid., pp. 381–82.

55. Ibid., p. 381.

56. Exelmans is a French general, Cavendish a British scientist, Habbakuk a Hebrew prophet Beckett had mentioned in his poem "Dortmunder." *Ecchymose* is a term in pathology signifying a skin discoloration due to the rupture of small blood vessels; the correct term is really *ecchymosis.*

57. Compare Bloom's "high grade ha" (*Ulysses*, p. 71). And in chapter 5 of *Finnegans Wake* we read: "He is my O'Jerusalem and I'm his Po" (*FW* 105.6-7). Mrs. Mathilde Finch, my editor, hears an echo of the old song "Annie Rooney"; "She's my Sweetheart, I'm her beau; She's my Annie, I'm her Joe."

58. Lionel Abel, "Joyce the Father, Beckett the Son," *Metatheatre* (New York: Hill and Wang, 1963), pp. 83-85.

59. Robinson, *The Long Sonata*, p. 105.

60. Hugh Kenner, *Flaubert, Joyce and Beckett: The Stoic Comedians* (Boston: Beacon Press, 1962).

61. Ibid., p. 64. Kenner writes that "Beckett has been the first writer to exploit directly the most general truth about the operations of a stoic comedian, that he selects elements from a closed set, and then arranges them inside a closed field" (pp. 92-94).

62. Compare *Murphy*: "Humanity is a well with two buckets. . . ."

63. Susan Field Senneff, "Song and Music in Samuel Beckett's *Watt,*" *Modern Fiction Studies* 11 (Summer 1964): 139.

64. Joyce, *Ulysses*, p. 37. The sound also suggests Aristophanes' frogs.

65. Senneff, "Song and Music," p. 149.

66. Ruby Cohn, "*Watt* in the Light of *The Castle,*" *Comparative Literature* 13 (Spring 1961): 161.

67. Susan Senneff even sees the Addenda as "circles surrounding a gear wheel" ("Song and Music," 146).

68. Ruby Cohn ("*Watt* in the Light of *The Castle,*" p. 161) writes that "if the line of narration is circular, it is a far cry from Browning's 'In heaven, a perfect round.' Rather, this circumference is riddled with gaps, and it is little short of a miracle if the circle closes at all."

69. Compare *Finnegans Wake*: ". . . the rite words by the rote order" (167.33).

70. Beckett used to read Fritz Mauthner's *Beiträge zu einer Kritik der Sprache* to Joyce (Ellmann, *James Joyce*, p. 661).

71. Hoefer, "Watt," p. 75 (original italics).

72. Ludwig Wittgenstein, *Tractatus Logico-Philosophicus*, trans. D. F. Pears and B. F. McGuinness, with an introduction by Bertrand Russell (London: Routledge & Kegan Paul; New York: The Humanities Press, 1961), p. 150.

73. John Fletcher, *The Novels of Samuel Beckett* (London: Chatto & Windus, 1964), pp. 87-88.

74. Fritz Mauthner, *Beiträge zu einer Kritik der Sprache* (Stuttgart, 1901–2), 1: 1–2, quoted in Gershon Weiler's book *Mauthner's Critique of Language* (London and Colchester: Cambridge University Press, 1970), p. 296 (italics mine).

75. Weiler, *Mauthner's Critique*, p. 142 n. 5. There is also, as Weiler points out, a possible reference to Mauthner in *Finnegans Wake*: "Mister Maut" (*FW* 319.9).

76. It is significant that in "Circe" Joyce represents the descent into man's primitive nature, his subconscious, by a return to gesture. Stephen uses his ashplant to shiver the lamp image, "so that gesture, not music, not odours, would be a universal language" (*Ulysses*, p. 432), and subsequently he makes a "movement" to "illustrate the loaf and jug of bread and wine in Omar" (*Ulysses*, p. 433).

77. Joyce, "The Study of Languages," *Critical Writings*, p. 28. Beckett would probably agree with this.

78. Joyce, *Ulysses*, p. 76.

79. William Butler Yeats, "The Song of the Happy Shepherd," *The Collected Poems of W. B. Yeats* (New York: The Macmillan Company, 1966).

80. Richard Coe, *Samuel Beckett* (New York: Grove Press, Inc., 1968), p. 11.

81. Harvey, *Samuel Beckett*, p. 379.

82. Nathan A. Scott, Jr., "The Recent Journey into the Zone of Zero: The Example of Beckett and His Despair of Literature," *Centennial Review* 6 (Spring 1962): 179.

83. Federman, *Journey to Chaos*, p. 117.

84. Cohn, *The Comic Gamut*, p. 93.

85. See pp. 93 and 253 on which a "Knott family" is alluded to or mentioned.

86. Joyce, *Ulysses*, p. 731.

87. Federman, *Journey to Chaos*, p. 131.

88. Samuel Beckett, *Mercier and Camier* (New York: Grove Press, Inc., 1974). Future references are to this edition, included parenthetically in the text after the identifying initials *M&C*.

89. Samuel Beckett, *Mercier et Camier* (Paris: Les Editions de Minuit, 1970), p. 172.

90. Hugh Kenner, "The Cartesian Centaur," in *Samuel Beckett: A Critical Study* (Berkeley and Los Angeles: University of California, 1968).

Chapter 4 The Voice of the Artist

1. Robinson, *The Long Sonata*, p. 141.

2. Samuel Beckett, "Dante . . . Bruno. Vico . . Joyce," *transition* 16–17 (June 1929) : 248.

3. William York Tindall, in a privately published pamphlet, *Beckett's Bums* (London, 1960), presents the theory that *Molloy* is a deliberate parody of *Ulysses*. "A wanderer like Ulysses in search of a home" (p. 10), Molloy meets his Circe in the person of Lousse (there is even a reference to moly) and later crawls into his mother's bed, much as Leopold Bloom crawls into Molly's. Moran, like Stephen Dedalus, seeks his true father, and is also told to set out on his quest by an agent. Other parallels are possible: the policeman who arrests Molloy could be meant to represent Cyclops, and the woman on the beach recalls the princess Nausicaa. John Fletcher further suggests the identification of Edith/Ruth, Molloy's partner in physical love, with Calypso ("Interpreting *Molloy*," in *Samuel Beckett Now*, ed. and intro. Melvin J. Friedman [Chicago & London: The University of Chicago Press, 1970], p. 161).

4. Niklaus Gessner, *Die Unzulänglichkeit der Sprache* (Zurich: Verlag, 1957), p. 32.

5. Tindall, *Samuel Beckett*, pp. 21–22.

6. *Molloy*, according to John Fletcher, represents a transitional stage in the process of cultural assimilation. Its dual Franco-Irish nature is evident in the names of the novel's characters, especially that of Jacques Moran. Some names, like those of Lousse, Father Ambrose, and the verger Joly, are entirely French in origin; others—Molloy, the Elsner sisters—recall Beckett's own Irish background (*The Novels of Samuel Beckett*, pp. 125–26).

7. George Steiner, *Language and Silence: Essays on Language, Literature and the Inhuman* (New York: Atheneum, 1970), pp. 168–69 (italics mine).

8. According to Ellmann, Joyce's worshipful elevation of art coincided with his break from organized religion (the Church) : "As his [Joyce's] faith in Catholicism tottered a counter-process began: his faith in art . . . grew great" (*James Joyce*, p. 50).

9. Joyce, *Portrait*, p. 221. •

10. Joyce, *Portrait*, p. 215.

11. Joyce, *Stephen Hero* (New York: New Directions, 1944), p. 80.

12. Samuel Beckett and Georges Duthuit, "Three Dialogues," in *Samuel Beckett: A Collection of Critical Essays*, ed. Martin Esslin (Englewood Cliffs, N.J.: Prentice-Hall, Inc., 1969), p. 21.

13. James Joyce, "James Clarence Mangan," in *The Critical Writings of James Joyce*, ed. Ellsworth Mason and Richard Ellmann (New York: The Viking Press, 1959), p. 83.

14. Beckett, *Molloy*, p. 16. Future references are to The Collected Works Edition and are included parenthetically in the text.

15. Joyce, "James Clarence Mangan."

16. Steiner, *Language and Silence*, p. 12.

17. Michel Foucault proposes a theory similar to that of Steiner. He, however, places the fall of language from its Olympian height somewhat later than the seventeenth century—indeed, in the nineteenth. (*Les mots et les choses: une archéologie des sciences humaines* [Paris: Editions Gallimard, 1966], p. 14).

18. Steiner, *Language and Silence*, pp. 13–14.

19. Ibid., pp. 24–25.

20. Ibid., p. 30.

21. Ibid,. p. 25.

22. Ibid., p. 7.

23. Frank Budgen testifies that "to Joyce words are more than a pleasurable material out of which agreeable patterns can be made, or thought and emotion communicated. They are quick with human history as pitchblends with radium, or coal with heat and flame. They have a will and life of their own and are not to be put like lead soldiers, but to be energised and persuaded like soldiers of flesh and blood" (*James Joyce and the Making of Ulysses* [Bloomington and London: Indiana University Press, 1970], p. 175).

24. William York Tindall, *A Reader's Guide to Finnegans Wake* (New York: Farrar, Straus and Giroux, 1969), p. 14.

25. Beckett's attitude toward the city is closer to Eliot's *Waste Land* than Joyce's *Ulysses*. Indeed, sitting with his back to the river, Macmann, like the Fisher King, contemplates the isolation and living death of metropolitan life: ". . . the people that throng the streets at this hour, their long day ended and the whole long evening before them. The doors open and spew them out, each door its contingent. For an instant they cluster in a daze, huddled on the sidewalk or in the gutter, then set off singly on their appointed ways. And even those who know themselves condemned, at the outset, to the same direction, for the choice of directions at the outset is not great, take leave of one another and part, . . . And God help him who longs, for once in his recovered freedom, to walk a little way with a fellow-creature" (Samuel Beckett, *Malone Dies*, Collected Works Edition [New York: Grove Press, Inc., 1970], p. 56. All further references are to this edition and are included parenthetically in the text after the identifying initials *MD*).

26. "The tragic figure represents the expiation of original sin . . . the sin of having been born" (*Proust*, p. 49).

27. Their loss and disappearance may also be a result of Beckett's interest, not in a particular person's case, but in the general situation of mankind. Thus his anti-realism—a reaction against Joyce—neces-

sitates "a standardization of object from work to work," a technique used to negate the specificity of any particular thing (E. M. Scarry, "Six Ways to Kill a Blackbird or Any Other Intentional Object: Samuel Beckett's Method of Meaning," *James Joyce Quarterly* 8 [Summer 1971]: 284.

28. Joyce, *Ulysses*, p. 37.

29. "Perhaps I had invented him [Molloy], I mean found him ready made in my head" (*Molloy*, pp. 152–53). This and other statements by Moran support the theory that his quest for Molloy is, in effect, the artist's effort to realize his vision by embodying it in a work of art.

30. Samuel Beckett, *How It Is*, Collected Works Edition (New York: The Grove Press, Inc., 1970), pp. 7, 147 (italics mine). Further references are to this edition and are included parenthetically in the text after the identifying initials *CC* (for the French title *Comment c'est*).

31. Samuel Beckett, *Stories and Texts for Nothing*, Collected Works Edition (New York: The Grove Press, Inc., 1970), p. 140 (italics mine).

32. Joyce, *FW* 14.16. This gap is the silence between A.D. 566 (ante deluvian) and A.D. 566 (anna dominant).

33. For an excellent discussion on this point see William York Tindall's *A Reader's Guide to James Joyce* (New York: Farrar, Straus & Giroux, 1959), pp. 73–82.

34. Krystyna Stamirowska, "The Conception of a Character in the Works of Joyce and Beckett," *Kwartalnik Neofilologiczny* 14, no. 4 (1967): 444.

35. David Hayman, "A Prefatory Note," *James Joyce Quarterly* 8 (Summer 1971): 175–76.

36. Joyce, *Portrait*, p. 215.

37. John Gross, *James Joyce*, Modern Masters series, ed. Frank Kermode (New York: The Viking Press, 1970), p. 13.

38. Cohn, *Samuel Beckett: The Comic Gamut*, pp. 131–32.

39. Patrick Bowles, "How Samuel Beckett Sees the Universe," *The Listener* 59 (19 June 1958): 1011.

40. Joyce, *FW* 20.13–16.

41. Robert Champigny, "Adventures of the First Person," in *Samuel Beckett Now*, p. 122.

42. Note too the parody of Molly Bloom's monologue in *Ulysses*: "alone in the mud yes the dark yes sure yes panting yes someone hears me no no one hears me no murmuring sometimes yes when the panting stops yes not at other times no in the mud yes to the mud yes my voice yes mine yes not another's no mine alone yes sure yes when the panting

stops yes one and off yes a few words yes a few scraps yes that no one hears no but less and less no answer LESS AND LESS yes" (*CC*, p. 146). Frances Doherty has discovered another parody on pp. 44–45, that of the Ballast Office Clock episode in *Stephen Hero* (*Samuel Beckett* [London: Hutchinson University Library, 1971], p. 124). But for Melvin J. Friedman, "*Comment c'est* might be interpreted, in fact, as a kind of implicit rejection of Joyce. The elaborate linguistic and musical cadences of *Finnegans Wake* have been reduced to the extreme of verbal barrenness and sparseness of vocabulary. The richness of Joyce's prose could not be more different than the staccato rumblings, with their many repetitions, of Beckett's narrator in *Comment c'est*" ("Preface," *Samuel Beckett*, Calepins de bibliographie no. 2 [Paris: Lettres Modernes, Menard, 1972], p. 6).

43. Bowles, "How Samuel Beckett Sees," p. 1011.

44. Beckett, "Dante . . . Bruno. Vico . . Joyce," p. 250.

45. Ibid., p. 253.

46. Walter A. Strauss, "Dante's Belacqua and Beckett's Tramps," *Comparative Literature* 11 (Summer 1959) : 260.

47. Samuel Beckett, *The Unnamable*, Collected Works Edition (New York: The Grove Press, Inc., 1970), p. 179. Future references are to this edition and are included parenthetically in the text after the identifying initials *Unn*.

48. See the discussion of "Ding-Dong" in chapter 1.

49. Federman, *Journey to Chaos*, p. 107.

50. Fletcher, *The Novels of Samuel Beckett*, pp. 242, 248. "The Expelled," "The Calmative," "The End," can all be found in *Stories and Texts for Nothing*, Complete Works Edition (New York: The Grove Press, Inc., 1970). Further references are to this edition and are included parenthetically in the text after the identifying initials *STFN*. *Premier Amour*, published separately and only in French at the time this was written (Paris: Les Editions de Minuit, 1970), is indicated by the initials *PA*.

51. Federman, *Journey to Chaos*, p. 136.

52. Again, much of what I term "Joycean" is not really that Dubliner's exclusive property. Cradle-grave polarities in literature go back as far as Sophocles and the Gilgamesh epic. However, in light of other Joycean similarities and allusions, it seems safe to assume that the presence of these motifs and themes in Beckett's writings is due *primarily* to Joyce's influence on him.

53. "Grace" is structured according to the three parts of Dante's *Divine Comedy*, and Tom Kernan's fall does represent inferno rather than infancy.

54. Confrontation with the law is a characteristic of Beckett's fiction (see *Murphy, Molloy*).

55. George Steiner, "Of Nuance and Scruple," *New Yorker* 44 (27 April 1968) : 173.

56. In an early short story of Beckett's, "Assumption," the artist-hero is each night destroyed and rebuilt by his creative efforts: "Thus each night he died and was God, each night revived and was torn . . ." (*transition* 16–17 [June 1929]: 271).

57. Bernard Pingaud, "*Molloy*, douze ans après," *Les Temps Modernes* 18 (January 1963) : 1287.

58. Dieter Wellershoff, "Failure of an Attempt at De-Mythologization: Samuel Beckett's Novels," in Martin Esslin, ed., *Samuel Beckett*, p. 92.

59. Robinson, *The Long Sonata*, p. 141.

60. Objective reality, according to existential theory, is finite and positive, an undifferentiated mass that, however, exists only when it is perceived (*"esse est percipi"* in the words of philosopher Berkeley). The perceiver is the Self, an infinite consciousness that is outside time, space, motion, and thought.

61. This too is an integral part of existentialist theory.

62. In existentialist terms, the objective reality, or *en-soi*, of such a fictional being is definite, limited, and as such cannot comprehend or apprehend the infinite, undefined nature of the artist-hero's *pour-soi* or Self.

63. Cohn, *The Comic Gamut*, p. 162.

64. Dan Davin, "Mr. Beckett's Everyman," *Irish Writing*, no. 34 (Spring 1956), p. 39 (italics mine). Joyce Carol Oates goes even further: *"The Unnamable* suggests as its central meaning . . . the relationships of the writer to his characters" ("The Trilogy of Samuel Beckett," *Renascence* 14 [Spring 1962]: 164). There is a somewhat similar problem in *Finnegans Wake*, where it is hard to establish "the identities in the writer complexus" (114.33) and "who . . . wrote the durn thing anyhow?" (107.36–108.1).

65. Gerald Jay Goldberg, "The Search for the Artist in Some Recent British Fiction," *South Atlantic Quarterly* 62 (Summer 1963) : 399.

66. Wayne C. Booth, *The Rhetoric of Fiction* (Chicago and London: The University of Chicago Press, 1961), p. 155.

67. The Unnamable uses this image in criticizing his (and Beckett's) previous creations: "Did they ever get Mahood to speak? It seems to me not. I think Murphy spoke now and then, the others too perhaps. I don't remember, but it was clumsily done, you could see the ventriloquist" (*Unn*, p. 85). And the "I" of *Texts for Nothing*

similarly separates himself from his creator: "here I'm a mere ventriloquist's dummy, I feel nothing, say nothing, he holds me in his arms
and moves my lips with a string . . ." (*STFN*, p. 113).

68. "The forms are many in which the unchanging seeks relief from
its formlessness" (*MD*, p. 21).

69. Tom F. Driver, "Beckett by the Madeleine," *Columbia University
Forum* 4 (Summer 1961): 23.

70. Robinson, *The Long Sonata*, p. 144.

71. A *limbo* existence differs from a purgatorial one in that it
implies no possible change or hope of one. Beckett's characters know
this; however, like the artist who knows he will fail and yet continues
to write in the hope of succeeding, all Beckett's heroes, despite their
certainty that there is none, continue in hope. Although they know
they are in limbo, condemned "to wander the last of the living in
the depths of an instant without bounds" (*MD*, p. 59), Molloy.
Malone, and the Unnamable all possess an instinctive and unquench-
able *purgatorial* hope of being redeemed, of somehow ending the
unendable. It is this irrational faith that makes Beckett's grotesque
characters so human, their plight so painful and real.

72. Samuel Beckett, "Dante . . . Bruno. Vico . . Joyce," p. 253.

73. William York Tindall, *James Joyce: His Way of Interpreting
the Modern World* (New York: Charles Scribner's Sons, 1950), p. 125.

74. In his essay on Proust, Beckett approvingly cites Schopenhauer's
definition of the "artistic procedure as 'the contemplation of the world
independently of the principle of reason'" (*Proust*, p. 66).

75. Beckett's description recalls Yeats's gyres.

76. Beckett, in a review of Denis Devlin's poems, prophesied his
own great series of novels when he praised "the art that condenses as
inverted spiral of need, that condenses in intensity and brightness
from the mere need of the angels to that of the seraphinns [*sic*], whose
end is its own end in the end and source of need" ("Denis Devlin,"
transition 27 [April–May 1938]: 290).

77. Vivian Mercier, "The Mathematical Limit," *The Nation* 188
(14 February 1959): 145.

Chapter 5 "Me to Play"

1. T. S. Eliot, "Four Quartets," *The Complete Poems and Plays:
1909–1950* (New York: Harcourt, Brace and Company, 1952), pp.
123–29.

2. Beckett echoes Eliot's phrase in *Endgame* (New York: Grove
Press, Inc., 1970), p. 69. Further references are to this edition and
are included parenthetically in the text after the identifying initial
E.

3. As defined by Beckett in his essay "Dante . . . Bruno. Vico . . Joyce," *transition* 16–17 (June 1929) : 242–53.

4. Samuel Beckett, *Happy Days*, Complete Works Edition (New York: Grove Press, Inc., 1970), p. 11. Further references are to this edition and are included parenthetically in the text after the identifying initials *HD*.

5. Samuel Beckett, *All That Fall*, in *Krapp's Last Tape And Other Dramatic Pieces*, Complete Works Edition (New York: Grove Press, Inc., 1970), p. 34. Further references are to this edition and are included parenthetically in the text after the identifying initials *ATF*.

6. Samuel Beckett, *Play*, in *Cascando and Other Dramatic Pieces* (New York: Grove Press, Inc., 1970), p. 54. Further references are to this edition and are included parenthetically in the text.

7. Both wear necklaces and open and close their blue eyes.

8. Alain Robbe-Grillet, "Samuel Beckett, or 'Presence' in the Theatre," in *Samuel Beckett*, ed. Martin Esslin, p. 113.

9. Hugh Kenner, *Samuel Beckett*, p. 136.

10. Beckett, *Waiting for Godot*, p. 10b. Further references are included parenthetically in the text after the initials *WFG*.

11. Marion Trousdale, "Dramatic Form: Tne Example of *Godot*," *Modern Drama* 11 (May 1968) : 1.

12. Alan Schneider, "Waiting for Beckett: A Personal Chronicle," *Chelsea Review*, no. 2 (Autumn 1958), p. 3.

13. Gabor Mihalyi, "Beckett's 'Godot' and the Myth of Alienation," *Modern Drama* 9 (December 1966) : 280.

14. Herbert Blau, "Notes from Underground," *Casebook on Waiting for Godot*, ed. Ruby Cohn (New York: Grove Press, Inc., 1967), p. 117.

15. Ludovic Janvier, "Cyclical Dramaturgy," in *Casebook on Waiting for Godot*, ed. Ruby Cohn (New York: Grove Press, Inc., 1967), p. 167.

16. Armand Salacrou, "I Is Not an Accident But a Triumph," in *Casebook on Waiting for Godot*, ed. Ruby Cohn (New York: Grove Press, Inc., 1967), p. 14.

17. In act 1 the speakers are reversed.

18. Colin Duckworth, ed., *En Attendant Godot* (London: George G. Harrap, 1966), p. lxxxix.

19. Janvier, "Cyclical Dramaturgy," p. 168.

20. Robinson, *The Long Sonata*, p. 244.

21. Ibid., p. 237.

22. Murray Schumach, "Why They Wait for Godot," *New York Times Magazine*, 21 September 1958, p. 36.

23. Martin Esslin, *The Theatre of the Absurd* (Garden City, N.Y.: Doubleday, Anchor Books, 1961), p. 52.

24. Richard Lee Francis, "Beckett's Metaphysical Tragicomedy," *Modern Drama* 8 (December 1965) : 262.

25. Kenner, *Samuel Beckett*, p. 139.

26. Vivian Mercier, "A Pyrrhonian Eclogue," *Hudson Review* 7 (Winter 1955) : 621. Mercier also considers the often-advanced possibility that Godot does come, for he is Pozzo: "If Pozzo is Godot and Godot is God, we get a Viconian cycle in which history repeats itself every evening" (p. 623).

27. Jeremy Beckett, "Compte rendu de *Waiting for Godot*," *Meanjin* 15 (Winter 1956): p. 218. See Appendix A for a more complete discussion of Beckett's relationship to Irish literature.

28. Lawrence E. Harvey, "Art and the Existential in 'Waiting for Godot,'" in *Casebook on Waiting for Godot*, ed. Ruby Cohn (New York: Grove Press, Inc., 1967), p. 149.

29. Robinson, *The Long Sonata*, pp. 250–51.

30. Compare Moran's uncertainty over Molloy's name.

31. Samuel Beckett, "Assez," *Têtes-Mortes* (Paris: Les Editions de Minuit, 1967), p. 39.

32. Cohn, *Samuel Beckett*, p. 221.

33. G. S. Fraser, *The Modern Writer and His World* (Baltimore, Md.: Pelican Books, 1964), p. 63. Hamm voices a similar sentiment: "The bastard! He doesn't exist!" (*E*, p. 55).

34. Critic Frederick Hoffmann disagrees: "Godot is no more God than is the Mr. Knott whom Watt serves. The suggestions of a remote theological being fail to attract the inhabitants of Beckett's world, who choose the metaphors and techniques of transcendence that are to their own liking. . . . The Christian beliefs are turned to secular metaphors; and the great line of progress in time is toward death rather than either a secular or a theological perfection" (*Samuel Beckett*, p. 146).

35. Samuel Beckett, "Lessness," *Evergreen Review* 80 (July 1970): 35–36.

36. The very fact that Beckett continues to write as he does, faithful to his vision of the inevitable failure but moral necessity of art, is testimony to Joyce's influence: "Joyce had a moral effect on me—he made me realize artistic integrity" (Ruby Cohn, *Back to Beckett* [Princeton, N.J.: Princeton University Press, 1973], p. 14).

Appendix A: Beckett and Irish Literature

1. Vivian Mercier, *The Irish Comic Tradition* (London: Oxford University Press, 1969), pp. 75–76.

2. Ibid., p. 5.

3. Samuel Beckett, *All That Fall*, in *Krapp's Last Tape And Other*

Dramatic Pieces, Collected Works Edition (New York: Grove Press, Inc., 1970) , p. 74.

4. Mercier, *Irish Comic Tradition,* pp. 53–56.

5. Joyce, *Portrait,* p. 139.

6. Joyce, *Ulysses,* p. 28.

7. Ibid., p. 161.

8. Mercier, *Irish Comic Tradition,* p. 71.

9. Joyce, *Ulysses,* p. 753.

10. Joyce, *Portrait,* p. 171 (italics mine) .

11. Ibid., p. 172.

12. Richard Ellmann comments that Boylan is an "example of malign fleshliness" *(Ulysses on the Liffey* [New York: Oxford University Press, 1972], p. 75) .

13. Joyce, *Ulysses,* p. 553.

14. Ellmann, *Ulysses on the Liffey,* p. 174.

Appendix B: Joyce and the Jews

1. Joyce, *Ulysses,* p. 94.

2. Ellmann, *James Joyce,* p. 393.

3. Joyce, *Ulysses,* p. 94.

4. Ellmann, *James Joyce,* p. 39n.

5. Ibid., p. 722.

Works Cited

I. By Samuel Beckett:

The Collected Works of Samuel Beckett. New York: Grove Press, Inc., 1970. This includes all of Beckett's works cited in this study except the following:

"Assumption." *transition* 16–17 (June 1929) : 268–71.

"Dante . . . Bruno. Vico . . Joyce." *transition* 16–17 (June 1929): 242–53.

"Denis Devlin." Review of Denis Devlin's *Intercessions. transition* 27 (April–May 1938) : 289–94.

"Gnome." *Dublin Magazine* 4, no. 3 (July–September 1934) : 8.

"Home Olga." *Contempo* (Chapel Hill, N.C.) 3 (15 February 1934) : 3.

"Lessness." *Evergreen Review* (July 1970) : pp. 35–36.

et al. *Our Exagmination round his Factification for Incamination of Work in Progress.* Paris: Shakespeare & Co., 1929.

Premier Amour. Paris: Les Editions de Minuit, 1970.

"Sedendo et Quiescendo." *transition* 21 (March 1932) : 13–20.

Têtes-Mortes. Paris: Les Editions de Minuit, 1967.

"Text." *The New Review* 5 (April 1932) : 57.

and Duthuit, Georges. "Three Dialogues." In *Samuel Beckett: A Collection of Critical Essays.* Edited by Martin Esslin. Englewood Cliffs, N.J.: Prentice-Hall, Inc., 1965.

II. By James Joyce:

The Critical Writings of James Joyce. Edited by Ellsworth Mason and Richard Ellmann. New York: The Viking Press, Inc., 1968.

Dubliners. Compass Edition. New York: The Viking Press, Inc., 1964.

Finnegans Wake. New York: The Viking Press, Inc., 1966.

Letters of James Joyce. Vol. 1. Edited by Stuart Gilbert. New Edition. New York: The Viking Press, Inc., 1966.

Letters of James Joyce. Vols. 2, 3. Edited by Richard Ellmann. New York: The Viking Press, Inc., 1966.

The Portable James Joyce. Edited by Harry Levin. New York: The Viking Press, Inc., 1967.

A Portrait of the Artist as a Young Man. Edited by Chester G. Anderson. New York: The Viking Press, Inc., 1968.

Stephen Hero. Edited by Theodore Spencer, with additional manuscript pages edited by John J. Slocum and Herbert Cahoon. New York: New Directions Publishing Corp., 1963.

Ulysses. New Edition. New York: Random House, 1961.

III. By Others:

Abbott, H. Porter. *The Fiction of Samuel Beckett: Form and Effect.* Berkeley: University of California, 1973.

Abel, Lionel. *Metatheatre: A New View of Dramatic Form.* New York: Hill & Wang, 1963.

Arp, Hans, et al. "Poetry is Vertical." *transition* 21 (March 1932) : 148–49.

Atherton, J. S. "More on 'An Anecdote of Beckett's.'" *A Wake Newslitter.* n.s. (October 1966) : 109.

d'Aubarède, Gabriel. Interview. *Les Nouvelles Littéraires,* February 16, 1971, pp. 1, 7.

Barnard, G. C. *Samuel Beckett: A New Approach.* New York: Dodd Mead & Co., Inc., 1970.

Bataille, Georges. "Le Silence de *Molloy*." *Critique* 7 (May 15, 1951) : 387–96.

Beckett at 60: A Festschrift. London: Calder and Boyars, 1967.

Beckett, Jeremy. "Compte rendu de *Waiting for Godot*." *Meanjin* 15 (Winter 1956) : 216–18.

Blau, Herbert. "Notes from the Underground." *Casebook on Waiting for Godot*. Edited by Ruby Cohn. New York: Grove Press, Inc., 1967.

Booth, Wayne C. *The Rhetoric of Fiction*. Chicago and London: The University of Chicago Press, 1961.

Bowles, Patrick. "How Samuel Beckett Sees the Universe." *The Listener* 59 (June 19, 1958) : 1011–12.

Brick, Allan. "The Madman in his Cell: Joyce, Beckett, Nabokov and the Stereotypes." *Massachusetts Review* 1 (Fall 1959): 40–55.

Budgen, Frank. *James Joyce and the Making of Ulysses*. Bloomington and London: Indiana University Press, 1967.

————. *Further Recollections of James Joyce*. London: Shenval Press, 1955.

Champigny, Robert. "Adventures of the First Person." *Samuel Beckett Now*. Edited by Melvin J. Friedman. Chicago and London: The University of Chicago Press, 1970.

Chevigny, Bell Gale. "Introduction." *Twentieth Century Interpretations of Endgame*. Edited by Bell Gale Chevigny. Englewood Cliffs, N.J.: Prentice-Hall, 1969.

Coe, Richard. *Samuel Beckett*. New York: Grove Press, Inc., 1964.

Cohn, Ruby. *Samuel Beckett: The Comic Gamut*. New Brunswick, N.J.: Rutgers University Press, 1962.

————. "*Watt* in the Light of *The Castle*." *Comparative Literature* 13 (Spring 1961) : 154–66.

————, ed. *Casebook on Waiting for Godot*. New York: Grove Press, Inc., 1967.

————. "Joyce and Beckett: Irish Cosmopolitans." *James Joyce Quarterly* 8 (Summer 1971) : 385–91.

————. *Back to Beckett*. Princeton, N.J.: Princeton University Press, 1973.

Colum, Mary and Padraic. *Our Friend James Joyce*. Gloucester, Mass.: Peter Smith, 1968.

Cowley, Malcolm. *Exile's Return: A Literary Odyssey of the 1920's.* New York: The Viking Press, 1969.

Curran, C. P. *James Joyce Remembered.* New York and London: Oxford University Press, 1968.

Davin, Dan. "Mr. Beckett's Everyman." *Irish Writing* 34 (Spring 1956) : 36–39.

Doherty, Frances. *Samuel Beckett.* London: Hutchinson University Library, 1971.

Driver, Tom. "Beckett by the Madeleine." *Columbia University Forum* 4 (Summer 1961) : 21–25.

Duckworth, Colin, ed. *En Attendant Godot.* London: George G. Harrap, 1966.

Eliot, T. S. *The Complete Poems and Plays: 1909–1950.* New York: Harcourt, Brace & Co., 1952.

Ellmann, Richard. *James Joyce.* New York: Oxford University Press, 1959.

———. *Ulysses on the Liffey.* New York: Oxford University Press, 1972.

Esslin, Martin. *The Theatre of the Absurd.* Garden City, N.Y.: Doubleday, Anchor Books, 1961.

———. "Samuel Beckett." *The Novelist as Philosopher.* Edited by John Cruikshank. London: Oxford University Press, 1962.

———, ed. *Samuel Beckett: A Collection of Critical Essays.* Englewood Cliffs, N.J.: Prentice-Hall, 1965.

Farrell, Patric. Letter to Barbara Gluck, July 1970.

Federman, Raymond. *Journey to Chaos: Samuel Beckett's Early Fiction.* Berkeley and Los Angeles: University of California Press, 1965.

Fletcher, John. "Interpreting *Molloy.*" *Samuel Beckett Now.* Edited by Melvin J. Friedman. Chicago and London: University of Chicago Press, 1970.

———. *The Novels of Samuel Beckett.* London: Chatto and Windus, 1964.

———. "The Private Pain and the Whey of Words." *Samuel Beckett: A Collection of Critical Essays.* Englewood Cliffs, N.J.: Prentice-Hall, 1965.

Foucault, Michel. *Les Mots et les choses: une archéologie des sciences humaines.* Paris: Editions Gallimard, 1966.

Francis, Richard Lee. "Beckett's Metaphysical Tragicomedy." *Modern Drama* 8 (December 1965) : 259–67.

Fraser, G. S. *The Modern Writer and His World*. Baltimore, Md.: Penguin Books, 1964.

Freund, Gisele, and Carleton, V. B. *James Joyce in Paris: His Final Years*. New York: Harcourt, Brace and World, 1966.

Friedman, Melvin J. *Samuel Beckett Now*. Chicago and London: University of Chicago Press, 1970.

————. "Preface" to *Samuel Beckett*. Calepins de bibliographie, no. 2. Paris: Lettres Modernes, Menard, 1972.

Frye, Northrop. "The Nightmare Life in Death." *Hudson Review* 13 (Autumn 1960) : 442–49.

Gessner, Nicholas. *Die Unzulänglichkeit der Sprache*. Zurich: Verlag, 1957.

Glasheen, Adaline. "Home Olga." *A Wake Newslitter*. n.s. (April 1966) : 45.

Gogarty, Oliver St. John. *As I Was Going Down Sackville Street*. Dublin: Rich and Cowan, 1937.

Goldberg, Gerald Jay. "The Search for the Artist in Some Recent British Fiction." *South Atlantic Quarterly* 62 (Summer 1963): 387–401.

Goldberg, S. L. *The Classical Temper: A Study of James Joyce's Ulysses*. New York: Barnes and Noble, 1961.

Gross, John. *James Joyce*, Modern Masters series. Edited by Frank Kermode. New York: The Viking Press, 1970.

Guggenheim, Marguerite. *Confessions of an Art Addict*. London: André Deutsch, 1960.

————. *Out of this Century: the Informal Memoirs of Peggy Guggenheim*. New York: Dial Press, 1946.

Halper, Nathan. "On an Anecdote of Beckett's." *A Wake Newslitter*. n.s. (June 1966) : 55–56.

Harvey, Lawrence. "Art and the Existential in *Waiting for Godot*." *Casebook on Waiting for Godot*. Edited by Ruby Cohn. New York: Grove Press, Inc., 1967.

————. *Samuel Beckett: Poet and Critic*. Princeton, N.J.: Princeton University Press, 1970.

Hassan, Ihab. *The Literature of Silence: Henry Miller and Samuel Beckett*. New York: Alfred A. Knopf, 1967.

Hayman, David. "A Meeting in the Park and a Meeting on the

Bridge." *James Joyce Quarterly* 8 (Summer 1971) : 372–83.

———. "A Prefatory Note." *James Joyce Quarterly* 8 (Summer 1971) : 275–77.

Hemingway, Ernest. *A Moveable Feast.* New York: Charles Scribner's Sons, 1964.

Heppenstall, Rayner. *The Fourfold Tradition.* New York: New Directions, 1961.

Hoefer, Jacqueline. "Watt." In *Samuel Beckett: A Collection of Critical Essays.* Edited by Martin Esslin. Englewood Cliffs, N.J.: Prentice-Hall, 1965.

Hoffmann, Fredrick J. *Samuel Beckett: The Language of Self.* London and Amsterdam: Southern Illinois University Press, 1962.

Hutchins, Patricia. *James Joyce's World.* London: Methuen & Co., Ltd., 1957.

Janvier, Ludovic. "Cyclical Dramaturgy." *Casebook on Waiting for Godot.* Edited by Ruby Cohn. New York: Grove Press, Inc., 1967.

Jolas, Eugene. "Literature and the New Man." *transition* 19–20 (June 1930) : 13–19.

———. "Preface." *transition* 21 (March 1932) : 284.

———. "Revolt Against the Philistine." *transition* 6 (September 1927) : 176–79.

———, et al. "Suggestions for a New Magic." *transition* 3 (June 1927) : 178–79.

———. "Super-Occident." *transition* 15 (February 1929) : 11–16.

Jolas, Maria. "A Bloomlein for Sam." *Beckett at 60: A Festschrift.* London: Calder and Boyars, 1967.

Kastor, Robert. Letter to Barbara Gluck, 7 November 1970.

Kennedy, Sighle. *Murphy's Bed: A Study of Real Sources and Surreal Associations in Samuel Beckett's First Novel.* Lewisburg, Pa.: Bucknell University Press, 1971.

Kenner, Hugh. *Flaubert, Joyce and Beckett: The Stoic Comedians.* Boston: Beacon Press, 1962.

———. *Samuel Beckett: A Critical Study.* Berkeley and Los Angeles: University of California Press, 1968.

———. *A Reader's Guide to Samuel Beckett.* New York: Farrar, Straus and Giroux, 1973.

Knowlson, James. *Samuel Beckett:* catalog of an exhibition

held at Reading University Library, May to July 1971. London: Turret Books, 1971.

Knuth, Leo. "Beckett's 'Come In.'" *A Wake Newslitter*. n.s. (December 1970) : 96.

Le Sage, Laurent. *The French New Novel: An Introduction and a Sampler*. University Park, Pa.: Pennsylvania State University Press, 1962.

Leventhal, A. J. "The Beckett Hero." *Samuel Beckett: A Collection of Critical Essays*. Edited by Martin Esslin. Englewood Cliffs, N.J.: Prentice-Hall, 1965.

———. "The Thirties." *Beckett at 60: A Festschrift*. London: Calder and Boyars, 1967.

Lidderdale, Jane, and Nicholson, Mary. *Dear Miss Weaver: Harriet Shaw Weaver 1876–1961*. New York: Viking Press, 1970.

Litz, A. Walton. "Ithaca," in *James Joyce's Ulysses: Critical Essays*. Edited by Clive Hart and David Hayman. Berkeley: University of California Press, 1974.

Lombardi, Thomas W. "Who Tells Who *Watt*." *Chelsea* 22–23 (June 1968) : 170–79.

Mercier, Vivian. "The Mathematical Limit." *The Nation,* 14 February 1959, pp. 144–45.

———. "A Pyrrhonian Eclogue." *Hudson Review* 7 (Winter 1955) : 620–24.

———. *The Irish Comic Tradition*. London: Oxford University Press, 1969.

Mihalyi, Gabor. "Beckett's *Godot* and the Myth of Alienation." *Modern Drama* 9 (December 1966) : 277–82.

Morse, J. Mitchell. "The Contemplative Life According to Samuel Beckett." *Hudson Review* 15 (Winter 1962–63) : 512–24.

———. "The Ideal Core of the Onion: Samuel Beckett's Criticism." *French Review* 38 (October 1964) : 23–29.

———. "The Choreography of the New Novel." *Hudson Review* 3 (Autumn 1963) : 396–419.

Oates, J. C. "The Trilogy of Samuel Beckett." *Renascence: A Critical Journal of Letters* 14 (Spring 1962) : 160–65.

O'Connor, Ulick. *The Times I've Seen: Oliver St. John Gogarty —A Biography*. New York: Ivan Obolensky, Inc., 1963.

Pingaud, Bernard. *"Molloy,* douze ans après." *Les Temps Modernes* 18 (January 1963) : 1283–1300.

Pritchett, V. S. "An Irish Oblomov." *New Statesman.* n.s., 59 (2 April 1960) : 489.

Putnam, Samuel. *Paris Was Our Mistress.* New York: Viking Press, 1947.

Reid, Alec. *All I Can Manage, More Than I Could: An Approach to the Plays of Samuel Beckett.* Chester Springs, Pa.: Dufour Editions, 1968.

Ricks, Christopher. "The Roots of Samuel Beckett." *The Listener* 72 (17 December 1964) : 963–64, 980.

Robbe-Grillet, Alain. "Samuel Beckett or 'Presence in the Theatre.'" *Samuel Beckett: A Collection of Critical Essays.* Edited by Martin Esslin. Englewood Cliffs, N.J.: Prentice-Hall, 1965.

Robinson, Michael. *The Long Sonata of the Dead: A Study of Samuel Beckett.* New York: Grove Press, Inc., 1969.

Salacrou, Armand. "It Is Not an Accident but a Triumph." *Casebook on Waiting for Godot.* Edited by Ruby Cohn. New York: Grove Press, Inc., 1967.

Scarry, E. M. "Six Ways to Kill a Blackbird or Any Other Intentional Object: Samuel Beckett's Method of Meaning." *James Joyce Quarterly* 8 (Summer 1971) : 278–85.

Schneider, Alan. "Waiting for Beckett: A Personal Chronicle." *Chelsea Review* 2 (Autumn 1958) : 3–20.

Schumach, Murray. "Why They Wait for Godot." *New York Times Magazine,* 21 September 1958, pp. 36, 38, 41.

Scott, Nathan A., Jr. "The Recent Journey into the Zone of Zero: The Example of Beckett and His Despair of Literature." *Centennial Review of Arts and Science* 6 (1962) : 144–81.

Senneff, Susan Field. "Song and Music in Samuel Beckett's *Watt.*" *Modern Fiction Studies* 10 (Summer 1964) : 137–49.

Shenker, Israel. "Moody Man of Letters." New York *Times.* Interview, 6 May 1956.

Simpson, Alan. *Beckett and Behan and a Theatre in Dublin.* London: Routledge and Kegan Paul, 1962.

Stamirowska, Krystyna. "The Conception of a Character in the Works of Joyce and Beckett." *Kwartalnik Neofilologiczny* 14, no. 4 (1967) : 443–47.

Steiner, George. *Language and Silence: Essays on Language, Literature and the Inhuman.* New York: Atheneum, 1970.

———. "Of Nuance and Scruple." *New Yorker,* 27 April 1968, pp. 164–74.

Strauss, Walter A. "Dante's Belacqua and Beckett's Tramps." *Comparative Literature* 11 (Summer 1959) : 250–61.

Tallmer, Jerry. "A Nobel Prize Is . . . Waiting for Beckett." New York *Post,* 1 November 1969.

Tindall, William York. *Beckett's Bums.* Privately printed by the author. London, 1960.

———. *James Joyce: His Way of Interpreting the Modern World.* New York: Charles Scribner's Sons, 1950.

———. *A Reader's Guide to Finnegans Wake.* New York: Farrar, Straus & Giroux, 1969.

———. *A Reader's Guide to James Joyce.* New York: Noonday Press, 1959.

———. *Samuel Beckett.* New York: Columbia University Press, 1964.

Trousdale, Marion. "Dramatic Form: The Example of *Godot.*" *Modern Drama* 11 (May 1968) : 1–9.

Waidner, H. Frew, III. "*Ulysses* by Way of *Culture and Anarchy,*" in *Approaches to Ulysses: Ten Essays.* Edited by Thomas F. Staley and Bernard Benstock. Pittsburgh: University of Pittsburgh Press, 1970.

Warner, Frances. "The Absence of Nationalism in the Work of Samuel Beckett." *Theatre and Nationalism in Twentieth-Century Ireland.* Toronto: University of Toronto, 1972. Pp. 179–220.

Weiler, Gershon. *Mauthner's Critique of Language.* London and Colchester: Cambridge University Press, 1970.

Wellershoff, Dieter. "Failure of an Attempt at De-Mythologization: Samuel Beckett's Novels." *Samuel Beckett: A Collection of Critical Essays.* Edited by Martin Esslin. Englewood Cliffs, N.J.: Prentice-Hall, 1965.

Wilson, Colin. *The Strength to Dream: Literature and the Imagination.* Boston: Houghton Mifflin Co.; Cambridge: Riverside Press, 1962.

Wilson, Edmund. *Axel's Castle: A Study in the Imaginative*

Literature of 1870 to 1930. New York: Charles Scribner's Sons, 1931.

Wittgenstein, Ludwig. *Tractatus Logico-Philosophicus.* Translated by D. F. Pears and B. F. McGuinness with an introduction by Bertrand Russell. London: Routledge and Kegan Paul; New York: The Humanities Press, 1961.

Wordsworth, William. *Selected Poetry.* New York: Random House, Inc., 1950.

Yeats, William Butler. *The Collected Poems of W. B. Yeats.* New York: Macmillan Co., 1966.

Index

Abel, Lionel, 9, 151, 156

Act Without Words I and *II* Beckett): a mime, 165

A la recherche du temps perdu (Proust). 42; Oriane de Guermantes' bon mot, 43; Beckett's puns on names of characters in, 44

"Alba" (Beckett), 51

Alienation: the condition of Beckett's characters, 80, 105, 112-15, 122, 134, 184 n. 12; deeper in Beckett than in Joyce, 80. *See also* Exile

All That Fall (Beckett), 142, 165

Ambiguity: more fundamental in Beckett's work than in Joyce's, 98-99; in *Waiting for Godot*, 137-38, 153-54, 196 n.26

An die Musik (Schubert), 66

"Anna Livia Plurabelle" (Joyce), 26-27, 55; French translation of, 26-27; echoed in "Home Olga," 33

Anti-Semitism: and Sinclair-Gogarty libel suit, 35-37; no evidence of in Joyce, 169-70

Aquinas, Saint Thomas, aesthetic doctrine of, 108

Art, religion of: a Joycean creed, 108-9, 189 n. 8; rejected by Beckett, 109-10; neither Joyce nor Beckett adopts posture of Joyce's artist-God, 117, 128; Malone mocks concept of, 130

As I Was Going Down Sackville Street (Gogarty), 35

"Assez" (Beckett): published in French, 157; may reflect Joyce-Beckett relationship, 157

"Assumption" (Beckett): the author's first printed story, 25; recurrent death of artist-hero, 193 n. 56

Astrology: in "Whoroscope," 44-45; in *Murphy*, 74, 82; as closed system, 82

Aubarède, Gabriel d', 30

Augustine, Saint, 45; Beckett admires shape of sentence of, 145

Beillet, Adrien: biographer of Descartes, 44

Barnard, G. C., 66

Bataille, Georges, 184 n. 10

Baudelaire, Charles, 115

Bauke, Joseph, 96